G
FOR
INT
DISINTEGRATION?

EDITED BY
Franklin Allen
Elena Carletti
Saverio Simonelli

With a foreword by
Josep Borrell Fontelles

AUTHORS
Leszek Balcerowicz
Antonio Borges
Russell Cooper
Paul De Grauwe
Bruno De Witte
Charles Goodhart
Janet Kersnar
Friedrich K. Kübler
Brigid Laffan
Wolfgang Münchau
Victor Ngai
Pier Carlo Padoan
Richard Portes
Frank Smets
Paul van den Noord
Guntram Wolff
Jacques Ziller

European University Institute
Florence, Italy
and
Wharton Financial Institutions Center
University of Pennsylvania, Philadelphia, USA

Published by FIC Press
Wharton Financial Institutions Center
2405 Steinberg Hall - Dietrich Hall
3620 Locust Walk
Philadelphia, PA 19104-6367
USA

First Published 2012

ISBN 978-0-9836469-4-5 (paperback)
ISBN 978-0-9836469-5-2 (e-book version)

Cover artwork, design and layout by Christopher Trollen

Contents

The Contributors

Franklin Allen
University of Pennsylvania
Franklin Allen is the Nippon Life Professor of Finance and Professor of Economics at the Wharton School of the University of Pennsylvania. He has been on the faculty since 1980. He is currently Co-Director of the Wharton Financial Institutions Center. He was formerly Vice Dean and Director of Wharton Doctoral Programs and Executive Editor of the Review of Financial Studies, one of the leading academic finance journals. He is a past President of the American Finance Association, the Western Finance Association, the Society for Financial Studies, and the Financial Intermediation Research Society, and a Fellow of the Econometric Society. He received his doctorate from Oxford University. Dr. Allen's main areas of interest are corporate finance, asset pricing, financial innovation, comparative financial systems, and financial crises. He is a co-author with Richard Brealey and Stewart Myers of the eighth through tenth editions of the textbook Principles of Corporate Finance.

Leszek Balcerowicz
Warsaw School of Economics
Leszek Balcerowicz, born in 1947, graduated with distinction from Foreign Trade Faculty in Central School of Planning and Statistics in Warsaw (CSPS), now Warsaw School of Economics (WSE), in 1970. In 1974 he gained an MBA at St. John's University in New York; in 1975 he received his Ph.D. in economics at the CSPS. Since October 1992 Leszek Balcerowicz has been a Professor at WSE, and since 1993 a Head of Department of International Comparative Studies.

Since 2006, he has been a Corresponding Member of the History and Philosophy Class of the Polish Academy of Arts and Sciences. Leszek Balcerowicz designed and executed the radical stabilization and transformation of the Polish economy since the fall of communism in Poland. In September 1989, Leszek Balcerowicz became Deputy Prime Minister of Poland and Minister of Finance in the first non-communist government in Poland after the Second World War. He retained his positions in the government until December 1991. From April 1995 to December 2000, he was the president of the Freedom Union, a free market - oriented party and from 1997 to June 2000 he was Deputy Prime Minister, Minister of Finance. He is a member of the Washington-based financial advisory body, the Group of Thirty, a board member of Washington, D.C. think-tank, the Peterson Institute for International Economics. Leszek Balcerowicz is a Chairman and a founder of Civil Development Forum Foundation – FOR – based in Warsaw. In 2011, he has been appointed a member of the Advisory Scientific Committee providing advice and assistance on issues relevant to the work of the European Systemic Risk Board (ESRB).

Antonio Borges
Universidade Católica Portuguesa
António Borges is Professor of Economics at Universidade Católica Portuguesa, Lisbon. He was Director of the European Department of the International Monetary Fund until November 2011. Prior to that, he was the Chairman of ECGI (European Corporate Governance Institute), a post which he had held since the Institute was founded in 2002. In June 2008, he was appointed Chairman of the Hedge Fund Standards Board. Formerly, he was Vice Chairman of Goldman Sachs International, which he joined in September 2000. His responsibilities included investment banking, leadership development and strategy. Prior to this he was Dean of INSEAD between 1993 and 2000. He joined INSEAD's faculty in 1980 and also taught at the University of Lisbon, Portuguese Catholic University and Stanford University. Between 1990 and 1993, António Borges was Vice Governor of Banco de Portugal, where he took a leading role in the liberalization of Portugal's financial system. He also worked at the European level on the project of Economic and

Monetary Union. He graduated from the Technical University in Lisbon and holds his MA and PhD in Economics from Stanford University. He has been a Board member of several corporations and foundations.

Josep Borrell Fontelles
President of the European University Institute

Josep Borrell graduated in Aeronautical Engineering in 1969 and obtained his PhD in Economic Sciences in 1976. In 1983 he was Professor in Economic Analysis at Complutense University of Madrid. From 1984 to 1991, he was Spanish Secretary of State for Finance, and from 1991 to 1996 he was Spanish Minister for Public Works, Transport, Environment, Housing and Telecommunications. In the period 1999 – 2004 he was President of the European Affairs Committee of the Spanish Parliament (and between 2002 – 2003 Member of the European Convention). In 2004, he was elected President of the European Parliament, a position which he covered until 2007. From 2007, he was President of the Development Committee of the European Parliament and in 2010 he began his mandate as President of the European University Institute.

Elena Carletti
European University Institute

Elena Carletti is Professor of Economics at the European University Institute, where she holds a joint chair in the Economics Department and the Robert Schuman Centre for Advanced Studies. She is also Research Fellow at CEPR, Extramural Fellow at TILEC, Fellow at the Center for Financial Studies at CesIfo, and at the Wharton Financial Institutions Center. Her main areas of interest are financial intermediation, financial crises, financial regulation, corporate governance, industrial organization and competition policy. She has published numerous articles in leading economic journals, and has recently coedited a book with Franklin Allen, Jan Pieter Krahnen and Marcel Tyrell on Liquidity and Crises. She has worked as consultant for the OECD and the World Bank and participates regularly in policy debates and roundtables at central banks and international organizations.

Russell Cooper
European University Institute
Russell Cooper joined the Institute in September 2009 from the University of Texas, where he is the Fred Hofheinz Regents Professor of Economics. He was previously Professor of Economics at Boston University, Associate Professor of Economics at the University of Iowa and Assistant Professor at Yale University. He is Fellow of the Econometric Society. He has published in journals such as the American Economic Review, the Quarterly Journal of Economics, the Review of Economic Studies, and the Journal of Political Economy

Paul De Grauwe
London School of Economics
Prior to joining LSE, Paul De Grauwe was Professor of International Economics at the University of Leuven, Belgium. He was a member of the Belgian parliament from 1991 to 2003. He is honorary doctor of the University of St. Gallen (Switzerland), of the University of Turku (Finland), and the University of Genoa. He obtained his PhD from the Johns Hopkins University in 1974. He was a visiting professor at various universities - the University of Paris, the University of Michigan, the University of Pennsylvania, Humboldt University Berlin, the Université Libre de Bruxelles, the Université Catholique de Louvain, the University of Amsterdam, the University of Milan, Tilburg University, and the University of Kiel. He was also a visiting scholar at the IMF, the Board of Governors of the Federal Reserve, the Bank of Japan and the European Central Bank. He was a member of the Group of Economic Policy Analysis, advising President Barroso. He is also director of the money, macro and international finance research network of CESifo, University of Munich. He is a research fellow at the Centre for European Policy Studies in Brussels.

Bruno De Witte
Maastricht University
Bruno de Witte is Professor of European Union law at Maastricht University, and part-time professor at the Robert Schuman Centre of the European University Institute (EUI) in Florence. He is co-director of the Maastricht Centre for European Law. Previously, from 2000 to February 2010, he was professor of EU law at the EUI, and

co-director of the Academy of European Law there, and before that, from 1989 to 2000, he was professor at Maastricht University. He studied law at the University of Leuven and the College of Europe, and obtained a doctorate at the European University Institute in 1985 on 'The Protection of Linguistic Diversity through Fundamental Rights.' Bruno De Witte's principal interest is the constitutional law of the European Union, with a particular focus on the relation between international, European and national law, the protection of fundamental rights, law-making and treaty revision procedures, internal market law and non-market values. His second main field of interest is the law of cultural diversity, with a particular focus on language law, the protection of minorities and the relation between market integration and cultural diversity in European Union law. Bruno De Witte is also a member of the Ius Commune Research School. He is a member of the editorial board of the European Law Journal, the European Human Rights Law Review, the Revista Española de Derecho Europeo, and the Revista de Llengua I Dret. He is a member of the advisory board of the European Journal of International Law, the European Constitutional Law Review, the Maastricht Journal of European and Comparative Law, the European Journal of Law Reform, and the Zeitschrift für öffentliches Recht, and correspondent of the Rivista Italiana di Diritto Pubblico Comunitario. He currently teaches the course of Advanced EU law in the Master programmes of Maastricht University. He has supervised some 35 doctoral dissertations, partly at the European University Institute and partly at Maastricht University.

Charles Goodhart
London School of Economics
Charles Goodhart (b. 1936: London, UK) was appointed to the newly established Norman Sosnow Chair of Banking and Finance at the London School of Economics (LSE) in September 1985, which he held until his retirement in 2002, when he became Emeritus Professor of Banking and Finance. He has remained at LSE at the Financial Markets Group, initially as Deputy Director, 1987-2005, and now as member in charge of the research program in financial regulation, 2005-present. He was elected a Fellow of the British Academy in 1990, and awarded the CBE in the New Years Honours List for

1997, for services to monetary economics. During 1986, he helped to found, with Professor Mervyn King, the Financial Markets Group at LSE, which began operation at the start of 1987. For the previous 17 years he served as a monetary economist at the Bank of England, becoming a Chief Adviser in 1980. Following his advice on overcoming the financial crisis in Hong Kong in 1983, and the establishment of the link between the HK and the US $, he subsequently served on the HK Exchange Fund Advisory Committee for several years until 1997. Later in 1997, he was appointed for three years, until May 2000, as one of the four independent outside members of the newly-formed Bank of England Monetary Policy Committee. Between 2002 and 2004, he returned to the Bank of England as a (part-time) adviser to the Governor on Financial Stability. He is a graduate of Cambridge (B.A. 1960) and Harvard (Ph.D. 1963). After returning from Harvard to teach at Cambridge, where he was a Fellow of Trinity College (1963-65), he became an adviser in the Department of Economic Affairs (DEA) for a brief period (1965-66), before returning to academic life as a Lecturer in Economics at the LSE (1966-68), from whence he joined the Bank of England.

Janet Kersnar
SNL Financial
Janet Kersnar was recently appointed London Bureau Chief for business intelligence firm SNL Financial, having been Europe Editor of Knowledge@Wharton, the online publication of The Wharton School, since 2009. Prior to K@W, Janet was Editor-in-Chief for 11 years of The Economist Group's CFO Europe, which was part of a global portfolio of award-winning magazines for chief financial officers. Along with various other publishing roles in Berlin, Paris and San Francisco, she has also been an Editor at The Wall Street Journal and other Dow Jones International publications. With a BA in political science and German from the University of California, Santa Barbara, she also studied at the Georg-August University in Göttingen, Germany, and the Free University in Berlin.

Friedrich K. Kübler
Johann-Wolfgang-Goethe University & University of Pennsylvania
Friedrich Kübler is an expert on corporations, banking and mass media. He has written or co-written more than 20 books and other in-

dependent publications and has published more than 100 articles in contract and property law; corporations, banking and securities regulation; and mass media and legal theory, many of them comparing American with European legal structures. His textbook on German corporate law has seen six editions and was recently translated into Spanish. Last year, he published a textbook on German Mass Media Law. He is a member of the American Law Institute and has served on the boards of the Deutscher Juristentag (the German institution corresponding to the American Law Institute) and the German Association of Comparative Law. He was a Commissioner of the German Interstate Commission for the Regulation of Media Concentration and served on the board of the Hessian Public Service Broadcasting Entity. He is a member of the European Shadow Financial Regulatory Committee and of the Frankfurt Academy of Sciences.

Brigid Laffan
University College Dublin

Brigid Laffan PhD took office as the Principal of the College of Human Sciences, University College Dublin, in September 2004. In 1991, Professor Laffan was appointed as Jean Monnet Professor of European Politics in the Department of Politics, UCD. She was the founding Director of the Dublin European Institute UCD in 1999. In March 2004, she was elected as a member of the Royal Irish Academy. She is a member of the Research Council of the European University Institute (EUI) Florence, the National Economic and Social Council (NESC) and the Irish Government's High Level Asia Strategy Group. Professor Laffan is author of Integration and Cooperation in Europe, 1992, The Finances of the Union, 1997, and co-author of Europe's Experimental Union, 2000. She has published numerous articles in the Journal of Common Market Studies and the European Journal of Public Policy. Professor Laffan co-ordinated a six country cross national research project entitled Organising for Enlargement (2001-2004), financed by the EU Commission's Fifth Framework Programme, and is part of an integrated research project on New Governance in Europe.

Wolfgang Münchau
Eurointelligence

Wolfgang Münchau is an associate editor and European economic

columnist of the Financial Times. Together with his wife, the economist Susanne Mundschenk, he runs eurointelligence.com, an internet service that provides daily comment and analysis of the Euro area,
targeted at investors, academics and policy makers. Mr. Münchau
was one of the founding members of Financial Times Deutschland,
the German language business daily, where he served as deputy editor from 1999 until 2001, and as editor-in-chief from 2001 until
2003. The business daily is now a firmly established player in the
German media market with a daily circulation of more than 100,000
copies sold. Previous appointments include correspondent posts for
the Financial Times and the Times of London in Washington, Brussels and Frankfurt. He was awarded the Wincott Young Financial
Journalist of the Year award in 1989. Mr. Münchau has published
three German-language books. His book Vorbeben, on the financial
crisis, has received the prestigious GetAbstract business book award
in 2008, and is now published by McGraw Hill in the US. He holds
degrees from the Universities of Reutlingen and Hagen and an M.A.
in international journalism from City University, London.

Victor Ngai
University of Pennsylvania
Victor Ngai graduated summa cum laude in May 2012 from the
Huntsman Program in International Studies and Business at the
University of Pennsylvania. He received a Bachelor of Science in
Economics from the Wharton School with concentrations in Fi-
nance and Accounting, and a Bachelor of Arts from the College of
Arts of Sciences with a major in International Studies.

Pier Carlo Padoan
Organisation for Economic Co-operation and Development (OECD)
Mr. Pier Carlo Padoan took up his functions as Deputy Secretary-
General of the OECD on 1 June 2007. As of 1 December 2009,
he was also appointed Chief Economist while retaining his role as
Deputy Secretary-General. In addition to heading the Economics
Department, Mr. Padoan is the G20 Finance Deputy for the OECD
and also leads the Strategic Response, the Green Growth and Innovation initiatives of the Organisation and helps build the necessary
synergies between the work of the Economics Department and that
of other Directorates. Mr. Padoan is an Italian national and prior

to joining the OECD was Professor of Economics at the University La Sapienza of Rome, and Director of the Fondazione Italianieuropei, a policy think-tank focusing on economic and social issues. From 2001 to 2005, Mr. Padoan was the Italian Executive Director at the International Monetary Fund, with responsibility for Greece, Portugal, San Marino, Albania and Timor Leste. He served as a member of the Board and chaired a number of Board Committees. During his mandate at the IMF he was also in charge of European Co-ordination. From 1998 to 2001, Mr. Padoan served as Economic Adviser to the Italian Prime Ministers, Massimo D'Alema and Giuliano Amato, in charge of international economic policies. He was responsible for co-ordinating the Italian position in the Agenda 2000 negotiations for the EU budget, Lisbon Agenda, European Council, bilateral meetings, and G8 Summits. He has been a consultant to the World Bank, European Commission, and European Central Bank. Mr. Padoan has a degree in Economics from the University of Rome and has held various academic positions in Italian and foreign universities, including at the University of Rome, College of Europe (Bruges and Warsaw), Université Libre de Bruxelles, University of Urbino, Universidad de la Plata, and University of Tokyo. He has published widely in international academic journals and is the author and editor of several books.

Richard Portes
London Business School
Richard Portes is Professor of Economics at London Business School (since 1995); President of the Centre for Economic Policy Research (which he founded in 1983); and Directeur d'Etudes at the Ecole des Hautes Etudes en Sciences Sociales in Paris (since 1978). He was a Rhodes Scholar and a Fellow of Balliol College, Oxford, and has also taught at Princeton, Harvard (as a Guggenheim Fellow), and Birkbeck College (University of London). In 1999-2000, he was the Distinguished Global Visiting Professor at the Haas Business School, University of California, Berkeley, and in 2003-04 he was Joel Stern Visiting Professor of International Finance at Columbia Business School. Professor Portes is a Fellow of the Econometric Society and a Fellow of the British Academy. He was Secretary-General of the Royal Economic Society 1992-2008. He is Co-Chairman of

the Board of Economic Policy. He is a member of the Group of Economic Policy Advisers to the President of the European Commission and of the Bellagio Group on the International Economy. He has written extensively on sovereign debt, European monetary and financial issues, international capital flows, centrally planned economies and transition, macroeconomic disequilibrium, and European integration. His work on collective action clauses in sovereign bond contracts, on the international role of the Euro, on international financial stability and on European bond markets has been directed towards policy as well as academic publications. Richard Portes was created CBE in the Queen's New Year Honours List 2003.

Saverio Simonelli
University of Naples

Saverio Simonelli is Assistant Professor of Economics at the University of Naples Federico II. He is also Research Fellow at CSEF, EABCN and Fellow at the European University Institute. He obtained his PhD from the University of Naples Federico II, and a Master in Economics from University Pompeu Fabra. His current research focuses on real business cycle, fiscal policy and short-term forecasting. Recently he has published in the Review of Economic Dynamics, Scandinavian Journal of Economics, and Journal of Economic Dynamics and Control.

Frank Smets
European Central Bank

Frank Smets is Director General of the Directorate General Research of the European Central Bank. He is professor of international economics at the Centre for Economic Studies at the KU Leuven and an honorary professor in the Duisenberg chair at the Faculty of Economics and Business of the University of Groningen. He is a Research Fellow of the Centre for Economic Policy Research in London and CESifo in Munich. He has written and published extensively on monetary, macroeconomic, financial and international issues mostly related to central banking in top academic journals such as the Journal of the European Economic Association, the American Economic Review and the Journal of Monetary Economics. He has been managing editor of the International Journal of Central Banking from

2008 till 2010. Before joining the European Central Bank in 1998, he was a research economist at the Bank for International Settlements in Basel, Switzerland. He holds a PhD in Economics from Yale University.

Paul van den Noord
Organisation for Economic Co-operation and Development (OECD)
Paul van den Noord, who is Dutch, is Counsellor to the Chief Economist in the Economics Department of the OECD since September 2010. He assists the Chief Economist in the Finance Ministers' track of the G-20 and represents the OECD in the Framework Working Group of the G-20. Between March 2007 and September 2010, he was seconded as adviser to the European Commission in Brussels. Prior to his secondment, Mr. Van den Noord has worked both in the Country Studies and Policy Studies Branches of the Economic Department of the OECD. In the Country Studies Branch, he has covered many OECD countries and, between 2000 and 2005, was Head of the European Union Desk. In the Policy Studies Branch he has been in charge of the assessment of fiscal policy and the General Assessment of the Macroeconomic Situation, the leading chapter of the semi-annual OECD Economic Outlook. Mr. Van den Noord has published extensively on fiscal policy, economic and monetary union and the political economy of structural reforms. He holds a PhD from the University of Amsterdam (Netherlands), where he was also a lecturer and research fellow before joining the OECD in 1989.

Guntram Wolff
Bruegel
Guntram Wolff is the Deputy Director of Bruegel. His research focuses on the Euro area economy and governance, on fiscal policy, global finance and Germany. He joined Bruegel from the European Commission, where he worked on the macroeconomics of the Euro area and the reform of Euro area governance. Prior to joining the Commission, he was an economist at the Deutsche Bundesbank, where he coordinated the research team on fiscal policy. He also worked as an adviser to the International Monetary Fund. He holds a PhD from the University of Bonn, studied economics in Bonn,

Toulouse, Pittsburgh and Passau and taught economics at the University of Pittsburgh. He has published numerous papers in leading academic journals. Guntram is fluent in German, English, French and has good notions of Bulgarian and Spanish. His columns and policy work are published and cited in leading international media such as the Financial Times, the New York Times, Wall Street Journal, El Pais, La Stampa, FAZ, Financial Times Deutschland, BBC, ZDF, WDR, Die Welt, CNBC and others.

Jacques Ziller
University of Pavia
Born in 1951, of French nationality, Professor of European Union Law at the University of Pavia, Faculty of Political Sciences. Studied at Paris II and Paris IV Universities as well as at the Paris Institute of Political Studies (Sciences Po.). Doctor's degree in law from Paris II University (Doctorat d'Etat en droit), post-graduate diplomas (Diplômes d'Etudes supérieures) in law and political science, the graduate diploma of the Paris Institute of Political Studies, as well as a graduate diploma (Licence ès lettres) in German language and literature. Has been teaching French public law and comparative public law, European community law and international law, as well as public administration as an assistant professor at Paris II University (1980-1985), as an associate professor at ESSEC Business School (Cergy-Pontoise, 1980-1985) and later as a professor at the University of French West-Indies and Guyana (Guadeloupe-FWI, 1989- 1991) and at Uni. Paris 1, Panthéon-Sorbonne (1992-2007 – on secondment from 1/09/1998 to 30/09/2007). Professor of Comparative Public Law at the European University Institute, Florence from September 1st 1998 until 2008. Head of the Law Department from 1 October 1999 to 31 October 2003. Specialized in research and training for senior civil servants in the fields of comparative public administration and management and also in the field of European affairs and regional integration when working as a lecturer and later an associate professor at the European Institute of Public Administration (IEAP/EIPA-Maastricht, The Netherlands, 1986-1989) and Director of research and publications at the International Institute of Public Administration (IIAP, Paris, France, 1992 -1995). Chief Editor of the Revue française d'Administration publique from Janu-

ary 1992 to September 1995. Visiting Professor at the College of Europe (Bruges, Belgium) from 1993 to 1998, and at the Universitat Autonoma (Barcelona, Spain) from 1994 to 1997. Consultant to OECD (Puma and Sigma programs). Consultant to the European Commission and to the Committee of the Regions of the European Union. He has been a member of the Scientific Advisory Board of the European Center for Development Policy Management (ECDPM -Maastricht); he has also been a member of the Program Committee of the International Association of Schools and Institutes or Administration (AIEIA/IASIA) and of the Steering Committee of the European Group of Public Administration (EGPA/GEAP) which he chaired in 1995-96. Member of the Scientific Council of the Institute for Research on Public Administration of the German School of Hochschule für Verwaltungswissenschaften Speyer) since May 2005. Member of the the Steering Committee of ELSNIT-Euro-Latin Study Network on Integration and Trade, of the advisory board of the Institut der Regionen Europas (IRE), Salzburg and of the Centro Interdipartimentale di Ricerca e di Formazione sul Diritto Pubblico Europeo e comparato (DIPEC), Siena.

Acknowledgments

As last year, we would like to thank all the people and institutions that have helped to make the conference and the book possible. Our special thanks go to Tina Horowitz, Christopher Trollen, Julia Valerio and the Presidential Office at the European University Institute. This book is produced as part of the project "Politics, Economics and Global Governance: The European Dimension" (PEGGED) funded by the European Commission under its Seventh Framework Programme for Research (Collaborative Project), Contract no. 217559. We would also like to thank the Wharton Financial Institutions Center for financial support.

FOREWORD

It is with great pleasure that I write the foreword to this e-book "Governance for the Eurozone: Integration or Disintegration?" – above all because it is the second publication in this series, following last year's "Life in the Eurozone: With or Without Default?".

In the foreword to last year's publication, I referred to the sovereign debt crisis and its implications as not only a severe economic problem, but also a major challenge to European society that has stark impacts on the broader European integration process. Furthermore, I put into question the claim that European political leaders have obtained a "successful grand bargain" and I hinted to the fact that numerous commentators have instead accused the decision-makers of only dangerously "muddling through" and "kicking the can down the road". Unfortunately, these accusations still hold true, and one year after the workshop "Life in the Eurozone: With or Without Default?", which was held at the European University Institute (EUI) in April 2011, we are still far from having found a substantial solution to the crisis.

The 2012 edition of the workshop and this e-book very appropriately raise the question "Governance for the Eurozone: Integration or Disintegration?" The survival of the Eurozone in its current form is as much at stake as it was a year ago and the publication of this e-book comes at a very timely moment. Once again, the individual chapters cover topics that dominate the political, economic and academic discussion in and on Europe and I think this e-book has the potential to make a significant contribution to the current debates – as much as last year's e-book did, which was a great success.

While many important changes in the economic governance of the Euro and regarding bail-out mechanisms have been made in the last two years (such as the European semester, the European Financial Stability Facility, the European Stability Mechanism, the Euro Plus Pact and lately the Fiscal pact), we still seem far away from reaching a proper and sustainable solution. The markets were not to be convinced, and while the heavy interventions of the European Central Bank were able to calm the markets for a short while, the crisis is now back in full force. And as much as the markets are not convinced, European citizens and politicians are increasingly uncertain about the benefits the common currency brings and about how far they are willing to reach for a proper design of the Eurozone that tackles the current crisis and prevents future crises. From an economic and political point of view, it seems clear to me that the only way out of this severe crisis is through proper economic governance with a proper fiscal union, but member states seem unable or unwilling to make the needed steps towards this direction.

This e-book describes how such steps and proper economic governance of the Eurozone and its institutions could look. In three sections, the individual chapters consider the role of public financial institutions in dealing with the crisis and discuss the possibilities and limits of fiscal policy support. Furthermore, the various authors reflect on the reform of the political and economic architecture and on the crucial question of how to reform the growth and stability pact and how to construct sound mechanisms for providing liquidity to governments and financial institutions. Finally, the contributions analyse how the European Union and the EU can coexist, whether Europe is developing towards a two-speed Europe and what the consequence of such a development would entail for the governance of the Eurozone. Overall, I think the chapters and their topics concentrate on some of the most crucial elements of the sovereign debt crisis, the future of the Euro and the Union.

At the time of writing this foreword, the future looks rather grim and the probability of "disintegration" seems to be growing. Unable to form a government after the Parliamentary elections in May, the Greeks are being called to the polling stations again and the prospects of a dramatic exit from the Eurozone are openly discussed. Although Germany and France have repeated - at the first meeting between the new President Hollande and Chancellor Merkel - their willingness to keep Greece in the Euro, words and affirmations are no longer enough and convincing action is needed. At the same time, the successive increases of the public deficit, the ever-growing banking crisis and the rising spreads in Spain, make it increasingly probable that a European intervention will be required to at least recapitalise parts of the Spanish banking system. These events and other problematic on-going developments make it very difficult to imagine what the situation will be when this e-book is published. However, this publication will certainly provide a very important intellectual contribution to the problems we are facing and to the analysis of the crisis' implications and the different ways out of the Eurozone crisis.

To conclude, I would like to thank and congratulate the editors of this e-book. The workshop that Professors Elena Carletti, Franklin Allen and Saverio Simonelli organised, and on which this e-book is based, was a huge success in several regards and I can speak for all participants when I say that it was a pleasure to attend this event. The workshop, which was held in the framework of the PEGGED project (Politics, Economics and Global Governance: The European Dimensions) and which was co-organised with the Wharton Financial Institutions Center, brought together leading academics from various disciplines and policymakers and I am very satisfied that the workshop's presentations and results are being published in this e-book.

Finally, as much as I hope the sovereign debt crisis in the Eurozone will be contained soon, I think the tradition of this workshop should be continued to annually discuss the state and the challenges of the Eurozone. The EUI is certainly the right place to hold such an event. The Institute was created to study the problems of European societies and the construction of Europe at the highest intellectual level.

And without any doubt, the current Eurozone crisis is one of the biggest problems that Europe and its societies are facing today. This means that these past and future workshops contribute to one of the EUI's core missions by being an excellent example for the European focus of the Institute's research activities.

May 2012

Josep Borrell Fontelles

President of the European University Institute

PREFACE

The European University Institute (EUI) and the Wharton Financial Institutions Center (FIC) organized a conference entitled "Governance for the Eurozone: Integration or Disintegration?" The event, which was held at the EUI in Florence, Italy, on 26 April 2012, was financed by the PEGGED project (Politics, Economics and Global Governance: The European Dimension). The conference brought together leading economists, lawyers, political scientists and policymakers to discuss the current situation in the Eurozone with particular emphasis on its governance. The goal was to have an open and multidisciplinary discussion on this important topic to understand better where the Eurozone is going and what is needed to preserve it.

The President of the European University Institute, Josep Borrell Fontelles, opened the event, which consisted of three panels, a keynote speech and a dinner speech.

The first panel considered the role of public financial institutions. Antonio Borges (Catolica-Lisbon School of Business and Economics) discussed the various responses of the European Central Bank (ECB) and the International Monetary Fund (IMF) in dealing with the European sovereign debt crisis; and the structure of the European Financial Stability Facility (EFSF) and the European Financial Stability Mechanism (EFSM). Paul De Grauwe (London School of Economics) discussed the role of the European Central Bank (ECB) during the crisis, and argued in favor of the ECB acting as the lender of last resort also in the government bond market. Friedrich Kübler (Johann-Wolfgang-Goethe University & University of Pennsylvania) discussed different scenarios of integration/disintegration for the Eurozone, stressing the responsibility of the public institutions designed to provide additional financial support for needy Euro Member States. Frank Smets (European Central Bank) focused on the role of the ECB as market maker of last resort to alleviate the risk that funding problems translate into a deep credit crunch and a systemic collapse.

In the keynote address, Richard Portes (London Business School) focused on the choice of the international reserve currency in the international monetary system. He stressed that markets normally choose the dominant currency, except for the Bretton Woods exchange-rate system in the period 1944-1971, and had to adjust to the creation of the Euro as a major new international currency. The role of the Euro may change now in light of the recent crisis and following the emergence of China with its currency RMB as a powerful nation.

The second panel discussed the reform of the political and economic architecture. Leszek Balcerowicz (Warsaw School of Economics) pointed out the importance of structural reforms to manage and prevent the Euro crisis. Russell Cooper (EUI) analyzed the exit from a monetary union as a punishment for an unsuccessful reform and thus as incentive mechanism for the reform to be implemented. Pietro Carlo Padoan (OECD) discussed the contribution of structural reforms to solving the Euro area crisis together with the need to progress in fiscal consolidation. Jacques Ziller (University of Pavia) presented a legal perspective on the most recent reforms of the Eurozone architecture.

The third panel analyzed whether the Eurozone is diverging into two groups and the potential consequence of a two tier Europe for the governance of the Eurozone. Bruno De Witte (Maastricht University) focused on the function of treaties as an attempt of the EU institutions and governments to deal with the sovereign debt crisis during the past two years. Charles Goodhart (London School of Economics) discussed the role of the UK under three possible scenarios for the future of the Eurozone: (i) more political, fiscal and financial centralisation; (ii) Eurozone break-up; (iii) Eurozone and the EU collapse. Brigid Laffan (University College Dublin) discussed the implications of the policy responses to the Euro crisis for the dynamics of European integration. Guntram Wolff (Bruegel) pointed out that solving the Euro area crisis would require more integration steps, in particular in the financial and banking field.

At dinner, Wolfgang Münchau (Eurointelligence) presented his view on the German approach of fighting the crisis through a combination of fiscal discipline and structural reforms. He suggested that this approach is flawed because it does not take into account the interaction between austerity and growth. He argued that the likely success of Francois Hollande will change the crisis "narratives," in that eurobonds or bank resolution regimes, for example, may no longer be a taboo subject.

The book ends with a postscript entitled "Europe's Tragedy Nears the End of Act One, but the Drama Continues," written by Janet Kersnar as an article for Knowledge@Wharton. This summarizes the various views expressed at the conference.

The book contains also an appendix including a piece written by Victor Ngai (University of Pennsylvania) on the history of the Stability and Growth Pact and the conference program.

The conference follows last year's event entitled "Life in the Eurozone With or Without Sovereign Default?" As on the previous occasion, the debate at the conference was very lively and many different views on the need of further reforms were presented. Again, we prefer not to take a stance but rather present all of them in this book and let the readers draw their own conclusions.

A color e-book is available for free download at the following links:
http://www.eui.eu/Personal/Carletti/
http://www.eui.eu/DepartmentsAndCentres/Economics/SeminarsEvents/Conferences/GovernancefortheEurozoneIntegrationorDisintegration.aspx
http://finance.wharton.upenn.edu/FIC/FICPress/goveuro.pdf

Last year's e-book is available for free download at the following links:
http://www.eui.eu/Personal/Carletti/
http://www.eui.eu/DepartmentsAndCentres/Economics/ResearchTeaching/Conferences/Lifeinthe Eurozone/Index.aspx
http://finance.wharton.upenn.edu/FIC/FICPress/eurozone.pdf

Franklin Allen, Elena Carletti and Saverio Simonelli

1
The Role of Public Financial Institutions

Antonio Borges

1. Foundations of Monetary Union

When the project of European monetary union was conceived and agreed to, there was little dissent with respect to its model: Europeans agreed to the German approach to monetary and financial stability. We were all going to behave like the Germans, adopt price stability as a fundamental pillar of prosperity and put in place a central bank that would be single-mindedly focused on that goal. For this purpose, the central bank had to be fully independent from politicians, have a clear cut mandate with only one objective in mind and never engage in monetary financing of governments, let alone bail out any country.

It is most likely that, in the absence of agreement along these lines, the Germans would not have considered abandoning their beloved Deutschmark. But that was not the real issue: Europeans – or at least those who opted to join – were fully convinced of the merits of the German model of monetary policy, and embraced it without hesitation. And indeed it is a fact that the countries of the Eurozone started behaving more like the Germans, in the sense that they eliminated their propensity to let inflation flare up, and quickly converged on the German definition of price stability across the Eurozone.

Apart from the focus on price stability, this model was extremely specific about the separation between fiscal and monetary policy: governments would never be allowed to use central bank funding – monetary financing – irrespective of any crisis or emergencies they might face; furthermore, anything that might look like a bailout of a government by the monetary authorities was specifically ruled out, in a form that could be enforced by the courts.

The model also included a strict definition of the modus operandi of the central bank: funding to the banks within the union had to be based on sound collateral; banks should not be too dependent on the central bank for their funding needs; and any excessive growth of monetary aggregates should be a source of concern, to be fought with all the weapons of the central monetary authority.

Today, these conditions might be considered too rigid. There are many appeals to change the mandate of the European Central Bank, many demands that these restrictions be relaxed. Under the current emergency, many find it hard to believe that the central bank has to limit its action because of some rules devised at a time when no emergency existed or was foreseen. Furthermore, many well-known and highly reputed economists defend the view that Europe, and especially Germany, should accept a relatively high rate of inflation, as the simplest way to sort out the Eurozone crisis. This is, of course, in complete contradiction with the whole spirit under which monetary union was created and is certainly contrary to Germany's tradition of price stability as a fundamental pillar of prosperity.

This is a more serious problem than most commentators tend to admit. First, the single-minded focus on price stability is enshrined in the Maastricht Treaty, which was ratified by all member states and cannot be overlooked. Not only a deviation from the Treaty may be challenged in the courts, but, more importantly, the political legitimacy of such a break would be seriously questioned. It is not difficult to argue that the various countries agreed to a project of monetary union which was well defined and subject to political ratification; a material change in the rules of the game would be a rather dramatic violation of democratic principles.

Secondly, this is not simply a matter of disagreement among economists. In Germany – and to a certain extent in other neighboring countries - the principles of monetary stability, fiscal rectitude and robust financial policies are regarded as absolutely fundamental. Given their post-war experience, the Germans consider that their economic and financial success is due to the adherence to those principles and will not easily tolerate substantial deviations from them. Therefore, a change of policy, away from the principles enshrined in the Treaty, is not something that the German political leadership can accommodate as a matter of expediency. They would most likely face a real backlash from German public opinion. In this sense, it is fair to predict that the project of monetary union – however important for Germany – may very well not survive a demand for a change in the mandate of the European Central Bank.

2. The Need for Coherent Policies

The current crisis brings to broad daylight the consequences of incoherent economic policies across the Eurozone. From the beginning, it was clear that monetary union required some degree of restraint on the part of the member states, because of serious externalities in the conduct of their economic policies. But this restraint was initially limited to fiscal discipline. The stability and growth pact was designed to prevent what was perceived as free-riding temptation: the incentive to adopt lax fiscal policies because the cost would be diluted across the union, since interest rates would not rise nearly as much as if monetary policy remained a domestic affair.

What the current crisis showed is that the externalities went far beyond what was initially expected. Since the framework did not allow for any kind of bailout of countries with financial difficulties, governments were expected to adopt responsible fiscal policies. But not enough attention was paid to other perverse effects of inconsistent policies, beyond fiscal recklessness. In fact, without bailouts, debt sustainability was bound to become a central concern, simply because, if a government ever became insolvent, it might have no option but to leave the union and return to its own currency. Debt sustainability is not only a question of fiscal deficits, but also of interest rates and growth rates. This became only too apparent went the Greek crisis exploded in early 2010, proving that doubts about debt sustainability called into question the integrity of the Eurozone.

The first decade of monetary union went too well. Monetary integration proceeded at a fast pace, credit began flowing in larger and larger amounts across borders, interest rates converged almost perfectly and it seemed that the Eurozone had become like the United States of America: monetary conditions were pretty much the same, credit went to where it was in demand, exchange rate risk was eliminated, and the future looked very bright.

With large credit inflows, some countries on the periphery of the Eurozone seemed to be booming. Access to very cheap credit led to a spectacular increase in spending, both private and public. The most important consequence of this was a dramatic reduction in savings rates. These countries – Greece, Portugal, Spain and even Ireland – moved towards large current account deficits, funded through credit inflows, and reflecting a level of domestic demand far in excess of GDP. For a while, this looked like a new phase of prosperity, entirely justified by the need to catch up, relative to other members of the Eurozone. There were even some positive elements to this process: Spain had budget surpluses for quite a few years, Greece had significant productivity increases, and Ireland kept expanding its export base. But the negative components became dominant: most of the growth in spending benefited essentially the non-tradable sector, whose prices kept rising steadily, relative to tradables. This is exactly equivalent to real exchange rate appreciation and made these countries less and less competitive. Their current account deficits became not just a matter of excessive spending, but a more structural and permanent reality.

In Ireland and Spain, the wave of excessive credit and spending turned into a massive real estate bubble, with huge implications for their banking sectors. In Portugal and Greece, where the real estate problem was far less severe, the excessive level of indebtedness, coupled with a bloated non-tradable sector, also put the banks in a vulnerable position. As a result, when the process finally came to an end – that is, when credit stopped flowing to these countries, as the financial world realized that after all they were not as financially sound as Germany – it became clear that the situation was unsustainable. Saddled with too much foreign debt, having lost competitiveness and now facing a deadly serious banking situation, these countries became very problematic, because the sustainability of their public debt was no longer convincing. The particular situation of each country was not exactly the same; but all of them found it very difficult to attract investor interest, because the structural problems that had developed raised very serious questions about growth prospects, which made it impossible to convince investors that they would ever be able to pay back.

Thus, the real cause of the Eurozone crisis became not so much an issue of fiscal profligacy, but rather a much more serious issue of competitiveness and growth. Fiscal deficits can be cut rather quickly; restoring growth is much more difficult if the obstacles to growth are structural, that is, are caused by a misallocation of resources, with excessive growth in the non-tradable sector, an overvalued real exchange rate and a very fragile situation in the banking sector.

As investors became more and more aware of the dimension of the problem and of its long term implications, policymakers also realized that the challenge they faced was huge. Adjustment programs, funded by the European countries and the IMF became inevitable; but those programs could not simply adopt the typical IMF recipe of restoring fiscal discipline and regaining competitiveness through devaluation. Under fixed exchange rates, rebalancing the economy by transferring resources from non-tradables to tradables was much more difficult to do. Serious resistance from all those vested interests which had benefited from the previous policy was going to prove quite strong, and the financial sector was not in a position to finance in attractive conditions the investments necessary to restore the tradable sector back to a healthier and more competitive situation.

Policymakers realized that monetary union required much more than fiscal discipline. It became clear that systematic losses of competitiveness, massive foreign borrowing to finance consumer spending and real estate investment, and illusory growth based on non-tradables were all elements of an incoherent policy stance, which created very deeply entrenched obstacles to growth, justified serious doubts about debt sustainability and spooked investors who moved away from these countries. It dawned on all of them that monetary union would only be sustainable if policies were brought back in line, not only in fiscal terms, but also in regard to what concerned competitiveness, openness and potential growth.

3. Financial Support and Policy Conditionality

To avoid catastrophic outcomes that would put monetary union at risk, financial support became crucial. Taking Greece, Ireland and Portugal out of the markets, in order to provide them with the breathing space necessary to put their economies back on track, was inevitable. But the programs had, above all, to restore credibility; in other words, it was fundamental that investors recovered their confidence in the prospects of these countries, so that they would be ready to finance them again, when the programs were over.

Financial support may be needed even when the policies a country is following are not out of line in terms of long term debt sustainability. If an acute crisis of confidence raises fears about the prospects of a particular country, investors will demand a premium to hold that country's debt. If the premium is high enough, that may be sufficient to make the situation unsustainable. In other words, even a country where debt would normally be sustainable may find itself in a situation of insolvency, because a decline in investor confidence may make its debt too expensive. This is what is called a bad equilibrium, generated by a kind of self-fulfilling prophecy: if markets think debt is unsustainable, then debt will become unsustainable, irrespective of what would otherwise be relatively benign conditions in terms of the fiscal situation.

Thus, financial assistance has to restore confidence in the prospects of a country to regain debt sustainability, which most of the time requires confidence that economic growth will return. And therefore, the policy conditionality associated with assistance programs has to emphasize structural reforms and financial strengthening, in order to create the conditions to make growth possible. Much of the debate about the success or failure of these adjustment programs reflects controversy around the issue of growth. Since there is a need for fiscal consolidation, given the inability to keep on borrowing in the markets, many economists believe that these programs will only generate economic decline. But the fundamental goal of the programs has to be economic recovery, so that debt can be paid back and investors come back to the market for these countries' debt.

The last two years show that an obsessive focus on fiscal accounts is clearly not sufficient. The authorities have sometimes put too much emphasis on the immediate achievement of the standards of the Stability and Growth Pact, in particular through front loaded corrections of budget imbalances. Restoring the credibility of public finances is a requirement to recover investor confidence; but it is not sufficient. If there are no prospects for economic growth, debt will most likely never be sustainable again. And the programs fail in their ultimate goal of restoring credibility. Since growth requires the removal of deeply entrenched obstacles to growth, their nature has to be quite different from previous programs of adjustment, and their political component also becomes far more decisive.

This situation also creates a difficult dilemma: if the right policies are not adopted, the programs will fail. If there is a perception that programs fail, then financial assistance makes no sense. Not only will political opposition increase – both from taxpayers in Europe, but also at the IMF – but also countries at risk may resist asking for a program. This is now the case in Spain and Italy, where any kind of assistance from outside is seen as counterproductive because it is perceived as a step down a path of no return, with limited or no impact on market credibility.

4. Cooperation Between EFSF, ESM and IMF

The adjustment programs negotiated with the so-called Troika – the European Commission, the European Central Bank and the IMF – require a convergence of approaches and an understanding of the role of each of these institutions, which is hard to put in place. The three institutions have different perspectives and priorities: the European Commission attaches enormous priority to the fiscal adjustment process, with a focus on the Maastricht criteria; it prefers frontloaded adjustment and monitors closely budget execution, on the assumption that, if the fiscal problem is solved, everything else will fall in place. The European Central Bank also insists on frontloaded fiscal adjustment but adds to it a concern with the health of the banking sector. Beyond fiscal austerity, the ECB typically requires substantial deleveraging of the banking system, higher capital ratios and no losses imposed on holders of bank debt. The IMF is traditionally less focused on speedy fiscal consolidation and puts more emphasis on structural policies, designed to restore economic growth; but, given the Fund's previous focus on more straightforward stabilization programs, its experience in the area of structural reforms in advanced economies is rather limited.

Where the IMF plays a crucial role, which actually makes it indispensable, is in the credibility it has acquired over decades with respect to its ability to negotiate with the countries involved, and also to monitor rigorously the execution of the programs, their funding requirements and their impact on debt sustainability. European governments have repeatedly toyed with the idea that they could run the whole process themselves, relying only on the Commission and the ECB. But this has proven politically impossible. All governments have found that their tax-payers have serious doubts about the approach of throwing more money at the countries in trouble; and so, even the most hard line of them have realized that the support of the IMF had become crucial, not because of the amounts of money the Fund could contribute – which were always going to be small, relative to the total – but because they could convince their tax-payers that the money was going to be well spent, thanks to the kind of conditionality which the Fund could impose better than anyone else.

As the Greek program unfolded and began running into problems – during roughly the first half of 2011 – the position of the IMF became more and more uncomfortable. Since the program was not being properly executed, the whole credibility effect was losing its value, with considerable implications for the rest of the IMF's activity. But many throughout Europe were not prepared to accept the natural consequence of these developments, which was that the program should be terminated and no further disbursements should be authorized. Greek politicians skillfully exploited this divergence, by always promising to correct their slippage in program execution; and, with the financing guarantees provided by the European governments, it was possible to keep the program running and to maintain the myth that Greek debt was sustainable.

Another very difficult area for cooperation within the Troika related to debt restructuring. Based on their long experience with less developed economies, many at the IMF started early in 2011 proposing some kind of debt restructuring, certainly for Greece, perhaps also for Ireland and Portugal. This was strongly resisted by the European Commission and the ECB, who feared that the precedent would prove devastating for the cohesion of the Eurozone. The ECB, in particular, always argued that debt restructuring would place the countries in default, which prevented the Central Bank from continuing lending to banks in those countries and lead to a collapse of their banking sectors. As these discussions went on, the Greek Government obviously followed them with great interest, which led it to put much less emphasis on program execution.

The debate around debt restructuring eventually led to the concept of Private Sector Involvement, or PSI, which was essentially politically driven. Many countries, starting with but not limited to Germany, found it impossible to admit to their tax-payers that they were pouring money into Greece only to see private sector investors bailed out. Given that the program was proving to be less likely to succeed, it looked like the only benefit from foreign assistance was captured by private sector investors. Keeping them involved became a political necessity, so much so that the European Commission and especially the ECB, had to swallow their reservations and accept the idea, although dressing it up under the pretense of a voluntary negotiation, which was to have only a minor and temporary impact on ratings.

Over time, the PSI project became closer and closer to full blown debt restructuring. But, all things considered, it actually has only a very limited impact on Greek debt sustainability. It provides some liquidity relief, since the cash payments to investors were substantially delayed. But debt sustainability still depends crucially on the ability to get some degree of economic growth in Greece. Without it, the losses imposed on private investors will be only a down-payment for what is to come.

As everyone became more and more worried about the absence of progress in the Greek program, and as fears began spreading to Italy, the position of the IMF also changed and the differences of opinion with the European authorities became more pronounced. The Fund began putting more emphasis on decisive action to put an end to the catastrophic risk of a Eurozone collapse. In this new approach, the Fund began defending a change in the stance of the ECB, a more generalized adoption of debt restructuring and the creation of a huge firewall, designed to scare markets and restore a good equilibrium. This was bound to create tensions with the European authorities, or with those within Europe who had fundamental reservations about this plan. The level of tension increased steadily, leading the Fund to adopt a more reserved position with respect to support for the Eurozone. In the second Greek program, the Fund reduced its level of financial commitment to a minimum, in a gesture that many interpreted as an indication that the Fund was not happy to see its positions rejected.

In the end, the European authorities moved partially in the direction of what the Fund wanted. The ECB adopted a policy of large scale liquidity injections into the European banking system, designed to facilitate the purchase of sovereign debt by European banks, while also trying to eliminate liquidity risks across the European economy. The European governments agreed to provide additional funding to the IMF, to help shore up the financial resources required by a firewall. But the adoption of more radical measures – such as changing the EFSF or the ESM so that they could lend to banks, or asking the ECB to impose a ceiling on the yields of Italian debt – were firmly resisted.

Apart from the issue of fundamental differences of views on the model of monetary union, as described above, there is also a technical reason for the European resistance to the concept of a huge fire-wall. The European experience of 1992, at the time of the great currency crisis which almost destroyed the European Monetary System, shows that markets will always beat the authorities, if the issue is who can mobilize more money. The attempt to win a battle on a position which the market believes is untenable simply by displaying a large war chest will usually fail. The resources the authorities can mobilize for a firewall, no matter how large, will always be limited. And there is general consensus that they will never be sufficient to take Italy or Spain out of the markets. Therefore, if the issue becomes whether the firewall is large enough to deter the markets, the answer will always be negative, since markets can mobilize for all practical purposes an unlimited amount of funds. In other words, in the case of Italy and Spain, either the credibility battle is won, or a firewall, no matter how large, will never solve the problem. In fact, it can be argued that a large firewall is actually destabilizing, because it only makes the bet larger – this is exactly how George Soros and others looked at the UK defense of the Pound Sterling in the fall of 1992.

Of course, the proponents of a large firewall will always argue that it can be made all powerful if it is financed by the ECB. But this would require quite a change in the role and mandate of the ECB, which, as argued above, is not very likely.

5. The Limited Role of the ECB

The fact that the ECB has substantial constraints in its action does not mean that it has no possible contribution to helping to solve the Eurozone crisis. The Central Bank has been experimenting with several types of initiatives, with mixed results. A certain consensus seems to be emerging, even though this is a rather controversial area.

The key concern relates to the fact that every type of intervention has to have a certain degree of policy conditionality. Every expression of support must be based on the conviction that the country in question is moving in the right direction. And if that movement is not serious, whatever support is provided must be stopped. This is a simple principle, but very difficult to enforce by the ECB.

First, the very fact that the ECB has unlimited weaponry reduces the credibility of conditionality. The IMF may say that, if programs are not executed, the Fund must interrupt them, because otherwise it risks very large losses, since its money is at stake and a failed program makes repayment very unlikely. In the case of the ECB, it is easy to argue that, if the program is not working well, more money from the Central Bank will always allow the country to gain time and provide it with the means to overcome short term difficulties and get back on track. Since the ECB, unlike the IMF, can create unlimited amounts of money, it is easy to give credence to this argument, which obviously undermines the whole idea of conditionality.

Put more simply, when the ECB was intervening in Italian debt markets in the fall of 2011, Silvio Berlusconi could always argue that a little more money from the ECB would be enough to deal with market pressures; and if the ECB had accepted the argument, Berlusconi would still be Prime Minister of Italy, independently of the policies he would or would not put in place.

A second problem has to do with the kind of intervention the ECB can conduct and the way it is influenced by the attempt to impose conditionality. The same episode of intervention in Italian debt markets illustrates this point. The ECB was trying to limit the yields in Italian sovereign bonds, restore confidence, and bring investors back into the market. As the discussions with the Italian government became more and more difficult, the ECB found it necessary to condition its purchases of Italian bonds on the willingness of the Government to adopt the right policies. Given the Italian hesitations and frequent reversals of agreed policies, the ECB found itself in the uncomfortable position of intervening intermittently in the market. This created huge uncertainty and very high volatility, in fact scaring investors away, instead of bringing them back to the market. The ECB must have found this episode extremely frustrating.

This does not mean that there are no circumstances under which ECB intervention would be helpful and stabilizing. The Securities Market Program remains in the armory of the ECB and can and should have a role in stabilizing monetary conditions across the

Eurozone. There are occasions when erratic events or acute crises lead to very destabilizing effects in the markets for government bonds. It is quite appropriate that the SMP be used to control those situations and provide a degree of stability that leads investors to consider the markets for government bonds as stable, mature and reliable, something of enormous importance in every economy. But keeping this kind of intervention separate and distinct from a bail-out or a form of monetary financing is not always simple. The stabilizing role of the ECB in moments of crisis depends very much on its ability to work around this dilemma.

6. Financial Regulation, Incomplete Monetary Union and the Prisoner's Dilemma

Two more issues deserve a great deal of attention, when discussing the role of financial institutions in the unfolding of the Eurozone crisis. One is the fact that monetary union is still a work in progress across Europe. The other one deals with the incongruence of trying to put in place monetary union and maintaining a nationally regulated banking sector.

When compared with a proper monetary union, as in the case of the United States of America, the European project shows how incomplete it is. In Europe, the only form of capital that flows freely across borders is credit. Monetary integration has led to very large – even excessive – flows of credit across borders, but other forms of capital are not so easy to invest in other countries. This is particularly the case with equity, when it involves changes of control. In reality, in spite of monetary union and of several decades of freedom of capital flows, many European countries still resist the idea that foreign capital can buy their assets and can gain control of their large corporations. This is especially acute in the case of banks.

The main consequence of this restriction, which is essentially political, is that one of the most important mechanisms of self-correction of problems within the union is eliminated. In a proper monetary union, if, because of reckless policies in certain parts of the union, resulting in high levels of indebtedness, assets are discounted, then investors from other parts of the union will quickly step in and take advantage of the arbitrage opportunities to grab those assets. This allows conversion of debt into equity, with considerable mitigation of the excessive indebtedness problem. If cross-border mergers and acquisitions are not allowed, monetary union will be unbalanced, because credit flows cannot be compensated by equity flows when necessary. As long as corporate control remains protected and change of control is not allowed or seriously discouraged, excessive credit flows will be more destabilizing than otherwise.

A similar, but even more serious argument can be made with respect to the imprudence of trying to run monetary union without a central approach to banking regulation. As banking systems remain regulated at the national level, with resolution schemes and financial backstops also national, whenever a large scale banking problem emerges, monetary union becomes very unstable. This was evidently the problem in Ireland, but potentially could still happen in many other countries in the Eurozone. First, banks are typically very substantial investors in sovereign debt, so they become the first victims of any impairments related to the credibility of sovereign debt. But if in trouble, they can only turn to their own government for support. This creates the infamous vicious circle of excessive sovereign debt, which leads to solvency problems in the banking system, which in turn drives the public sector further into bankruptcy.

Furthermore, when these developments take place, monetary union tends to unravel. Regulators will insist that the banks they are responsible for must abandon exposure to the countries in difficulty, which only makes the problems of these countries worse. As the crisis advances, banking systems become more and more focused on domestic markets, and monetary conditions diverge more and more across Europe.

This then develops into a typical prisoner's dilemma. Under uncertain conditions for sovereign debt sustainability and bank solvency, every national regulator and every large bank will only think of solving its own problem. In the process they generate a final outcome which is a collective disaster. Only a cooperative solution creates the conditions to overcome the dilemma, and yet European institutions – national regulators – as well as the Commission, the ECB, and even the IMF will not be prepared to lead such a cooperative process, because it is outside of their traditional mandate.

The problem of retrenchment on the part of European banks, as a reaction to the inability of the European authorities and the IMF to find a solution to this prisoner's dilemma, is one of the biggest obstacles to economic recovery in Europe, since credit is not flowing and monetary conditions are extremely onerous in the countries which most need more relaxed access to credit. And yet, no solution seems to be in sight or is even being studied.

2
The European Central Bank: Lender of Last Resort in the Government Bond Markets?*

Paul De Grauwe

Introduction

In October 2008, the ECB discovered that there is more to central banking than price stability. This discovery occurred when the ECB was forced to massively increase liquidity to save the banking system. The ECB did not hesitate to exert its function of lender of last resort to the banking system, setting aside all fears of moral hazard and inflation, and concerns about the fiscal implications of its lending.

Things were very different when the sovereign debt crisis erupted in 2010. Then the ECB was gripped by hesitation. A stop-and-go policy ensued in which it provided liquidity in the government bond markets at some moments only to withdraw it at other times. When the crisis hit Spain and Italy in July 2011, the ECB was compelled again to provide liquidity in the government bond markets.

Is there a role for the ECB as a lender of last resort in the government bond market? This is the question I want to analyze in this paper.

* Paper prepared for the conference "Governance for the Eurozone. Integration or Disintegration?" organized at the European University Institute, 26 April, 2012.
I am grateful for the many comments formulated by the participants at the conference, and more particularly by Frank Smets.

Fragility of a monetary union

It is useful to start by describing the weakness of government bond markets in a monetary union. National governments in a monetary union issue debt in a "foreign" currency, i.e., one over which they have no control. As a result, they cannot guarantee to the bondholders that they will always have the necessary liquidity to pay out the bond at maturity. This contrasts with "stand-alone" countries that issue sovereign bonds in their own currencies. This feature allows these countries to guarantee that the cash will always be available to pay out the bondholders. Thus, in a stand-alone country there is an implicit guarantee that the central bank is a lender of last resort in the government bond market.

The absence of such a guarantee makes the sovereign bond markets in a monetary union prone to liquidity crises and forces of contagion, very much like banking systems that lack a lender of last resort. In such banking systems, solvency problems in one bank may lead deposit holders of other banks to withdraw their deposits. When everybody does this at the same time, the banks will not have enough cash. This sets in motion a liquidity crisis in many sound banks, and degenerates into a solvency crisis as banks try to cash in their assets, thereby pulling down their prices. As asset prices collapse, many banks find out that they are insolvent. This banking system instability was solved by mandating the central bank to be a lender of last resort – and the neat thing about this solution is that, when deposit holders are confident that it exists, it rarely has to be used.

The government bond markets in a monetary union have the same structure as the banking system. When solvency problems arise in one country (Greece), bondholders, fearing the worst, sell bonds in other bond markets. This triggers a liquidity crisis in these other markets, only because there is a fear that cash may not be available to pay out to bondholders. But this selling activity leads to an increase in government bond rates and turns the liquidity crisis into a solvency crisis. There is an interest rate high enough that will make any country insolvent. The characteristic feature of these dynamics is that distrust can push a country in a self-fulfilling way into a bad equilibrium.[1] The latter is characterized by high interest rates, recessionary forces, increasing budgetary problems, and an increased probability of insolvency. In a bad equilibrium, it is also likely that domestic banks will experience funding problems that can degenerate into solvency problems.

The single most important argument for mandating the ECB to be a lender of last resort in the government bond markets is to prevent countries from being pushed into a bad equilibrium. In a way, it can be said that the self-fulfilling nature of expectations creates a coordination failure, i.e., the fear of insufficient liquidity pushes countries into a situation in which there will be insufficient liquidity for both the government and the banking sector. The central bank can solve this coordination failure by providing lending of last resort.

Failure to provide lending of last resort in the government bond markets of the monetary union carries the risk of forcing the central bank into providing lending of last resort to the banks of the countries hit by a sovereign debt crisis. In fact, this happened in December 2011 and February 2012 when the ECB was forced to pour a total of one trillion Euros into the banking system that had become infected by the sovereign debt crises. And this lending of last resort is almost certainly more expensive. The reason is that most often the liabilities of the banking sector of a country are many times larger than the liabilities of the national government. This is shown in Figure 1. We observe that the bank liabilities in the Eurozone represented about 250% of GDP in 2008. This compares to a government debt to GDP ratio in the Eurozone of approximately 80% in the same year.

---

1 See De Grauwe (2011) where this point is elaborated further. See also Kopf (2011). For formal theoretical models see Calvo (1988) and Gros (2011). This problem also exists with emerging countries that issue debt in a foreign currency. See Eichengreen, et al. (2005). The problem is also similar to self-fulfilling foreign exchange crises (Obstfeld(1994)).

Figure 1: Bank liabilities as percent GDP (2008)

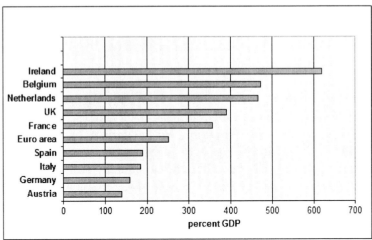

Source: IMF, Global Financial Stability Report 2008

While the argument for mandating the ECB to be a lender of last resort in the government bond markets is a strong one, the opposition to giving the ECB this mandate is equally intense. Let me review the main arguments that have been formulated against giving a lender of last resort role to the ECB.

Risk of inflation

A popular argument against an active role of the ECB as a lender of last resort in the sovereign bond market is that this would lead to inflation. By buying government bonds, it is said, the ECB increases the money stock thereby leading to a risk of inflation. Does an increase in the money stock not always lead to more inflation as Milton Friedman taught us? Two points should be made here.

First, a distinction should be introduced between the money base and the money stock. When the central bank buys government bonds (or other assets), it increases the money base (currency in circulation and banks' deposits at the central bank). This does not mean that the money stock increases. In fact, during periods of financial crises, both monetary aggregates tend to become disconnected. An example of this is shown in Figure 2. One observes that, prior to the banking crisis of October 2008, both aggregates were very much connected. From October 2008 on, however, the disconnect became quite spectacular. In order to save the banking system, the ECB massively piled up assets on its balance sheets, the counterpart of which was a very large increase in the money base. This had no effect on the money stock (M3) (see Figure 2). In fact, the latter declined until the end of 2009. The reason why this happened is that banks piled up the liquidity provided by the ECB without using it to extend credit to the non-banking sector. A similar phenomenon has been observed in the US and the UK.

Another way to understand this phenomenon is to note that when a financial crisis erupts, agents want to hold cash for safety reasons. If the central bank decides not to supply the cash, it turns the financial crisis into an economic recession and possibly a depression, as agents sell assets in their scramble for cash. When instead the central bank exerts its function of lender of last resort and supplies more money base, it stops this deflationary process. That does not allow us to conclude that the central bank is likely to create inflation.

All this was very well understood by Milton Friedman, the father of monetarism, who cannot be suspected of favoring inflationary policies. In his classic book co-authored with Anna Schwartz, A Monetary History of the United States, he argued that the Great Depression was so intense because the Federal Reserve failed to perform its role of lender of last resort, and did not increase the US money base sufficiently (see Friedman and Schwartz (1961). In fact, on page 333, Friedman and Schwartz produce a figure that is very similar to Figure 2, showing how, during the period 1929-33, the US money stock declined, while the money base ("high powered money") increased. Friedman and Schwartz argued forcefully that the money base should have increased much more and that the way to achieve this was by buying government securities. Much to the chagrin of Friedman and Schwartz, the Federal Reserve failed to do so. Those who today fear the inflationary risks of lender of last resort operations should do well to read Friedman and Schwartz (1961).

This unfounded fear of inflationary consequences of lender of last resort activity continues to affect policymaking. For example, when the ECB recently decided to start buying Spanish and Italian government bonds, it announced that it would sterilize the effect these purchases have on the money base by withdrawing liquidity from the market. This was an unfortunate decision. There was absolutely no need to do so. Since the start of the banking crisis in October 2008, the yearly growth rate of M3 in the Eurozone has only been 1%, much below the growth rate of 4.5% the ECB has previously announced would stabilize the rate of inflation at 2%. If Friedman were alive today, chances are that he would berate the ECB for making the same mistakes as the US Fed during the Great Depression.

Figure 2: Money Base and M3 in Eurozone (2007=100)

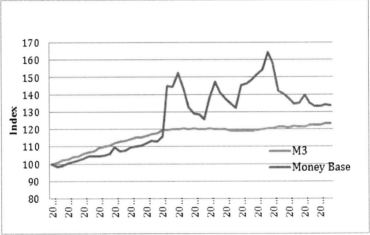

Source: ECB, Statistical Data Warehouse

Fiscal consequences

A second criticism is that lender of last resort operations in the government bond markets can have fiscal consequences. The reason is that if governments fail to service their debts, the ECB will make losses. These will have to be borne by taxpayers. Thus, by intervening in the government bond markets, the ECB is committing future taxpayers. The ECB should avoid operations that mix monetary and fiscal policies (see Goodfriend (2011)).

All this sounds reasonable. Yet it fails to recognize that all open market operations (including foreign exchange market operations) carry the risk of losses and thus have fiscal implications. When a central bank buys private paper in the context of its open market operation, there is a risk involved, because the issuer of the paper can default. This will then lead to losses for the central bank.[2] These losses are in no way different from the losses the central bank can incur when buying government bonds. Thus, the argument really implies that a central bank should abstain from any open market operation. It should stop being a central bank. The truth is that a central bank should perform (risky) open market operations. The fact that these are potentially loss making should not deter the central bank. Losses can be necessary, even desirable, to guarantee financial stability.

There is another dimension to the problem that follows from the fragility of the government bond markets in a monetary union. I argued earlier that financial markets can, in a self-fulfilling way, drive countries into a bad equilibrium, where default becomes inevitable. The use of the lender of last resort can prevent countries from being pushed into such a bad equilibrium. If the intervention by the central banks is successful there will be no losses, and no fiscal consequences.

Moral hazard

Like with all insurance mechanisms, there is a risk of moral hazard. By providing a lender of last resort insurance, the ECB gives an incentive to governments to issue too much debt. This is indeed a serious risk. But this risk of moral hazard is no different from the risk of moral hazard in the banking system. It would be a terrible mistake if the central bank were to abandon its role of lender of last resort in the banking sector because there is a risk of moral hazard. In the same way, it is wrong for the ECB to abandon its role of lender of last resort in the government bond market because there is a risk of moral hazard.

The way to deal with moral hazard is to impose rules that will constrain governments in issuing debt, very much like moral hazard in the banking sector is tackled by imposing limits on risk-taking by banks. In general, it is better to separate liquidity provision from

2 The same is true with foreign exchange market operations that can lead to large losses, as has been shown by the recent Swiss experience.

moral hazard concerns. Liquidity provision should be performed by a central bank -- the governance of moral hazard by another institution, the supervisor. This has been the approach taken in the strategy towards the banking sector: the central bank assumes the responsibility of lender of last resort, thereby guaranteeing unlimited liquidity provision in times of crisis, irrespective of what this does to moral hazard; the supervisory authority takes over the responsibility of regulating and supervising the banks.

This should also be the design of the governance within the Eurozone. The ECB assumes the responsibility of lender of last resort in the sovereign bond markets. A different and independent authority takes over the responsibility of regulating and supervising the creation of debt by national governments. To use a metaphor: When a house is burning, the fire department is responsible for extinguishing the fire. Another department (police and the justice system) is responsible for investigating wrongdoing and applying punishment if necessary. Both functions should be kept separate. A fire department that is responsible both for fire extinguishing and punishment is unlikely to be a good fire department. The same is true for the ECB. If the latter tries to solve a moral hazard problem, it will fail in its duty to be a lender of last resort.

The Bagehot doctrine

Ideally, the lender of last resort function should only be used when banks (or governments) experience liquidity problems. It should not be used when they are insolvent. This is the doctrine as formulated by Bagehot (1873). It is also very strongly felt by economists in Northern Europe (see Plenum der Ökonomen(2011)). The central bank should not bail out banks or governments that are insolvent. This is certainly correct. The problem with this doctrine, however, is that it is often difficult to distinguish between liquidity and solvency crises. Most economists today would agree that Greece is insolvent and therefore should not be bailed out by the European Central Bank. But what about Spain, Ireland, Portugal, Italy and Belgium? The best and the brightest economists do not agree on the question of whether these countries' governments are just illiquid or whether they suffer from a deep solvency problem. How would markets know?

As argued earlier, when sovereign debt crises erupt, these are very often a mix of liquidity and solvency problems. Liquidity crises raise the interest rate on the debt issued by governments and therefore quickly degenerate into solvency problems. Solvency problems often lead to liquidity crises that intensify the solvency problem. It is therefore easy to say that the central bank should only provide liquidity to governments or banks that are illiquid but solvent. It is most often very difficult to implement this doctrine.

In fact it is even worse. The doctrine leads to a paradox. If it were easy to separate liquidity from solvency problems, the markets would also find it easy to do so. Thus if a government came under pressure, financial markets would be able to determine whether this government suffered from a liquidity or solvency problem. If they determined it was a liquidity problem, they would be willing to provide credit to the government. The central bank would not have to step in. If they determined it is a solvency problem, they would not want to provide credit, and rightly so. The Bagehot doctrine would come to the same conclusion: the central bank should not bail out the insolvent government. The conclusion is that if solvency and liquidity crises can be separated, there is no need for a lender of last resort. Financial markets would take care of the problems. Who wants to believe this these days?

There is one way in which the Bagehot doctrine could be used by the ECB. As will be remembered, Bagehot put forward the principle that, in times of crisis, the central bank should provide unlimited liquidity at a penalty rate. The latter was seen by Bagehot as a way to take care of the moral hazard problem. The ECB could apply this principle by committing itself to providing unlimited liquidity as soon as the government bond rate of country A exceeds the risk free rate (say the German bond rate) by more than, say, 200 basis points (it could also be another number). This could be a way in which the ECB takes care of moral hazard concerns.

Legal objections

It is often said that the ECB's decision to buy government bonds represents a violation of its statutes, which, it is claimed, forbid such operations. A careful reading of the Treaty, however, makes clear that this is not the case. Article 18 of the "Protocol on the Statute of the European System of Central Banks and the European Central Bank" is very clear when it states that "the ECB and the national central banks may operate in financial markets by buying and selling (..) claims and marketable instruments." Government bonds are marketable instruments, and nowhere is it said that the ECB is forbidden to buy and sell these bonds in financial markets.

What is prohibited is spelled out in article 21: the ECB is not allowed to provide "overdrafts or any other type of credit facilities" to public entities, nor can the ECB purchase directly "debt instruments" from these public entities.

The distinction between these two types of operations is important and is often confused. According to its statute, the ECB is allowed to buy government bonds in the secondary markets in the context of its open market operations. In doing so, the ECB does not provide credit to governments. What it does is to provide liquidity to the holders of these government bonds. These holders are typically financial institutions. In no way can this be interpreted as a monetary financing of government budget deficits.

In contrast, the prohibition on buying debt instruments directly from national governments is based on the fact that such an operation provides liquidity to these governments and thus implies a monetary financing of the government budget deficit.

Conclusion

The ECB has been unduly influenced by the theory that inflation should be the only concern of a central bank. Financial stability should also be on the radar screen of a central bank. In fact, most central banks have been created to solve an endemic problem of financial system instability. With their unlimited firing power, central banks are the only institutions capable of stabilizing the financial system. It is time that the ECB recognizes this old truth instead of fleeing from its responsibility.

In order for the ECB to be successful in stabilizing the sovereign bond markets of the Eurozone, it will have to make it clear that it is fully committed to exerting its function of lender of last resort. By creating confidence, such a commitment will ensure that the ECB does not have to intervene in the government bond markets most of the time, very much like the commitment to be a lender of last resort in the banking system ensures that the central bank only rarely has to provide lender of last resort support.

While the ECB's lender of last resort support in the sovereign bond markets is a necessary feature of the governance of the Eurozone, it is not sufficient. In order to prevent future crises in the Eurozone, significant steps towards further political unification will be necessary. Some steps in that direction were taken recently when the European Council decided to strengthen the control on national budgetary processes and on national macroeconomic policies. These decisions, however, are insufficient and more fundamental changes in the governance of the Eurozone are called for. These should be such that the central bank can trust that its lender of last resort responsibilities in the government bond markets will not lead to a never-ending dynamics of debt creation.

References

Bagehot, W., (1873), Lombard Street, 14th ed., Henry S. King and Co., London
http://www.econlib.org/library/Bagehot/bagLom1.html

Calvo, G. (1988), Servicing the Public Debt: The Role of Expectations, American Economic Review, Vol. 78, No. 4, pp. 647-661.

De Grauwe, P., (2011), The Governance of a Fragile Eurozone, Economic Policy, CEPS Working Documents, May
http://www.ceps.eu/book/governance-fragile-eurozone

Eichengreen, B., Hausmann, R., Panizza, U., (2005), "The Pain of Original Sin", in Eichengreen, B., and Hausmann, R., (eds), Other-People's Money: Debt Denomination and Financial Instability in Emerging Market Economies, Chicago University Press.

Friedman, M., and Schwartz, A., (1961), A Monetary History of the United States, Princeton University Press.

Goodfriend, M., (2011), Central Banking in the Credit Turmoil: An Assessment of Federal Reserve Practice, Journal of Monetary Economics, January.

Gros, D., (2011), A Simple Model of Multiple Equilibria and Default, CEPS Working Document.

Kopf, C., (2011), Restoring Financial Stability in the Euro Area, 15 March, CEPS Policy Briefs.

Obstfeld, M., (1994), The Logic of Currency Crises
http://elsa.berkeley.edu/~obstfeld/ftp/currency_crises/cc.pdf

Plenum der Ökonomen, (2011), Stellungnahme zur EU-Schuldenkrise
http://www.wiso.uni-hamburg.de/lucke/?p=581

3
Institutional Aspects of the Eurozone Crisis

Friedrich Kübler

In last year's conference, Charles Calomiris started by saying that he would "place more stock in arithmetic than in the legalities of what countries supposedly are or are not permitted to do."[1] This is an elegant way to claim the final say in what my German colleague Ernst-Joachim Mestmäcker has called the "power struggle between the primacy of the economic and the primacy of the political,"[2] clearly leaning to the primacy of the economic. In my contribution, I should like to confront this position with some questions. The normative framework of our social compact is more than formal rules generated by politics; our basic institutions are deeply rooted in the beliefs and expectations of people who – as we know from behavioural economics – often prefer fairness to maximizing their profits.

I should like to proceed in three parts. First, I wish to cast a closer look at what European integration or disintegration might be in the context of our discussions (A.). In the second part, I want to present some views on the system of the European Central Bank (ECB) and the stability mechanisms called EFSF and ESM (B.). At the end, I should like to come back to some open questions (C.).

---

1 Exiting the Euro Crisis, in: Allen/Carletti/Corsetti (eds.), Life in the Eurozone With or Without Sovereign Default? p. 115.
2 Der Schamfleck ist die Geldverachtung, FAZ vom 18. 11. 2011 (Nr. 269) p. 33.

A. Integration versus Disintegration

I. The notion of integration – at least in the present context – can have two different meanings. The first would be that we stay with the status quo in the Eurozone and in the European Union (EU); nobody leaves and the rules remain very much what they are. But we can equally look for more integration, in particular to a more federal, political, and fiscal union. Such an agenda raises two legal or institutional issues. The German Federal Constitutional Court has – in two lengthy opinions – rather narrowly defined the limits of European integration under the existing German constitution.[3] There is no time to go into details, but I should like to mention that the Court so far has shied away from any big conflict with the European Union or the German Parliament, always showing considerable flexibility in specific cases. The second issue is related, but refers to the internal structure of the EU. Its major institutions – Parliament, Council and Commission – are shaped by what is sometimes called "regressive proportionality." This is to say that in all these institutions, the smaller Member States are overrepresented and the bigger ones underrepresented. In the Parliament, the vote of a citizen from Luxembourg has about 15 times the weight given to the vote of a German citizen. This is explained as a device which should balance the power the big Member States are exercising outside the formal institutions. But this may cut both ways: as the formal institutions lack democratic legitimacy, more of the decisions are taken outside. In any case, the existing system would hardly be acceptable for a fiscal union or a fiscal pact which would empower the EU to raise taxes. The old adage, "no taxation without representation," requires equal representation for all citizens. At this moment, it is an open question how far the European Fiscal Compact[4] will confer taxing powers to the EU institutions and thus intensify the problems of "degressive proportionality."

---

3 BVerfGE 89, 155 (Maastricht), 123, 267 (Lissabon).
4 Adopted by 25 Member States January 30, 2012, to be ratified before January 1, 2013.

II. Let me move to disintegration. In a very rough and certainly not exhaustive way, I should like to distinguish five scenarios:

— a Member State is leaving the Eurozone;

— this Member State also leaves the EU;

— several Member States are leaving, splitting the Eurozone into a southern and a northern part (in early capital market regulation we used to call this Club Med versus North Sea Alliance);

— the Eurozone is falling apart;

— and finally: this is happening to the EU itself.

III. At first sight, these appear to be events of very different significance. In fact, at the present time we do not have a clear idea how the exit of a Member State from the Eurozone will affect the other Member States. But the falling apart of the Eurozone and, still much more so, of the EU itself, would be a disaster for Europe and a shock for other parts of the world. One of the problems here is that one event may trigger others. If a Member State leaves the Eurozone and returns to its own currency, it may have to impose a rigid capital control regime incompatible with the free movement of capital guarantees of the European treaty framework; therefore it may have to leave the EU as well.[5] Or, the loss of one Member State will have a domino effect: others will have to follow and this could lead to the Club Med/North Sea Alliance scenario.

IV. Finally, we have to see that integration and disintegration are not mutually exclusive. It is at least conceivable that one Member State could leave the Eurozone (and perhaps even the EU), and that the remaining Member States then form a closer fiscal or political union.

---

5 See Alphandéry, The Economic Consequences of the Euro Pact, in: Allen / Carletti/Corsetti, p. 104.

B. Structure and Role of Public Institutions

I. The European Central Bank (ECB)

1. Under Articles 130 and 282 of the Treaty on the Functioning of the EU (TFEU), the ECB and the national central banks of the Eurozone countries are independent from the other EU institutions as well as from the Member State governments. This constitutional guarantee of independence is cut in stone; any amendment of the TFEU requires the consent of all 27 Member States. Germany could not agree with such an amendment without amending its own constitution (the "Basic Law"). Even without these legal constraints, it is extremely unlikely that Germany would ever go along with any amendment weakening the independence of the European System of Central Banks (ESCB).

2. The ECB is in at least three ways involved in the present crisis:

   a) It buys sovereign debt instruments which have been issued by the governments of heavily indebted Euro Member States. It is very controversial whether this activity is compatible with the "no bailout" clause of Art. 125 TFEU. With regard to this provision, the ECB never buys from the issuing Member States but from commercial banks. This has been nice for them, but they are much less pleased by the fact that the ECB has declined to participate in the restructuring of the Greek sovereign debt.

   b) The second involvement of the ECB is Target2. This is a network designed to circulate liquidity in the Eurozone by allowing cross-border transfers of money between central banks of Euro Member States. The need for these transfers arises from cross-border payments executed by commercial banks. Normally it is assumed that these transfers will stay in balance. But as the interbank market has been seriously affected by the loss of trust between banks, Target2 has been and is being used as a substitute. As a consequence, the positions have ceased to be balanced. The "periphery" Member States have by now debt positions of 750 billion Euros.[6] The biggest creditor is Germany with claims against the system of more than 500 billion Euro. This is normally no risk as repayment is guaranteed by the ESCB. But if a Member State were to leave the Eurozone, the others would have to bear its debt positions. If the Eurozone were to blow up, Germany would completely lose its claims. Jens Weidmann, the new head of the Bundesbank, views this as unconceivable, but he still argues for ending the use of Target2 as an instrument of monetary state financing.

c) Finally, the ECB continues to provide huge amounts of liquidity to the European commercial banks; the sum appears to be well beyond a trillion Euro. This is – at least in part – again a consequence of the weakness of the interbank market. This is confirmed by the fact that, at the same time, the banks maintain huge deposits with the ECB.

3. It is obvious that there are new challenges for the ECB, and it appears that they affect the self-understanding and the functioning of the institution. The Bundesbank and the ECB in its early years followed the rule that internal conflicts were never disclosed to the public. This has changed: Jürgen Stark, the former chief economist of the ECB, left the institution, as he strongly disagrees with the continuing acquisition of sovereign bonds issued by financially weak Member States. For the same reason, Axel Weber withdrew his application to become President of the ECB. And more recently, the media reported disagreements between Mario Draghi, the new President of the ECB, and Jens Weidmann from the Bundesbank regarding Target2. It can be assumed that these conflicts reflect some fundamental differences.

---

6 The most recent figures are given by Weidmann, Was steckt hinter den Target2-Salden? FAZ from 12. 3. 2012 (Nr. 62) p. 11.

Under Wim Duisenberg as President and Otmar Issing as Chief Economist, the ECB largely followed the philosophy of the Bundesbank that monetary stability was the primary responsibility of central banking. Today, many observers feel that the majority of the Governing Board thinks other objectives like growth, employment and the preservation of the Eurozone in its present shape are no less important.

II. Public institutions are not only the ECB but also the bodies designed to provide additional financial support for needy Euro Member States.

1. We have to distinguish the European Financial Stability Mechanism (EFSM), organized in the European Financial Stability Facility (EFSF), from the European Stability Mechanism (ESM).

   a) EFSM was started in May 2010 as a preliminary measure. EFSF is a stock corporation under the laws of Luxemburg; shareholders are the Euro Member States. The program will end in June 2013. EFSM has a volume of 750 billion Euros, divided into three parts (or "pots"). All three are designed to provide loans:

— 60 billion are contributions by Euro Member States;

— 440 billion are loans provided by the Euro Member States to EFSF;

— 250 billion are loans provided by the IMF.

   b) ESM was agreed to and formed by the Euro Member States in June 2011. It will be based on a new para. 3 of Art. 136 TFEU. It will, however, not be a program of the EU but a joint venture formed by the Euro Member States under the rules of international public law. ESM is designed to replace EFSM as a more long term facility. For the moment, it is unclear how far EFSM and ESM can both be used at the same time (this would considerably increase the amount of available funds).[7] The most important organ of both is the

---

7 Mussler, Unterschiedliche Berechnungen der Brandmauer, FAZ from 29 March 2012 (No. 76) p. 13.

Board of Governors where every Euro Member State is represented. Loans to needy Member States require the unanimous consent of the Board. German citizens brought constitutional complaints against EFSM and ESM that have been rejected by the Federal Constitutional Court.

2. The structure and the volume of ESM is quite similar to EFSF; again we find the three "pots":

— 80 billion are contributions from the Euro Member States; these funds can be lent to needy countries;

— 420 billion are authorized debt capital. The ESM Fund can issue bonds; the repayment is guaranteed by the participating Member States. These guarantees cover 120% of the face value of the loans. This is designed to allow a triple A rating of the bonds. At the same time, the ESM can buy sovereign bonds from issuing Euro Member States; this is not allowed to the EFSM.

— 250 billion are again loans from the IMF.

The claims of ESM against borrowing Euro Member States enjoy priority over all other creditors, but they are subordinated to the claims of the IMF. The EFSF and ESM have been characterized as "bad banks in Luxemburg."[8]

III. It is obvious that the ESM increases financial risks for the Euro Member States; but it is much less clear to what extent this will happen. The following chart is designed to present a summary of the figures for all Euro Member States and for Germany. It is based on the assumption that 200 billion Euro of the EFSF funds which have already been allocated will be added to ESM. The figures indicate billions of Euro.

---

8 Jakobs, Deutschland wird erpressbar, Südd. Zeitung from 31 March/ April 2012 (No. 77) p. 25.

Source of Financial Risk	for all Euro MS	for Germany
IMF	250	15
ESM (cash)	80	22
ESM (guarantees)	620	168
EFSF (already allocated)	200	50
IMF (direct aid to Greece)	30	2
EU (direct support for Greece)	80	27
ECB (buying sovereign debt)	96	32
Target2	500	466
Sum	1,856	782

I am unable to check how far these figures are accurate and up to date. In any case, they look staggering. But they represent very different degrees of risk. This is particularly true for Target2. For the reasons explained, it is very unlikely that these accounts will not be settled, even if this will take some time. Time may be an important factor for other items, too. When several of the risks on the list mature, it is assumed that this will not happen at the same time.

C. Some Open Questions

In the last part of my presentation, I should like to address some open questions.

I. I should like to start with the critical reactions to ESM. We can distinguish objections to substance and to procedure.

1. As to substance, the Bundesbank, in an official statement, has expressed concerns with regard to the extension of the safety measures introduced by ESM.[9] This is seen as a big step towards a regime of common liability of the Euro Member States for national debt. The Bundesbank is afraid that this will further weaken market discipline with-

---

9 Bundesbank.de: Stellungnahme von Dr. Jens Weidmann, Präsident der Bundesbank (http://www.bundesbank.de/Redaktion/DE/Pressemitteilungen/ BBK/2011/2011_09_19_stellungnahme_weidmann_haushaltsausschuss.html?nsc =true&templateQueryString=stellungnahme&searchIssued=0&searchArchive=0& view=render[Druckversion]).

out providing effective tools of control and supervision of the financial behaviour of the Euro Member States. At the same time, there are concerns that the burden accepted by the creditor Member States will exhaust their financial capacity and produce a general recession.[10] And there are fears that the situation will deteriorate even more by the decline of monetary stability.[11] So far, the Euro has shown considerable strength; the recent increase of the inflation rate to 2.7 % appears to be primarily due to rising prices for energy. But, so far, the stabilizing facilities have hardly been used; there will be more stress in the future.

2. As to procedure, the German Council of Economic Advisers thinks that the process is not sufficiently controlled by economic events; sovereign insolvency will still be triggered by political decisions.[12] At the same time, there is criticism that the ESM is neither subject to parliamentary control nor to the supervision of any official accounting institution.[13]

II. On the other hand, there is no clear perception and still much less agreement as to the costs of disintegration.

1. Let us assume that a Member State is persuaded or forced to leave the Eurozone and to return to its own currency. What does this mean in technical terms? How much time will it take to replace the Euro with a new national currency? Will the Member State be able to achieve this by its own administrative resources or will it need the assistance of the EU, in particular the ECB, and/or of other Member States? In order to improve its competitiveness and to maintain its essential functions, this country will have to

---

10 Handelsblatt, May 20 2010: "Fehlentscheidung": Ifo-Institut verdammt Euro-Rettungsschirm (http://www.handelsblatt.com/politik/konjunktur/nachrichten/fehlentscheidung-ifo-institut-verdammt-euro-rettungsschirm/3440846.html).
11 see Mestmäcker (FN 2).
12 Sachverständigenrat, "Verantwortung für Europa wahrnehmen", p. 144(2) (http://www.sachverstaendigenrat-wirtschaft.de/fileadmin/dateiablage/an2011/ga11_ges.pdf).
13 Die Pressse: Euroschirm: Der nächste problematische Vertrag (http://diepresse.com/home/wirtschaft/international/694692/Euroschirm_Der-naechste-problematische-Vertrag).

devalue its currency step by step and to print money for paying its teachers and policemen and for maintaining at least a fraction of its social security system. This is very likely to trigger heavy inflation; and this will affect people even more. How will they react? Will we experience a wave of migration to other Member States? Will we see undesirable changes in the political system, moving it away from the democratic model? Could or should this be a reason for the EU to suspend membership rights under Art. 7 of the Treaty on European Union (TEU)? Could this be a reason for the country to leave the EU?

2. A final question is how this might affect the political substance of the EU. It is true that it started as the European Economic Community (EEC), and we normally discuss the benefits of the Internal Market and of Monetary Union in economic terms: how much has the union contributed to growth and to the improvement of the living standard in the old and the new Member States? But this is only a part of the story. The European Community (EC) has had an enormous impact on bringing down the fascist regimes in Spain and Portugal, the military government in Greece and the Soviet system in Eastern Europe. In spite of huge problems, the institutional setting so far has proved to be able to peacefully mitigate conflicts between Member States, to balance differing interests of peoples, and to present common European positions in global affairs. This might be still more important in the future as other parts of the globe, e. g. the BRIC-States, gain economic strength and political power. And, the EU may be important in other parts of the world – e.g., the Near East or Southeast Asia – as the example of an organisation which is able to successfully deal with regional conflicts. And finally: the philosopher Jürgen Habermas has recently expressed the hope that the complex setting of the EU may serve as a blueprint for the emergence of more cooperative and democratic forms of interaction and organisation in international politics.[14] If it is true that the exit of any country from the Eurozone

14 Zur Verfassung Europas (2011) S. 39 ff.

and/or the EU could trigger a chain reaction, we have to balance the huge costs of stabilizing financially weak Member States against the equally huge benefits of the existing European institutions.

4
Imbalances In The Euro Area and the ECB's Response

Frank Smets[1]

"When the tide goes out, you can see the rocks"

Blinder (2010) used the above saying to make the point that the financial crisis of 2007-2009 has revealed fundamental weaknesses of the financial system and the need for regulatory and supervisory reform.[2] One can use the same image to argue that the sovereign debt crisis that broke out in the Euro area in May 2010 has laid bare some of the fault lines in the construction of the Economic and Monetary Union (EMU). In particular, it has made it very clear that the E of EMU, the economic governance of the monetary union, needs to be strengthened to avoid a recurrence of the growing intra-Euro-area imbalances and the subsequent systemic crisis that we have observed over the past decade.[3] This realisation has accelerated a broad European reform agenda which includes strengthening the fiscal policy

1 The views expressed are my own and should not be attributed to the ECB. This presentation was prepared for the workshop "Governance for the Eurozone: Integration or Disintegration," organised by Franklin Allen, Elena Carletti and Saverio Simonelli at the European University Institute in Florence on 26 April 2012. I would like to thank Rasmus Rüffer and many other ECB colleagues for their help and input.
2 See Blinder (2010), "It's broke, let's fix it: Rethinking financial regulation," International Journal of Central Banking, December 2010, 277-330.
3 Jean-Claude Trichet, former President of the ECB, repeatedly called for a "quantum leap" in economic governance. See, for example, Trichet (2011), "Reforming EMU: Time for Bold Decisions," Speech at the conference of the Group of the Progressive Alliance of Socialists and Democrats in the European Parliament, "What Future for the Euro?", Frankfurt, 18 March 2011.

framework, establishing a new European financial supervisory architecture, putting in place a crisis management framework, accelerating growth and adjustment, enhancing structural reforms in labour and goods markets, and creating a procedure for identifying and addressing newly emerging imbalances. In this contribution, I focus on the emergence of the intra-Euro-area imbalances, how their unravelling affected the core of the Euro area financial system, and the ECB's policy response. The ECB's response is not a solution to the underlying adjustment problem, but it has created breathing room for governments and supervisors to continue the necessary implementation of the restructuring and reform process.

In the new regulation governing the Excessive Imbalances Procedure (EIP), imbalances are defined as *"any trend giving rise to macroeconomic developments which are adversely affecting, or have the potential to adversely affect, the proper functioning of the economy of a Member State or of economic and monetary union, or of the Union as a whole"*.[4] This is not a very precise definition. Are we talking about financial imbalances as witnessed by the excessive accumulation of debt and leverage in financial and non-financial sectors leading up to the start of the financial crisis in 2007? Or does one have fiscal imbalances in mind, as many governments failed to build up sufficient buffers to deal with adverse macro-economic shocks and some of them hid a substantial deterioration in their explicit and implicit liabilities. Should the focus be on external imbalances as a number of countries experienced large current account deficits and built up a large net foreign debt which made them vulnerable to a sudden stop? Or does one need to look at imbalances in dual labour markets, where some segments of the workers are heavily protected and drive generous wage developments, whereas others, such as many young workers, are in a much more precarious situation. The scoreboard developed by the European Commission to help identify macroeconomic imbalances in the Euro area and the EU contains indicators in each of the fields mentioned above. This reflects the fact that excessive imbalances typically pop up in a number of sectors at the same time.

---

4 See Article 2 of the Regulation of the European Parliament and the Council on the prevention and correction of macroeconomic imbalances.

In the first section of this contribution, I describe the emergence of intra-Euro-area imbalances and how their unravelling affected not only government finances but also the core of the Euro area financial system. The imbalances took the form of a classic credit-fueled bubble in housing markets in a number of Euro area countries (most strongly in Ireland, Spain and Greece). It is well-known that financial crises following a combination of excessive growth in credit and real estate prices are particularly costly both in terms of the depth and persistence of the recession that accompanies the bust and the fiscal costs of dealing with the resulting banking crisis.[5] Indeed, the big financial crises in advanced economies over the last thirty years (such as the Nordic banking crises and the bursting of the Japanese bubble in the early 1990s) all featured such a combination. What was less appreciated is that these real estate booms, fueled by a combination of relatively low real interest rates and easy financing within the integrated European money and bond market, could ultimately put the proper working of the monetary union in danger. The crucial role of financial stability and a properly working, integrated financial system in a well-functioning monetary union has become crystal clear during the current crisis.

In the second part, I will describe the response of the ECB to the impairment of the transmission process and the threat of a credit crunch following renewed tensions in the sovereign debt and inter-bank money markets, and discuss some of the risks and criticisms associated with the non-standard measures that were taken. The ECB's actions as a market maker of last resort have prevented a systemic collapse, but can not address some of the more fundamental weaknesses in the construction of EMU now that the sovereign debt crisis has been unveiled. While the patient may have been removed from intensive care, the healing process has just started. It is therefore important that the breathing room provided by the ECB's actions is used for further implementing the necessary restructuring and reform process. Only in this way can the loss of confidence in banks'

---

5 See, for example, Borio, Claudio and Philip Lowe (2002), "Asset Prices, Financial and Monetary Stability: Exploring the Nexus," BIS Working Paper 114, July 2002; and Detken, Carsten and Frank Smets (2004), "Asset Price Booms and Monetary Policy," in Siebert, H. (ed), Macroeconomic Policies in the World Economy, Springer, for two early references.

and governments' finances and the doubts about the ability of countries to gradually adjust be addressed.

The unravelling of imbalances and systemic risk

The story of the emergence of intra-Euro-area imbalances is very visible in the heterogeneous developments in housing and credit markets across the Euro area. While in Spain, Ireland and Greece (and to a lesser extent Portugal), a house price bubble developed, the housing market remained very subdued in Germany and Austria. For each of the Euro area countries, Figure 1 shows the average annual growth of loans to the private sector and the average growth of residential investment in two sub periods since the start of EMU: the period leading up to the crisis from 1999 to 2007 and the period 2008-2010. Figure 2 shows the average increase in house prices. In Greece, Ireland and Spain, the picture of a classic house price boom and bust clearly emerges. The average growth of loans to the private sector exceeded 15 percent on an annual basis in the run-up to the crisis. This was accompanied by a big increase in residential investment and house prices. On average, house prices each year increased by more than 10 percent in the boom period in those countries. With the outbreak of the subprime crisis in the United States, this then turned into an enormous bust in 2007. Residential investment fell on average by more than 30 percent in Ireland, more than 20 percent in Greece and more than 15 percent in Spain in the period 2008-2010, triggering a deep recession. In contrast, during most of the EMU period, the German housing market was still recovering from the post-reunification boom, with real house prices actually falling on average.

Note: Color versions of all graphs in this publication are available for download at:
http://www.eui.eu/Personal/Carletti/
http://www.eui.eu/DepartmentsAndCentres/Economics/SeminarsEvents/Conferences/
GovernancefortheEurozoneIntegrationorDisintegration.aspx
http://finance.wharton.upenn.edu/FIC/FICPress/goveuro.pdf

Figure 1: Credit growth and residential investment in Euro area countries

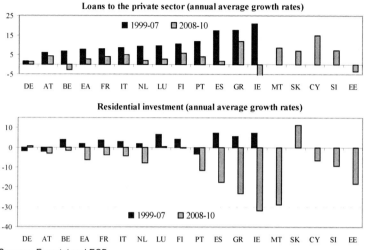

Sources: Eurostat and ECB.
Note: Countries are ranked in ascending order according to the average loans growth in 1999-2007.

Figure 2: Nominal house price growth in Euro area countries

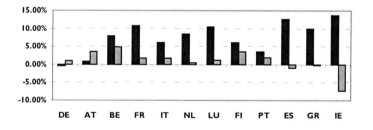

The real estate boom was mostly financed through a widening current account deficit, which in 2007 reached more than 10 percent of GDP in Spain, Greece and Portugal, and more than 5 percent in Ireland (Figure 3). As a result, the net foreign debt position of those countries reached around 100 percent of GDP in 2009 (Table 1). Until 2008, most of the foreign debt was financed by private capital inflows, often through the short-term interbank debt market.[6] As

6 See, for example, Merler, Silvia and Jean Pisani-Ferry (2012), "Sudden Stops in the Euro Area," Bruegel Policy Contribution 2012/06, March 2012.

domestic resources were reallocated to the real estate sector, a non-traded sector, these countries also experienced a loss of competitiveness and a rising deficit on the trade balance. Figure 4 shows that the average inflation rate was persistently higher in those countries than the average level of 2 percent in the Euro area. Also, the increase in unit labour costs in the bubble economies was more than double that of Germany (not shown). As a result, when the bubble burst, it left these countries not only with an internal and external debt overhang, but also with reduced competitiveness, an overvalued real exchange rate, and a need to reallocate resources back from the non-traded to the traded sector.

Figure 3: Current account balances in Euro area countries (% of GDP)

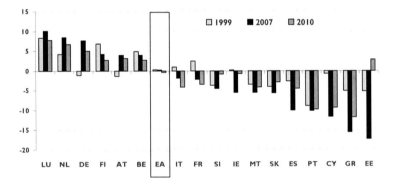

Figure 4: Inflation rates in Euro area countries (average annual percentage)

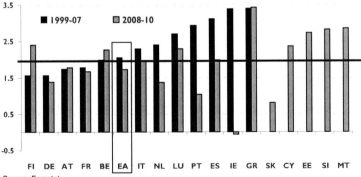

Source: Eurostat.
Notes: Countries are ranked in ascending order according to average HICP inflation in 1999-2007 (2001-2007 for GR). The new euro area countries have been added at the end of the chart. In the case of SK average. 2009-2010 is shown: in the case of EE only 2010 is shown.

Table 1

Net foreign investment position, % of GDP

	1999	2009
Belgium		44.6
Germany	4.5	37.3
Ireland	51.7	-98.4
Greece	-32.6	-85.7
Spain	-28.4	-92.1
France	-7.0	-13.2
Italy	4.4	-19.3
Netherlands	-8.2	17.4
Portugal	-31.6	-109.3
Slovenia	-11.7	-35.5
Slovakia		-68.0
Finland	-177.0	-5.4
Euro area	-6.1	-16.3

The bursting of the house price bubble and the sudden stop in private capital inflows led to a deep recession, sharply rising unemployment, and an exposed and fragile banking sector. As a result of automatic stabilisers, additional discretionary fiscal easing and government support measures for the financial sector, government finances in those countries quickly deteriorated. Figure 5 shows that in Ireland and Spain, a small surplus in 2007 rapidly turned into a large deficit of more than 10 and 6 percent of GDP, respectively, in 2011. As a result, the government debt to GDP ratio has skyrocketed over the past four years and has reached more than 100 percent of GDP in Ireland, Portugal and Greece. In Spain, the government debt almost doubled over the same period (Figure 6).

Figure 5: General government balance (% of GDP)

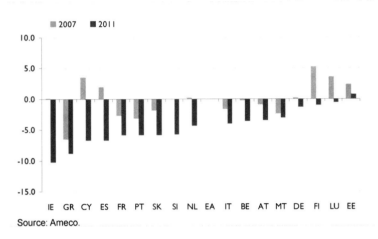

Source: Ameco.

Figure 6: General government gross debt (% of GDP)

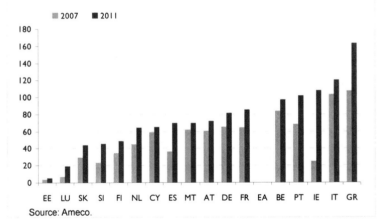

Source: Ameco.

Triggered by fiscal profligacy in Greece and the news that the Greek fiscal deficit and debt were much larger than originally announced, the rapidly rising government debt as well as the uncertainty regarding implicit government liabilities from guaranteeing the banking sector led to a confidence crisis in government finances and rising sovereign spreads in a number of the periphery countries (Figure 7). This set in motion a mutually reinforcing negative spiral between sovereign and banking risks all over the Euro area. On the one hand, weak banking sectors in a number of countries undermined the credibility of planned consolidation programmes, in particular in those countries with weak fiscal fundamentals. On the other hand, uncertainty about the involvement of the private sector in a possible restructuring of the Greek debt and the exposure of European banks to the sovereign risks led to rising costs of bank finance and banking risks across Europe. This tight link between sovereign and banking risks has been reflected in a large positive correlation between sovereign and bank bond premia in the Euro area.

Figure 7: Sovereign bond spreads in the Euro area (basis points)

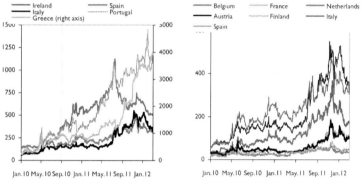

Source: Bloomberg, Reuters and ECB calculations

The self-fulfilling nature of the twin funding problems of the banking sector and the government became particularly acute towards the end of 2011, when it became obvious that both governments and banks were facing large refinancing needs in 2012. Against the background of an already weakened financial sector following the Lehman collapse, confidence in the banking sector evaporated as, for example, indicated by the widely used euribor/OIS spread indicator, a measure of the perceived credit risk in the banking sector. By the end of 2011, the 3-month euribor/OIS spread again reached 100 basis points, a level that had not been seen since the heat of the banking crisis following the Lehman collapse in early 2009 (Figure 8). While the stress in the banking sector following the collapse of Lehman Brothers in October 2008 was mostly related to the exposure of banks to the subprime crisis and toxic assets in the United States, the epicentre had moved to Europe in the Summer of 2011, as uncertainty regarding the exposure to European sovereign risks dominated. The systemic character of the sovereign debt crisis can also be seen in Figure 9, which shows the Composite Index of Systemic Stress (CISS) indicator, developed by Holló, Kremer and Lo Duca (2012).[7] The CISS covers stress in five different European financial markets and, in contrast to many other indicators, also takes into account the degree of correlation between those five markets, making it a particularly useful indicator of systemic stress. Also from this indicator, it is clear that the systemic stress in European financial markets breached its crisis threshold of 0.35 in early Summer of 2010 as the Greek debt crisis intensified and reached a new high towards the end of 2011.

Figure 8: Euribor/OIS spread

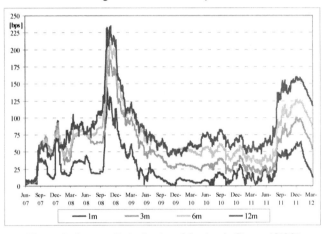

Figure 9: Composite Indicator of Systemic Stress (CISS)

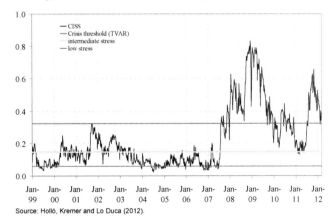

Source: Holló, Kremer and Lo Duca (2012).

---

7 Holló, Dániel, Manfred Kremer and Marco Lo Duca (2012), CISS - a Composite Indicator of Systemic Stress in the Financial System, ECB Working Paper 1426, March 2012.

In the second half of 2011, the rising spreads on government yields and bank funding costs started to affect the outlook for economic activity and price stability as the cost of finance of non-financial sectors increased and credit standards tightened. Also, actual monetary and credit developments in the private sector were exceptionally weak. It was clear that the intensification of the sovereign crisis was hampering the ability of banks to support the real economy. Moreover, quite a bit of heterogeneity in the pass-through of monetary policy across weak and stronger countries was observed.

Price stability and the ECB as a market maker of last resort

What has been the ECB's response? In line with its mandate of maintaining price stability over the medium term, the ECB has used both standard and non-standard monetary policy measures to alleviate the risk that bank funding problems translate into a credit crunch and endanger the gradual recovery and price stability. At the same time, these measures also prevented a systemic collapse.

Figure 10: ECB policy rates and EONIA (in percent)

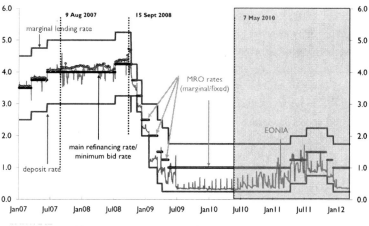

Note: The upper and lower band are respectively the ECB's marginal lending facility and deposit facility rates.

As depicted in Figure 10, in response to the increasing risk of a double-dip recession in the fourth quarter of 2011, standard monetary policy was eased by lowering the policy-controlled interest rates back to their previous low levels. The main refinancing rate was lowered to 1 percent, whereas the EONIA, the overnight interbank money market rate, dropped to close to the ECB's deposit rate of 25 basis points. Orphanides and Wieland (2012) have recently shown that this easing is consistent with the prescriptions of a simple policy rule whereby interest rates change in response to deviation of expected one-year ahead annual inflation from the inflation objective and the deviation of expected one-year ahead annual growth rate from estimated potential growth rate.[8]

In addition, in order to avoid bank funding problems mutating into excessive deleveraging, solvency problems, and a collapse of the financial system, the ECB also eased its non-standard policy measures. In line with the enhanced credit support measures taken since the start of the crisis in October 2008, the ECB changed the conditions of its refinancing operations to alleviate these funding problems. First, it announced two long-term refinancing operations (LTROs) with a maturity of three years (and the option to pay back after one year) to provide longer-term funding security and help banks with the maturity mismatch they were facing. Second, it broadened the eligible collateral base for those refinancing operations to ensure a wide set of banks would have access to these operations. Third, it reduced the reserve requirements for monetary and financial institutions from two to one percent to release some of the required reserves for bank funding. These measures aimed at improving confidence in the banking sector and thereby avoiding a credit crunch and neutralising the heterogeneity in the transmission of monetary policy that resulted from the fact that the weaker countries were much more affected by the negative confidence spiral between sovereign and bank risks.

Figure 12 gives a colourful picture of the most important elements of the monetary operations on the balance sheet of the ECB. Under the full allotment procedure, the expansion of the balance sheet (in net terms by about 530 billion Euros over the two three-year operations) reflects the increased demand for longer-term liquidity due to the tensions in the money market. The elastic supply of liquidity at a

---

8 See Orphanides, Athanasios and Volker Wieland (2012), "Complexity and Monetary Policy," paper presented at the conference on "Central Banking: Before, During and After the Crisis," sponsored by the Federal Reserve Board and the International Journal of Central Banking on March 23-24, 2012.

fixed interest rate and against collateral is a typical feature of central bank support during financial crises. In addition, the ECB had previously announced a second covered bonds purchasing programme and maintained its Securities Market Programme (SMP) geared at addressing malfunctioning in specific bond markets. Overall, the ECB has used its balance sheet to function as a market maker of last resort, taking up the intermediation role in the segmented money market. This way, it avoided an incipient credit crunch and a further deterioration of the economic outlook and the risks to price stability.

Figure 11: Monetary policy operations of the ECB

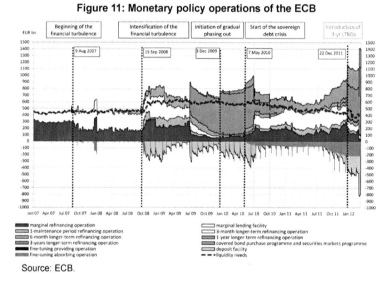

Source: ECB.

Figure 12: Euro-area corporate bond spreads (in basis points)

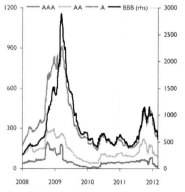
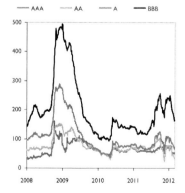

Source: Thomson Financial Datastream.
Note. Bonds of maturities of over one year are included in the indices.
Benchmark is EMU AAA government bond index calculated by Merrill Lynch

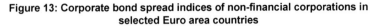

Figure 13: Corporate bond spread indices of non-financial corporations in selected Euro area countries

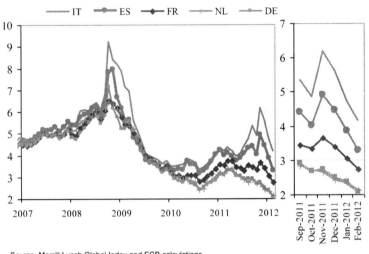

Source: Merrill Lynch Global Index and ECB calculations.
Note: Aggregated investment grade bonds by countries are displayed as unweighted averages.

Figures 8 and 9 show that the ECB's actions, as well as decisions to move towards a stronger economic union announced by the Heads of State and Government on 9 December 2011, have led to an easing of tensions in the interbank money market and in financial markets more generally. Nevertheless, the state of the financial sector is still very fragile as indicated by the fact that the level of the CISS still hovers around the critical level of 0.35. Figure 12 shows that corporate bond spreads have generally fallen since the announcement of the three-year LTROs. Figure 13 illustrates how the LTROs have also led to a more homogenous transmission of standard monetary policy in the Eurozone. Moreover, the incipient tightening of bank credit standards in the second half of 2011, as indicated in the ECB's bank lending survey, was reversed in the first quarter of 2012. Finally, the incipient drop in broad money growth was halted and gave rise to a moderate increase in the first quarter of 2012. Loan growth to the private sector, on the other hand, remained quite subdued partly due to continuing low demand.

Figure 14: Inflation and inflation expectations in the Euro area (in percent)

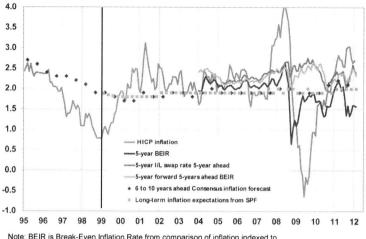

Note: BEIR is Break-Even Inflation Rate from comparison of inflation indexed to conventional sovereign bonds.

There have been various criticisms of the ECB's actions. Let me address some of them.[9] A first criticism is that the large expansion of the ECB's balance sheet and the associated big increase in the use of the deposit facility may hamper the ability of the ECB to contain inflationary pressures. In my view, in the short run, such inflationary risks are unlikely to materialise. The implications of higher central bank money for inflation very much depend on the underlying source of the monetary expansion. As in the simple framework of Poole (1970)[10], changes in the demand for liquidity, for example because of increased risk aversion, should be accommodated from a stabilisation perspective. Failing to do so would lead to a rise in money market interest rates and spreads, falling economic activity, and disinflation. In other words, rather than creating inflation risks, the ECB's liquidity accommodation avoided deflationary risks as discussed above. Figure 14 illustrates the stability of Euro area inflation expectations in bond markets and in surveys. It is also striking that the large increase in base money has not translated into an increase in broad money growth, which has been very subdued all through

9 See also the speech by Benoit Coeuré, member of the ECB's Executive Board, "Financing the Economy of the Euro Area: the ECB's Role," Association Française des Tresoriers d'Entreprises (AFTE), Paris, 11 April 2012.
10 Poole, William (1970), "Optimal Choice of Monetary Instruments in a Simple Stochastic Macro Model," Quarterly Journal of Economics 84 (May): 197-216.

the crisis. Does the expansion in the size of the balance sheet make a timely exit to counteract future incipient inflationary pressures less likely? Not necessarily -- both standard and non-standard policy easing can be easily reversed. First, the interest rate on the 3-year LTROs is at a variable interest rate, so the cost of central bank financing will automatically increase if policy rates increase. Second, the ECB has various instruments such as the issuance of debt certificates or increasing the reserve requirement, which can be used to mop up liquidity if that became an issue.

A second criticism is that generous liquidity provision to banks may reduce the incentives of national governments to restructure their banking sector and may lead banks to evergreen their non-performing loans and avoid (from a private perspective) costly recapitalisation. This may, first, further undermine an improvement of market confidence in the financial system and therefore generate higher spreads and, second, backfire when the central bank needs to increase interest rates to counteract risks to price stability as borrowers may go bankrupt and the risk of financial instability may return. To avoid this risk, it is essential for banks to strengthen their resilience by retaining earnings and further building up capital and for governments and supervisors to improve the transparency in the banking sector by removing bad assets and restructuring the banking sector where needed. The soundness of banks' balance sheets is a key factor in facilitating an appropriate provision of credit to the economy. On the other hand, central bank liquidity provision, while avoiding a disorderly deleveraging of the banking sector, will in itself not address the underlying weakness of the banking sector. It is therefore important that the process of bank restructuring and recapitalisation is completed as quickly as possible.

A third and related criticism is that the generous liquidity provision by the ECB may delay the necessary macro-economic adjustment to the external imbalances that we have described above. In addition, to the extent that banks have used central bank liquidity to buy sovereign debt, it may ease market pressure on governments to consolidate government finances. Indeed, as described in Merler and Pisani-Ferry (2012),[11] the intermediation through the ECB's balance

---

11 op. cit.

sheet has avoided that the sudden stop in private capital flows has further resulted in an abrupt closing of the current account deficit, and avoided an even larger recession in the weak countries. As originally pointed out by Sinn and Wollmershaeuser (2011), this has contributed to an explosion of Target 2 balances within the Eurosystem with a large positive asset position of the Bundesbank and some other northern NCBs and large deficit positions of the central banks of Spain, Ireland, Greece and Italy.[12] While the risks associated with these Target 2 balances are limited, given that they reflect the collateralised lending of the ECB, they do reflect the balance of payments problems faced by the weaker countries and the fact that banking markets are still segmented along national lines. This does not imply, however, that adjustment is not taking place. Over the last couple of years, the current account deficit has narrowed substantially in most of the deficit countries, and relative unit labour costs are gradually adjusting to improve the competitiveness of those countries. It is, however, also fair to say that this process is unduly slow, often reflecting rigidities in goods and labour markets with large costs in terms of high unemployment. It is therefore of utmost importance that the labour market reforms that have been agreed to in countries like Spain and Italy are implemented as quickly as possible to facilitate this adjustment process. Gains in competitiveness and a return of market confidence will then automatically also imply a reduced role for non-standard policy measures.

Finally, a fourth and somewhat separate source of criticism of the ECB's actions is that the ECB should address the liquidity problem where it arises, i.e., in the government bond markets. According to this view, the lack of a lender of last resort to governments (rather than to banks) in the monetary union creates the possibility of self-fulfilling speculative attacks, whereby expectations of future default lead to rising sovereign spreads, which in turn undermine the sustainability of the government debt, confirming those default expectations. An unconditional commitment to cap interest rates on government bonds would prevent such self-fulfilling attacks. This view is in contrast to the view mentioned above that central bank

---

12 See, for example, Sinn, Hans-Werner and Timo Wollmershaeuser (2011), "Target Loans, Current Account Balances and Capital Flows: The ECB's Rescue Facility," NBER Working Paper 17626, November 2011.

intervention in government bond markets may reduce the incentives of governments to consolidate and increase the risk of inflationary pressures arising from fiscal dominance. A number of arguments hold against direct unconditional intervention in government debt markets of this sort. First and foremost, such unconditional support would contradict the Treaty provisions on the prohibition of monetary financing to the extent that they provide the government with financing "on tap." This would undermine a cornerstone of the stability-oriented monetary and fiscal policy framework in the Euro area and may thereby backfire by creating instability in inflation expectations. The analogy between the lender of last resort function for banks and governments is misleading in a number of ways. First, banks are inherently susceptible to bank runs because of their explicit role in liquidity and maturity transformation. This explains the existence of deposit insurance and the historic role of central banks as lenders of last resort to the banking sector. This is not the case for governments which, in the European Union, typically have an average maturity of liabilities that lies between 4 and 12 years. Governments have become susceptible to speculative attacks because of weak fiscal fundamentals, which leads to questioning the notion that such episodes are only about liquidity.

Second, because banks are refinanced against collateral, such operations provide a double layer of protection for the central bank. Third, addressing liquidity provision through the banking system maintains a form of market discipline on governments, as the private sector will adjust its lending depending on the outlook for fiscal sustainability. Fourth, because of their shorter maturity structure, refinancing operations with the banking sector can more easily be unwound when needed. On the other hand, through its SMP, the ECB has directly intervened in specific government bond markets in order to alleviate the impairment of the transmission mechanism associated with malfunctioning bond markets. However, the ECB has frequently stressed that these interventions are both limited and temporary. They are commensurate with the degree of malfunctioning and conditional on governments taking the necessary actions to ensure debt sustainability, and thereby financial stability.

In sum, the ECB has acted forcefully with both standard and non-standard policies in accordance with its mandate given by the Treaty on Monetary Union. The ECB's actions are, however, no panacea. They do not directly address the need for adjustment that must take place following the unravelling of the imbalances. Stability in the monetary union will only return when confidence in the banking sector, government finances, and the ability of countries to adjust to imbalances is re-established. When that happens, the ECB's non-standard measures will automatically become superfluous and disappear. In this sense, the non-standard measures are temporary and limited.

5
Governance of the International Monetary System[1]

Richard Portes

Introduction

This essay will focus on the choice of the international reserve currency, the 'key currency' (or currencies) in the international monetary system. Whereas national governments typically impose the currency of legal tender, internationally the dominant currency is 'chosen' by the markets, except for the period of the Bretton Woods exchange-rate system, 1944-1971.

The level of development of domestic financial markets and institutions has always been central to this choice (Portes and Rey, 1998; Papaioannou and Portes, 2010; Chitu et al., 2012). With network

---

1 This essay is an extended version of my presentation on 'Governance of the international monetary system', given at the conference on 'Governance for the Euro Zone', held at the European University Institute on 26 April 2012. It draws extensively on my paper, 'The Triffin Dilemma and a Multipolar International Reserve System', forthcoming in J.-C. Koeune, ed., In Search of a New World Monetary Order, P.I.E. Peter Lang SA - Editions Scientifiques Internationales, Proceedings of a conference held in Brussels on 3-4 October 2011, to commemorate the 100th anniversary of the birth of Robert Triffin. I am grateful for comments from Maurice Obstfeld. I am also indebted to Tommaso Padoa Schioppa for many discussions of these issues over 25 years and to Hélène Rey for more recent extended discussions – even though, in both cases, we sometimes had to agree to disagree, as will be evident from the text.

externalities, there are multiple equilibria (Portes and Rey, 1998), and in such circumstances, history (inertia) matters. But shocks – e.g., the two world wars in the 20th century – and major policy changes by key actors in the system can nevertheless overcome inertia and provoke a move from one equilibrium to another. Sterling was the dominant (but not exclusive) international currency pre-1914, then sterling and the dollar alternated during the interwar period, then the Bretton Woods agreement enshrined the dollar from 1944 onwards. Subsequently, policy actions by the United States in the early 1970s clearly affected the international currency status of the dollar – both US monetary policies and the decision to break the link with gold were important here. And, at this point, the 'governance' of the system broke down, at least for exchange rates. All the efforts of the major countries and the IMF could not construct a new regime.

Many thought this was foreseen by Robert Triffin (1960). Some now agree with the Governor of the Peoples Bank of China that we currently face a version of the Triffin Dilemma (Zhou, 2009). There is an alternative hypothesis, that the gradual erosion of capital controls in the 1960s was incompatible with fixed exchange rates and monetary policy (the 'trilemma'), and the major countries were unwilling to sacrifice autonomy in monetary policy. We shall not elaborate on this (our preferred) view.

It is important to note, however, that some countries were either unwilling or unable to take on the key currency role. The Deutschmark and the yen seemed contenders, especially when reserve holders shifted away from dollars in the late 1970s, because of US inflation and dollar depreciation. But Germany (in particular, the Bundesbank) did not want what they perceived as the burdens associated with a key currency, and the Japanese financial system crashed, so that Japan's domestic financial markets and institutions could not support the international currency role.

The creation of the Euro in 1999 brought a major new international currency onto the scene. Until the current crisis, the Euro's share of international reserves was rising, along with its share in the issuance of international bonds, invoicing, and other international currency functions. This trend has now reversed somewhat, and meanwhile China is pushing for a greater international role for the RMB. But that development will be very slow indeed, limited again by the pace of development of China's financial markets. Again, markets will determine the outcome, and the dollar will not fall in importance necessarily because of a new, contemporary version of the Triffin Dilemma.

Recently, proposals for a multipolar reserve system have invoked such a supposed new form of the Triffin Dilemma (Farhi et al., 2011), as a reason for moving towards a multipolar reserve system. But the Triffin Dilemma did not describe the problems of the international monetary system in the late 1960s, and it does not describe the present day problems of that system. The world will move towards a multipolar reserve system, but for reasons unrelated to the Triffin Dilemma.

Triffin Dilemma Definitions

There are at least two rather different formulations of the Triffin Dilemma in recent discussions. The definition that is perhaps closer to what Triffin had in mind is that increasing demand for reserve assets strains the ability of the issuer to supply sufficient amounts while still credibly guaranteeing or stabilising the asset's value in terms of an acceptable numéraire (see Obstfeld, 2011, as well as Farhi et al., 2011). An alternative perspective from a policymaker is that the dilemma is founded on a tension between short-run policy incentives in reserve-issuing and reserve-holding countries, on the one hand, and the long-run stability of the international financial system on the other hand (Bini Smaghi, 2011).

The Triffin Dilemma of the 1960s

A dilemma is a difficult choice between alternatives. The first posited that the United States would stop providing more dollar balances for international finance. In that case, trade would stagnate and there would be a deflationary bias in the global economy – a global liquidity shortage. The second was that the United States would continue to provide more of the international reserve currency, leading ultimately to a loss of confidence in the dollar, as US obligations to 'redeem' foreign holdings with gold would be seen to be unsustainable.

Some writers have identified the second alternative with continued US current account deficits. But this is not correct, either empirically or conceptually.

Another interpretation of the 1960s

The US current account was actually in surplus throughout the 1960s. Moreover, much of the growth of dollar reserves from 1955 onwards was driven by foreign demand for money (recall the 'dollar shortage' of the late 1940s and early 1950s) and posed no threat to US liquidity (Obstfeld, 1993).

One analysis at the time took a different line (Despres et al., 1966) – a 'minority view'– as the authors put it. They argued that the US 'deficit' arose from its role as the world banker (see also Gourinchas and Rey, 2007). It borrowed short (issuing riskless assets) and lent long (buying risky assets). The source of the dollar balances accumulated abroad was net capital outflows, not current account deficits.

More generally, 'current accounts tell us little about the role a country plays in international borrowing, lending, and financial intermediation…' (Borio and Disyatat, 2011). Moreover, Despres et al., (1966) argued that the key issue was not external (global) liquidity but rather internal liquidity in Europe. That is, the United States was supplying financial intermediation to a Europe whose financial system was still incapable of providing that intermediation itself. The lack of 'confidence', they suggested, reflected a failure to understand this intermediary role. Hence, they argued, there was a straightforward policy response: develop and integrate foreign capital markets, while seeking to moderate foreign asset holders' insistence on liquidity. This minority view of 1966 was the correct one. It was put forward in the same year in which Valery Giscard d'Estaing spoke of the 'exorbitant privilege'. It resonates with today's policy discussions of global imbalances (Portes, 2009).

In sum, the 'dollar problem' of the 1960s was not founded on the Triffin Dilemma. Rather, it was simply a result of the US inability to convince dollar holders that the US would maintain a stable value of the dollar with appropriate monetary and fiscal policies. If the US had done that, then dollar holders would have had no incentive to demand gold. (Obstfeld, 1993) – unless it were to destroy the exorbitant privilege, as perhaps was the main French objective.

Is there a Triffin Dilemma now?

The leading current version of the Triffin Dilemma starts from the hypothesis that the global economy faces a chronic, severe shortage of reserve assets, which are identified with 'safe assets' (Caballero, 2006). The empirical evidence cited for this shortage is the persistently low level of real interest rates (Farhi et al., 2011, IMF, 2012).

There are several formulations of the problem which is supposed to be raised by the assumed shortage of safe assets. First, excess demand for safe assets is an incentive to create more. But this leads to a deterioration of the creditworthiness of the safe asset pool – in the period just before the 2008 financial crisis, we saw a wide range of assets rated at AAA that subsequently were revealed as very unsafe indeed.

Second, the supply of truly safe dollar assets – US Treasuries – rests on the backing of the US 'fiscal capacity'. But that grows only as US GDP grows, and US GDP grows slower than world GDP, which determines the growth of demand for those assets. Hence there must be a growing excess demand for safe assets.

Third, it is the 'ability to provide liquidity in times of global economic stress [that] defines the issuer of the reserve currency' (Farhi et al., 2011). This again rests on US fiscal capacity.

Fourth, global reserve growth requires an ongoing issuance of gross US government debt, which requires either fiscal deficits or issuing debt to buy riskier assets. Global reserve growth is therefore driven by fiscal deficits, not balance of payments deficits, and the resulting government debt will eventually outrun US fiscal capacity.

Farhi et al. do not define fiscal capacity, but they seem to mean the sustainability of government domestic debt or the solvency of a government. What debt level is 'sustainable' is a matter of considerable controversy, whether it applies to domestic or international debt (e.g., Mendoza and Ostry, 2008, Alogoskoufis et al., 1991), and it is not straightforward to make the intertemporal budget constraint operational in order to investigate this. In the sovereign debt and default literature, these are old issues, concerning the difficulties of distinguishing between a sovereign 'can't pay' from 'won't pay' or illiquidity from insolvency (Eichengreen and Portes, 1995).

Moreover, even setting these problems aside, the empirical evidence for this version of the Triffin Dilemma seems weak. We see no global liquidity shortage, no deflationary bias from that source. Even during the financial crisis of 2008-09, the only manifestation of inadequate global liquidity (as opposed to particular securities markets) was a short-run lack of dollars to finance dollar positions. This was met by short-term currency swaps, which briefly rose to high levels but were quickly wound down.

The main evidence cited for the shortage of safe assets is low real interest rates. It is indeed correct that real interest rates fell steadily from the 1980s and early 1990s to levels that seemed historically low in the 2000s. But they were not historically low – real interest rates were lower in the 1960s and 1970s (the average real interest rate on the sovereign borrowing of the 1970s was significantly negative). Are we supposed to believe that there was a shortage of safe assets both pre- and post-1971? Finally, the US is not the only source of safe assets – the government bonds of Germany, the United Kingdom, Norway, and Switzerland are also held in substantial amounts by foreign investors. A further critique of the 'safe asset shortage view' can be found in Borio and Disyatat (2011).

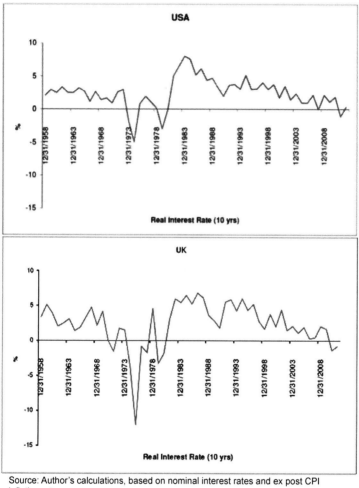

Source: Author's calculations, based on nominal interest rates and ex post CPI inflation rates.

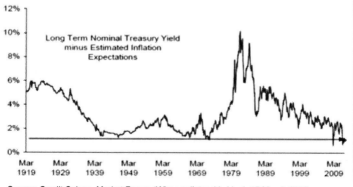

Source: Credit Suisse, Market Focus, 'When collateral is king', 15 March 2012

Current real interest rates are not clearly negative. For example, the Bund yield has moved in the range 1.40-2.20 % over the past several months, with 10-year inflation expectations in the range 1.90-2.05 %. Similar real rates are indicated by US TIPS. Moreover, the current low nominal rates on US Treasuries, Bunds, gilts and Japanese Government Bonds are likely due to aggressively loose monetary policies driving short rates close to zero with the prospect that short rates will stay there for an extended period of time. A standard expectations theory of the interest rate indicates that the long rate will then be low.

There was clearly a shortage of safe assets in late 2008, going into early 2009. No counterparty appeared trustworthy, all market participants were looking for 'safe havens'. But this was not a secular trend. And it is the private sector that seeks safe havens, rather than official sector reserve holders. Private sector capital flows in normal periods do not go into safe assets – e.g., flows from Germany and France to the 'periphery' countries in the Eurozone from 1999 to 2007, as well as US private investment in risky foreign assets (Gourinchas and Rey, 2007, Gourinchas et al., 2012).

Now suppose the United States had maintained the fiscal balance it achieved in 1999-2000. The net supply of US Treasuries was stable or falling, but private investment exceeded savings, so there was a current account deficit, with a rising foreign demand for reserves. What would the foreigners have bought? If the dominant source of safe assets was US Treasuries, then the constraint on the supply of these (reserve) assets would not have been US fiscal capacity, but US fiscal rectitude – no Triffin Dilemma, as set out by Farhi et al.

And finally, note that it is not clear that the US current account deficits of the 2000s were due to a demand for additional reserve assets from the rest of the world. That demand could have been met by net private capital outflows, as in the 1960s (with net private savings balancing any government deficits, and hence a zero current account).

All this is related to the 'global savings glut' hypothesis (Bernanke, 2005) and the 'global imbalances' controversies (Portes, 2009,

Obstfeld and Rogoff, 2010, Bernanke et al., 2011, Shin, 2011, Obstfeld, 2012). There is another relevant theme – that in a crisis, the 'world banker' offers insurance to other countries (Gourinchas et al, 2012). But pursuing these issues would take us too far away from our 'governance' theme.

The policy implications

The world will move towards a multipolar reserve system. But this will happen not because of the Triffin Dilemma and a shortage of safe assets in the current dollar-dominated system. It will happen because official reserve holders want to diversify their portfolios (see Papaioannou et al., 2006), especially in the light of trend dollar depreciation. And the correction of global imbalances will promote this.

For policymakers, the message is to try to convince surplus countries that reserve assets are not as safe as they think, so that they reduce their demand for these assets (China has already suffered a large capital loss because of dollar depreciation in the 2000s). The asymmetry between pressures on surplus and on deficit countries might be met by doing the opposite of creating more 'safe assets' – that is, by raising the risk premium on the supposedly safe assets, so that countries accumulating reserves cut their demand for them, shifting their portfolios towards other assets (for example sovereign wealth funds). (Goodhart, 2011, appears to be advocating policies that would have this effect.)

As the world moves towards a multipolar reserve system, emerging market countries will develop their domestic financial markets and will have less need for foreign financial intermediation (cf. Despres et al., 1966). Some emerging market countries may themselves become reserve suppliers. And the development of more international facilities centred on the IMF could reduce the demand for reserves for self-insurance (Farhi et al., 2011). All but the last can and will happen without major changes in the governance of the international monetary system. And this is just as well, because such changes are unlikely.

Perhaps surprisingly, the huge shock of the global financial crisis has not significantly changed the relative status of international currencies. It seems that only a true 'dollar crisis' or the disintegration of the Euro could do that. In any case, there is not now, nor is there a likely governance of the international monetary system that would manage the transition. National policymakers too can have little more effect on the process than can the IMF or the G20. The markets choose the international currency.

References

Alogoskoufis, G., L. Papademos, and R. Portes, eds., 1991, External Constraints on Macroeconomic Policy, Cambridge University Press for CEPR.

Bernanke, B., 2005, 'The Global Saving Glut and the Us Current Account Deficit', Homer Jones Lecture, St. Louis, Missouri, March 10, at http://www.federalreserve.gov/boarddocs/speeches/2005/20050414/default.htm.

Bernanke, B., C. Bertaut, L. DeMarco, and S. Kamin, 2011, 'International Capital Flows and the Returns To Safe Assets in the United States 2003-2007', FRB International Finance Discussion Paper 1014.

Bini Smaghi, L., 2011, 'The Triffin Dilemma Revisited', 3 October 2011, at http://www.ecb.int/press/key/date/2011/html/sp111003.en.html

Borio, C., and P. Disyatat, 2011, 'Global Imbalances and the Financial Crisis', BIS Working Paper 346.

Caballero, R., 2006, 'On the Macroeconomics of Asset Shortages', NBER Working Paper 12753.

Chitu, L., B. Eichengreen, and A. Mehl, 2012, "When Did the Dollar Overtake Sterling as the Leading International Currency? Evidence from the Bond Markets", ECB Working Paper 1433.

Despres, E., C. Kindleberger, and W. Salant, 1966, 'The Dollar and World Liquidity: A Minority View', The Economist, February 6.

Eichengreen, B., and R. Portes, 1995, 'Crisis? What Crisis?', CEPR.

Farhi, E., P.-O. Gourinchas, and H. Rey, 2011, Reforming the International Monetary System, CEPR e-Book, French version published by Conseil d'Analyse Economique.

Goodhart, C. A. E., 2011, 'Global Macroeconomic and Financial Supervision: Where Next?', forthcoming in R. C. Feenstra and A. M. Taylor, eds., Globalization in an Age of Crisis: Multilateral Economic Cooperation in the Twenty-First Century.

Gourinchas, P.-O., and H. Rey, 2007, 'From World Banker to World Venture Capitalist: The US External Adjustment and the Exorbitant Privilege', in R. Clarida, ed., G7 Current Account Imbalances: Sustainability and Adjustment, The University of Chicago Press for NBER.

Gourinchas, P.O., H. Rey, and K. Truempler, 2012, 'The Financial Crisis and the Geography of Wealth Transfers', Journal of International Economics, forthcoming.

IMF, 2012, Global Financial Stability Review, Ch. 3, April.

Mendoza, E., and J. Ostry, 2008, 'International Evidence on Fiscal Solvency: Is Fiscal Policy "Responsible"?', Journal of Monetary Economics 55(6), 1081-1093, September.

Obstfeld, M., 1993, 'The Adjustment Mechanism', in M. Bordo and B. Eichengreen, eds., A Retrospective on the Bretton Woods System, University of Chicago Press for NBER.

Obstfeld, M., 2011, 'The International Monetary System: Living with Asymmetry', forthcoming in R. C. Feenstra and A. M. Taylor, eds., Globalization in an Age of Crisis: Multilateral Economic Cooperation in the Twenty-First Century.

Obstfeld, M., 2012, 'Financial Flows, Financial Crises, and Global Imbalances', Journal of International Money and Finance 31, 469-480.

Obstfeld, M., and K. Rogoff, 2010, 'Global imbalances and the financial crisis', in R. Glick and M. Spiegel, eds., Asia and the Global Financial Crisis, Federal Reserve Bank of San Francisco.

Papaioannou, E., and R. Portes, 2010, 'The International Role of the Euro: A Status Report', in M. Buti et al., eds., The Euro: The First Decade, Cambridge University Press, 360-407.

Papaioannou, E., R. Portes, and G. Siourounis, 2006, 'Optimal Currency Shares in International Reserves: The Impact of the Euro and the Prospects for the Dollar', Journal of the Japanese and International Economies 20, 508-547.

Portes, R., 2009, 'Global Imbalances', in M. Dewatripont, X. Freixas, and R. Portes, eds., Macroeconomic Stability and Financial Regulation, CEPR.

Portes, R., and H. Rey, 1998, 'The Emergence of the Euro as an International Currency', Economic Policy 26, 305-343.

Shin, H. S., 2011, 'Global Banking Glut and Loan Risk Premium', Mundell-Fleming Lecture, IMF.

Triffin, R.,1960, Gold and the Dollar Crisis, Yale University Press.

Zhou X., 2009, 'Reform the International Monetary System', at http://www.bis.org/review/r090402c.pdf

6
On the Prevention of Crises in the Eurozone

Leszek Balcerowicz

This paper focuses on crisis prevention in the Eurozone. I start, however, with the management of the current crisis focusing on its main weaknesses and on its potential conflicts with crisis prevention. I distinguish then between two types of crises: the financial-fiscal and the fiscal-financial, and discuss their proximate and underlying causes. Based on this analysis, I discuss to what extent the initiatives taken so far have removed the root causes of both types of crisis.

Crisis Management Versus Crisis Prevention

The huge and ongoing debate on the crisis in the Eurozone is usually divided into two parts:

1. The discussion on how to cope with the current problems ("crisis management");

2. The discussion on how to prevent the occurrence of similar problems in the future, once – hopefully – the present ones are eliminated ("crisis prevention"). One can add to this category or treat as a separate issue the question of how to make the economies of the Eurozone better able to cope with future shocks.

In the next sections, I will focus on crisis prevention. In this section, I would like to mention certain weaknesses of the prevailing approach to crisis management in the Eurozone (if not more broadly). It is usually assumed that the fiscal and structural reforms which aim at strengthening longer-term economic growth, improving the fiscal health of a country or making its economy more flexible, are necessary or desirable, but can only produce these benefits in the long-run. What about, then, in the short-run? What is left are various kinds of official crisis lending (the official bail-out). The conventional discussion on short-run measures is then reduced to the question of what institutions are the best qualified in providing crisis lending and what size bail-out is sufficient to produce the "big bazooka" effect or to provide a large enough "firewall." Underlying these military or firefighting metaphors are some other metaphors like "contagion" or "domino effect." They express the view that once the financial markets are disturbed by a crisis in one country, they will act as a blind, violent and undiscriminating force, "attacking" other countries, regardless of their macroeconomic situation. On this basis it must follow that only a formidable countervailing power – massive official interventions ("the big bazooka") can break the presumed dynamics of the financial markets.

But the financial markets, even though disturbed, are not blind. They are capable of distinguishing, however imperfectly and belatedly, between the macroeconomic situations of various countries. That's why we can see the widening spreads on government bonds between Germany and other northern countries and those of the "problem" governments in the Eurozone.

Furthermore, the dynamics of yields on government bonds reflect to some extent the expected effects of the policies of countries affected by the crisis. One does not need, for example, to wait for the completion of a pension reform to see short-term benefits in the shape of reduced yields on government bonds. Markets react to the credible announcement of reforms and their implementation. A brief look at the countries that have been especially affected by the financial crisis, and that suffered a huge increase in the yields on their government bonds in 2009, is very illuminating. One group – Bulgaria, Estonia,

Latvia and Lithuania (the BELL group) – saw a surge in these yields in 2009, followed by a sharp decline. Another group – Portugal, Ireland, Italy, Greece and Spain (the PIIGS) – registered divergent developments: the yields on Greece's and Portugal's bonds have surged and so far have not declined, while those of Ireland have displayed, at least until recently, downward dynamics. These differences can be largely explained by the differences in the extent and structure of reforms in all these countries.

It is an important empirical question how the financial markets assess the expected effect of various packages of reforms under various initial conditions. However, there should be little doubt that the popular view, according to which reforms, however necessary, can produce the benefits only in the longer-run, thus leaving bail-outs as the only solution, should be rejected. Instead, one can propose that properly structured and implemented reforms produce two kinds of benefits:

1. The confidence effects, which appear in the short-run and take the form of reduced yields on government bonds (and on private agents' bonds, too).

2. The structural effects, which start appearing over a longer time frame and take the shape of strengthened economic growth (due to increased employment and/or productivity), reduced budget deficits, or a more flexible economy.

In the discussion of crisis management, one should not overlook a potential conflict between the availability and magnitude of official crisis lending and crisis prevention. There is a huge literature on this topic with respect to the IMF's lending: Lerrick and Meltzer (2001); Report of the International Financial Institutional Advisory Commission (2000); Dell'ariccia, Schnabel, and Zettelmeyer (2002); Jeanne and Zettelmeyer (2004); Roubini and Setser (2004); and Manasse and Roubini (2005). However, the problem is potentially present in any kind of official bail-out: the very prospect of easy availability of crisis lending can make countries' policies less prudent, thus increasing the number of policy-induced crises – and bail-outs (the moral hazard).

The easy availability of crisis lending may also prolong the crisis which has already started, by reducing politicians' incentives to engage in politically unpleasant but economically necessary reforms. Even if a country is blessed with a reformist prime minister who is immune to this danger, his political base may not be. The easy availability of crisis lending can, therefore, weaken political support for reformist leaders.

Both these risks – of increasing the frequency of policy-induced crisis and of crowding-out reforms once a crisis has already started – are especially severe in the case of bail-outs provided by central banks, as they can produce potentially unlimited funds. There are other longer-term risks and costs in this type of bail-out, which include the risks of asset bubbles and inflation, undercutting the credibility of a central bank and exposing it to the danger of politicization (see Balcerowicz, 2012).

Finally, official crisis lending to some extent replaces pressure from financial markets with pressure from experts and politicians of creditor nations. It is not difficult to see that the latter form of pressure is likely to have some unpleasant consequences for European cohesion, both in creditor and debtor countries. The bail-outs in the Eurozone, officially justified by European "solidarity" may, in fact, weaken European "solidarity"! This is especially likely if crisis lending turns into cross-country fiscal transfers or if such transfers, justified by the slogan of the "fiscal union," became prematurely institutionalized. Political tensions, partly generated by the inter-regional fiscal transfers in some EU countries (Italy, Spain, Belgium) should serve here as a warning. Fiscal union in the sense of a large common budget can only follow the process of the gradual build-up of a common identity. If fiscal transfers are rushed ahead of this process, they will undermine it. This is especially true in the case of fiscal transfers to countries affected by the crises caused by their own policies, as distinct from transfers whose aim is to help accelerate the real convergence of the poorer countries of the EU (the cohesion funds). However, the first type of transfers, if instituted, would tend to crowd-out the second type, thus generating another kind of political tension in the EU, this time between richer and poorer (i.e., new) members.

Crisis Prevention: the two types of crises which include fiscal distress

As a starting point in the discussion on crisis prevention, it is useful to distinguish two types of crises which include fiscal distress:

1. The financial (banking) crisis → fiscal crisis.
2. The fiscal crisis → the financial (banking) crisis.

In both cases, the proximate reason for the crisis (the "bust") is the previous spending boom, i.e., the positive demand shock, fuelled by the excessive growth of credit, extended to private actors (the financial-fiscal crises) or to governments (the fiscal-financial crises). There is not much disagreement about this. The true and much contested problems are the root causes of spending booms. And without a proper diagnosis of this problem, there is little hope for proper crisis prevention and great risk that the proposed measures would be ineffective or – even worse – counterproductive or capable of producing various negative side-effects.

The financial-fiscal crisis is currently exemplified by the developments in Spain and Ireland, and outside the Eurozone – by those in the U.S. and in Britain. The fiscal-financial crisis can be best illustrated by the situations in Greece and Portugal. Italy's fiscal problems stem not so much from expansionary fiscal policies during recent years but from high public debt in the presence of economic stagnation (due to the neglect of supply-side reforms) and external shocks.

Figure 1. The dynamics of the financial-fiscal crisis

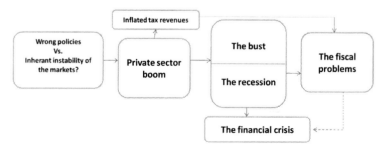

As indicated in Figure 1, there is a fundamental debate about the root causes of private sector credit booms – which are the proximate reason for the ensuing busts and the financial crises. Many observers blame what they consider to be an inherent instability of the "unregulated" financial sector – and call for more regulations. This is, however, a misguided view, as the most serious problems occurred in the most regulated parts of the financial sector (i.e., banks) and empirical research points to policy errors as important root causes of private sector booms (for more on this see: Balcerowicz, 2010; Calomiris, 2009; Taylor, 2009). Here is a list of some of these policies:

1. Politicized (or state-directed) credit allocation: it is usually driven by political considerations which dominate the economic risk assessment and, thus, leads to large banking losses and/or to sovereign debt distress. The activities of Fannie Mae and Freddie Mac in the US are recent examples.

2. Monetary policy, which occasionally leans "with the wind, i.e., fuels asset bubbles (the Fed's policy in the 2000s being the main recent example). It has been linked to a doctrine of monetary policy which narrows its goal to the short-term CPI inflation, and excludes from its purview asset price developments and related factors (e.g., the growth of monetary and credit aggregates).

3. Tax regulations which favor debt financing relative to equity finance.

4. Subsidies to mortgage borrowing.

5. Financial regulations which encouraged excessive securitization, e.g,. the risk-weights contained in Basel 1 and the mandatory use of credit rating by financial investors.

6. Generous deposit insurance which eliminates an important source of market discipline.

7. Regulations that limit shareholder concentration in large banks and thus increase agency problems and weaken market discipline (Calomiris, 2009). This may be an important source of managerial compensation schemes that favor short-term gains and disregard longer-term risks.

8. Policies which have resulted in the "too big to fail" syndrome, i.e,. financial markets' subsidization – via reduced risk premiums – of large financial conglomerates. This is another important instance of public interventions that weaken market discipline. The resulting concentration, in the face of financial crisis, exerts an enormous pressure upon decision makers to bail-out large financial companies again, thus creating a sort of vicious circle. The policies in question included an easy acceptance of the mergers of already huge financial companies and an easy-money policy that fueled the growth of already large financial conglomerates.

Let us now turn to the fiscal-financial crises.

The fiscal problems typically generated by systematic budgetary overspending spill over to the financial sector because financial institutions are big buyers of government bonds. And the domestic financial institutions own a disproportionally large part of their "own" Sovereign's debt – witness the present problems of the Greek banks. This home bias strengthens the link between the financial and fiscal crises in these countries.

Figure 2. The dynamics of the fiscal–financial crises

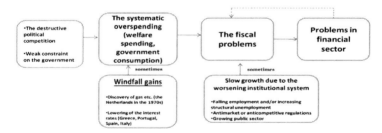

As shown in Figure 2, the windfall gains, or – more broadly – the easy money, are likely to fuel overspending and thus contribute to fiscal crises. The sharply lowered interest rates obtained by Greece, Portugal, Spain and Italy upon their entry in the EMU belonged in the category of windfall gains.

The fundamental question is: what are the driving forces behind modern political systems' systematic overspending. This issue belongs to political economy or public choice. Casual observation and empirical research point out the destructive nature of political competition (i.e., competing for votes with spending promises) and to the weak, if any, constraints on the expansion of budgetary spending. This diagnosis should not suggest that the right solution is to abolish open political competition, i.e., democracy, for rulers in non-democratic regimes tend to pacify the population with increased spending, not to mention various negative consequences of the lack of an open society. The solutions should be sought within a democratic system and aim at making the political competition economically more responsible, and at strengthening fiscal constraints on governments. On the first issue, there is no good substitute for the more active, more systematic and more professional engagement of these parts of civil society that understand that individual freedom and economic growth require keeping the size of government in check. Political leaders, both at the national and EU levels, should – at the minimum – stop equating the "European model" with a large (and usually badly structured) welfare state. On the second issue, constitutional constraints limiting the public debt/GDP ratio and other fiscal rules are necessary. However, in order to introduce and maintain them, a strong engagement of the appropriate parts of civil society is again required. This engagement is especially important in the larger EU countries, as they are less susceptible than the smaller ones to European pressures; instead they are largely behind these pressures. The European rhetoric should not mask the "Realpolitik" in the European Union. The sad story of the de facto emasculating of the Stability and Growth Pact in 2005 by Germany and France is a case in point.

Crisis prevention: what measures?

As spending booms, fueled by excessive growth of credit, are the proximate causes of the ensuing busts and crises, effective prevention must correctly address the root causes of these booms. This task goes beyond the Eurozone problems, but includes some issues that are specific to the Eurozone.

With respect to the private sector credit booms, I have presented an incomplete but long list of policies which have contributed to these booms in the past, by generating excessive credit growth and/ or reducing the perception of private risks. The natural question is then, to what extent have the post-crisis initiatives of national and institutional public bodies removed the danger of similar policies being adopted in the future. This would obviously require a more extensive discussion for which there is no place here. My short response would be that most of the indicated policies are still in place. They include tax regulations that favor debt financing relative to equity finance, subsidies to mortgage borrowing, generous deposit insurance that crowds out an important source of market discipline, and regulations that limit shareholders' concentration in large banks and thus increase agency problems. On a more positive note, I will note the Basel 3 initiative that increases the minimum capital ratios in banks and the ongoing work on the efficient insolvency procedures for big banks that would eliminate the "too big to fail" policies. On the latter, however, it is too early to say whether this work will yield practical results, especially with respect to large, international financial conglomerates.

There is very little debate on how to change the monetary policy doctrine so as to reduce the risk that monetary policy will occasionally lean "with the wind," i.e., fuel bubbles, as appears to have been the case with the Federal Reserves's and ECB's policies before the recent crisis (see Taylor, 2009). What is more, after this crisis the monetary policy of the main central banks has shifted for a long time period to very low interest rates, disregarding the potential negative impact of this policy on longer-run growth (for more on this see Cizkowicz and Rzonca, 2012).

There is one specific issue related to monetary policy in the Eurozone. By its very nature, there is only one level of the ECB interest rates, which cannot perfectly fit the conditions of all the various members. This problem has two aspects: temporal and structural. The first one is related to the different business cycle situations in the respective countries, due, for example, to asymmetric shocks. So far, the temporal problem has not been very serious due to the growing synchronization of the business cycle in the Eurozone. The structural aspect, which is widely ignored, results from different levels of natural interest rates in the different member countries that would make the ECB's rates too low for some members most of the time, thus fueling boom – bust cycles. (Ireland and Spain seem to belong to this group). The question is then what instruments of macroprudential regulation (e.g., varying the loan to value ratio), and to what extent, can neutralize this risk. This is one of the important open technical questions related to the prevention of future financial-fiscal crises in the Eurozone.

Let us now move to the prevention of the fiscal-financial crises that are driven by systematic fiscal overspending, leading to the accumulation of large public debt. This problem, again, goes well beyond the Eurozone, but has some aspects that are specific to the EMU.

In response to the crisis in the Eurozone, a number of European initiatives have been adopted that aim at preventing fiscal-financial crises: the European Semester, the Six Pack, and the Fiscal Treaty. There is no point in discussing them separately, as successive documents largely incorporate the previous ones. The main changes are the following ones:

1. The ex ante monitoring (by peer pressure) of budgets proposed by the respective countries;

2. Monitoring of medium term objectives regarding structural deficits;

3. More focus on reducing the public debt/GDP ratio;

4. The obligation to introduce fiscal rules (the debt brakes) into the national constitutions.

From a technical point of view, these changes, especially the last one, go in the right direction. However, one should remember that the main reason for the current crisis of the Eurozone was not the lack of constraints contained in the treaties but the fact that – due to the political forces in the respective member states – the treaties were not respected. Would the future be different, especially when the current crisis is – hopefully – over? A worrisome sign has been the strong and effective opposition of France against making sanctions for violating the Stability and Growth Pact more automatic. More fundamentally, there is no good substitute, I think, for the strong shift in public opinion, especially in the large countries of the Eurozone, in the direction of fiscal conservatism.

Besides, there are some important omissions regarding the technical changes that appear to be necessary to make the future fiscal-financial crises less likely. For example:

- Fiscal overspending and the related accumulation of public debt have been facilitated by easy financing provided by domestic banks, and this in turn was partly due to the Basel regulation that treats such lending as non risky (i.e., not absorbing the regulatory capital of the banks). This perverse regulation still remains in place and is contained in the proposed EU directive.

- The ECB has lowered the collateral standards in its cheap lending to banks which, in turn, lend to its own governments. What would be the best exit from this policy, and would it leave any lasting traces?

- The accounting rules for the governments in the EU leave much to be desired and so far have not been harmonized.

Concluding remarks

The prevailing approach to the current crisis in the Eurozone places an excessive emphasis on bail-outs to the detriment of attempts to prevent crises. It neglects the confidence effects of properly structured and implemented reforms and overlooks the potential detrimental impact of an easy availability of large crisis lending on policies of the affected countries, thus creating risks that the number of future crises will be increased, and the crises which have already started will be prolonged. It may also create increasing political tensions in the EMU.

Contrary to popular perception, the financial crises (that spill over into the fiscal sphere) are not a pure market phenomenon, as one can point to a number of policies that have contributed to them. Most of these policies are still in place. One challenge specific to the Eurozone is to work out and introduce macroprudential regulations that would reduce the risk of asset bubbles in countries with higher than average natural interest rates, i.e., those for which the ECB's interest rates will be too low most of the time. This is an argument against the proposed harmonization of macroprudential regulation in the EU.

The proximate cause of the fiscal crises that spill over from the financial sector is the systematic fiscal overspending ultimately driven by destructive political competition in the presence of weak or non-existent constraints on the fiscal activity of states. To prevent serious fiscal-financial crises one has, then, to effectively address their root causes. The recent initiatives in the EU appear to go in the right direction but can't substitute for a more active engagement of those parts of civil society in the respective countries that understand that individual freedom and economic growth require keeping the size of government in check.

References

Balcerowicz, Leszek. 2010. How to Avoid Another Serious Financial Crisis, mimeo.

Balcerowicz, Leszek. 2012. Eurozone I: Bail-outs are no Substitute for Reform, Europe's World (Spring).

Calomiris, Charles. 2009. Banking Crisis and the Rules of the Game. National Bureau of Economic Research (October). Cambridge, MA: National Bureau of Economic Research.

Cizkowicz, Piotr, and Andrzej Rzonca. 2012. Interest Rates Close to Zero, Post-Crisis Restructuring and Natural Interest Rate. MPRA Paper No. 36989 (February).

Dell'Ariccia, Giovanni, Isabel Schnabel, and Jeromin Zettelmeyer. 2002. Moral Hazard and International Crisis Lending: A Test. International Monetary Fund working paper (October). Washington: International Monetary Fund.

Jeanne, Olivier, and Jeromin Zettelmeyer. 2004. The Mussa Theorem (and other Results on IMF-Induced Moral Hazard). International Monetary Fund working paper (October). Washington: International Monetary Fund.

Lerrick, Adam, and Allan H. Meltzer. 2001. Beyond IMF Bailouts: Default without Disruption. Quarterly International Economics Report, Carnegie Mellon Gailliot Center for Public Policy (May).

Manasse, Paolo, and Nouriel Roubini. 2005. Rules of Thumb for Sovereign Debt Crises. International Monetary Fund working paper (March). Washington: International Monetary Fund.

Report of the International Financial Institutional Advisory Committee. 2000. Washington.

Roubini, Nouriel, and Brad Setser. 2004. Bailouts or Bail-ins. Responding to Financial Crises in Emerging Economies. Washington: Peterson Institute for International Economics.

Taylor, John B. 2009. Getting Off Track: How Government Actions and Interventions Caused, Prolonged, and Worsened the Financial Crisis. Hoover Institution Press.

7
Exit from a Monetary Union*

Russell Cooper

This paper studies the role of exit from a monetary union. The paper argues that Euroization, a monetary regime in which a country uses the Euro but is not part of the policy setting process, is an effective and credible punishment in response to the inability of a country to successfully reform.

1 Motivation

This paper contributes to the ongoing discussion of the potential disintegration of a monetary union. It focuses on a particular form: the role of exit from a monetary union. The role of exit is studied here in response to a country's failure to successfully implement reform policies. Here, reform is interpreted broadly to include: fiscal consolidation, the relaxation of regulation, repayment of debt, etc. The tension arises from the fact that the country is inside of a monetary union with an objective of reform in the country. The point of the analysis is to understand the role of exit as a punishment for an unsuccessful reform, thus providing an incentive for the reform to be implemented.

* I thank Franklin Allen, Elena Carletti and Saverio Simonelli for inviting this contribution.

A leading example is the role of the exit option during a debt crisis, as studied in Cooper (2012). In the event a country defaults on its debt obligation, which might include a bailout from other countries to partially cover its obligations, some form of exit should be an option for punishment. As recent events have made clear, existing mechanisms with the European Monetary Union (EMU) are insufficient to prevent excessive debt buildups and the consequent pressures for bail-out. It will be argued that in many cases, bailouts of countries are unavoidable: it is in the self-interest of existing countries to provide this assistance.

This paper argues in favor of a punishment mechanism that is **credible**. It involves a form of exit in which a country would remain within the Eurozone but not be part of the decision making process. This would exclude that country from receiving any favorable monetary interventions and from involvement in the debate on monetary policy.

This paper argues that Euroization is more credible than complete exit from a monetary union and provides incentives for repayment that do not exist if a country in default is allowed to continue within the monetary union.

This paper is complementary to Cooper (2012). That paper focuses on a debt crisis with particular attention on the incentives for bail-out. This paper highlights the Euroization dimension by providing further details about this option and exploring its robustness.

2 The Reform Game

We look at the strategic interaction between two players. The first is a single country, denoted country 1, which is in a reform process. A leading example would be a country in the midst of a debt crisis undertaking a fiscal reform. The reform might also include changes in regulations of labor and financial markets, removal of trade barriers, etc. As we see in the current situation in Greece, Italy and Spain, the choice of whether to reform or not has important political dimensions as well.

The second entity is a Central Authority representing the joint interests of a group of countries. As the paper proceeds, the identity of this central authority will be made clearer. At this point, it is sufficient to understand that this authority has the means to determine the status of country 1 within the monetary union.

The following events occur in each period of time. The country 1 government, representing its households (agents), chooses to reform or not. Cooper (2012) studies country 1 in a debt crisis in which "reform" entails a decision on default followed by a bailout decision by the Central Authority. Here we study reform more generally.

The game also includes two exit options. The first is the continued use of the common currency of the union without the ability to influence monetary policy. This regime is Euroization. The second possible form of exit is to force a country to adopt and create its own currency. In addition, the country could be allowed to remain in the monetary union without any additional actions taken against it.

This central authority includes the central bank as well as a representation of the countries in the federation. The game builds upon the one studied in Cooper, Kempf, and Peled (2010) to allow other options, including Euroization and exit from a monetary union, which form the basis of this essay.

In the next section, we present a model of a monetary union. This model is used to explain the options of Euroization as well as complete exit from a monetary union. Once these two options are delineated, we return to the key question of this essay: what is the role of exit in a monetary union?

3 A Two Country Model

In order to characterize the equilibrium of the "Reform Game," we need a model of a monetary union as well as the other options. Without such a model, it is impossible to be precise about incentives for exit. We build upon the model of Cooper and Kempf (2003). Once these options are set out, we return to the "Reform Game" and include the choice of reforming or not in the analysis.

Figure 1: The Game

The Reform Game

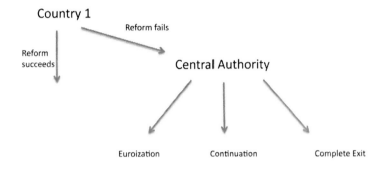

3.1 Environment

The different types of monetary arrangements share a common economic structure. The economy is composed of two regions, indexed $i=1,2$. To be clear, a region can be a state within a country or a country within a federation, such as a monetary union.

The model has overlapping generations. Agents live for two periods. They produce a good in their youth, sell it and then consume goods produced in each of the two countries in old age. Thus there is trade across the countries. What types of currency demands arise from this trade will depend on the underlying monetary structure.

There are also central banks, which determine the stocks of money in the two countries. In the case of a monetary union, the country banks operate according to the rules set by a central monetary authority.

3.2 Multi-currency Outcome

We start with a multi-currency world economy. This serves as a benchmark to appreciate the potential gains from monetary union and to value the outcome in the event there is exit from a monetary union.

3.2.1 Household Optimization

Agents born in period t in the "home" country produce good h when young, and consume both the home and foreign good when old. A key component of the Cooper and Kempf (2003) model is that tastes over the consumption goods are not known to agents at the time of their labor supply choice when young. Moreover, agents face a cash in advance constraint which means that they must hold money specific to the countries before being able to make a purchase. This choice of currency portfolio is also made prior to knowing the tastes for final goods.

This abstraction serves two purposes. First, it generates a demand for the multiple currencies. Second, the timing implies a mismatch between agent tastes and their portfolio of currencies. It is a simple device to model illiquidity.

Formally, a generation t home household solves:

$$max_{m_t^h, m_t^f, n_t} E_\theta[\theta ln(c_{t+1}^h) + (1-\theta)ln(c_{t+1}^f) - g(n_t)] \qquad (1)$$

subject to

$$p_t n_t = m_t^h + e_t m_t^f \qquad (2)$$

and

$$c_{t+1}^h = \frac{m_t^h + \tau_{t+1}}{p_{t+1}} \qquad c_{t+1}^f = \frac{m_t^f}{p_{t+1}^*} \qquad (3)$$

The taste shocks are represented by the random variable θ in (1). These shocks are iid across agents and have a mean of $\bar{\theta}$.

3.2.2 Central Banks Constraints

In the multi-currency setting, there are two central banks representing the two countries. The home and foreign central banks each independently control the growth rate of the money supply. Newly created money is provided as lump sum transfers to private households in each period: these transfers to home agents of generation t are represented as τ_{t+1} in (3).

Note that transfers by the home (foreign) central bank are given to home (foreign) agents. Thus transfers by the home central bank increase the nominal wealth of home agents, relative to foreign agents.

If the home country sets its money growth at σ, then the evolution of the money supply is given by (4) along with the transfers. Note that a constant growth rate gives rise to increasing nominal transfers.

$$M_{t+1} = M_t(1 + \sigma) \qquad \tau_{t+1} = M_t\sigma \qquad (4)$$

3.2.3 Steady State Equilibria

Cooper and Kempf (2003) study steady state equilibria. Given the money growth rates of the home and foreign central banks, denoted (σ, σ^*) respectively, a steady state equilibrium satisfies the conditions for household optimization. Further, in each period, the markets for goods and monies clear.

Given the growth rate of money of the foreign central bank, the home central bank selects to maximize the lifetime expected utility of a representative home household. The home central bank recognizes the effect of home money growth on the consumption and labor supply choices of all agents, both home and foreign. The same is true for the foreign central bank.

In an equilibrium, the two central banks have chosen their respective money supply growth levels optimally, given the choice of the other central bank. Given these choices of money growth rates, the actions of the private agents determine the equilibrium outcome.

The equilibrium rate of inflation is characterized in this proposition from Cooper and Kempf (2003) where $Z = \frac{1-\bar{\theta}}{\theta} > 0$ is a constant.

Proposition 1 *The symmetric equilibrium of the game between governments entails positive money growth rates:* $\sigma = \sigma^* = Z$.

Proof. See Cooper and Kempf (2003).

The proposition implies that there is positive inflation in equilibrium. One interpretation is that each of the central banks imposes an inflation tax on the currency held by households outside of the country. A second interpretation is that the inflation is a means of reducing output and thus influencing terms of trade.

The level of inflation depends on the openness of the economies. A lower $\bar{\theta}$ means that home agents spend on average more of their income on goods produced in the foreign country. From Proposition 1, the lower $\bar{\theta}$ also translates into higher inflation in the two countries.

For later reference, let the lifetime expected utility of a household in the multiple currency case be given by W^{LC}. Note that this is an expected utility as it accounts for uncertainty in tastes. Further, this utility is independent of the country of birth given the focus on symmetric equilibria.

3.3 Model of a Monetary Union

An alternative monetary structure entails a single currency, the Euro, within a monetary union. In this case, there is a single currency and thus the constraint that households hold currency in advance of purchasing goods is not binding. Instead, households produce goods when young and make consumption decisions in old age, given their realized tastes.

In addition, there are no longer multiple central banks. Instead, the money supply is controlled by a single central bank.

3.3.1 Optimization

In a monetary union, the optimization problem of a household becomes:

$$max_{c^h_{t+1}(\theta),c^f_{t+1}(\theta),n_t} E_\theta[\theta ln(c^h_{t+1}) + (1-\theta)ln(c^f_{t+1}) - g(n_t) \quad (5)$$

Here the household chooses how much to work in youth, saves all the income in the form of money and then purchases goods in old age once θ is known. The budget constraint is

$$c^h_{t+1}(\theta)q^h_{t+1} + c^f_{t+1}(\theta)q^f_{t+1} = q^h_t n_t + \tau^{MU}_{t+1} \quad (6)$$

To distinguish this from the multiple currency cases, the prices of goods in country i on period t are denoted q^i_t. Note that (6) is given in money terms.

3.3.2 Central Bank

In a monetary union, there is a single central bank that prints money at a rate σ^{MU} and transfers the newly created money to old agents. The evolution of the money supply is given by

$$M^{MU}_{t+1} = M^{MU}_t(1+\sigma^{MU}) \qquad \tau^{MU}_{t+1} = M^{MU}_t\sigma^{MU} \quad (7)$$

As before, the transfers are part of the household budget constraint (6).

3.3.3 Steady State Equilibrium

As in the multiple currency case, all markets must clear and all agents act in an optimally fashion in a steady state. But, unlike the multiple currency case, in the monetary union regime there is a single central bank representing the interests of *all* agents in the federation. As a consequence, the inflation created in the multiple currency case coming from attempts of each country to tax money holdings is gone. Cooper and Kempf (2003) find

Proposition 2 *The optimal monetary policy in a common currency area is $\sigma^{CC} = 0$.*

Proof. See Cooper and Kempf (2003).

Let W^{MU} represent the lifetime expected utility of an agent in the monetary union regime. Compared to the outcome with multiple currencies, $W^{MU} > W^{LC}$. These gains from a monetary union come from two sources: the ability of the households to respond to variations in tastes and the absence of an inflation tax.

3.4 Euroization

There is a third monetary design to consider. It arises when one country (a proxy for a group of countries) sets monetary policy without regard to the welfare of the agents in the other country. Yet, there is a common currency. This is of course not just a abstract idea but one that has been used in a number of instances around the world.[1] This is termed "Euroization" here since the Euro is the common currency of the two countries.

Here, country 1 is using the Euro without being part of the decision process. The Central Bank is then acting in the interest of country 2. Of course, it is possible to think of country 2 as itself a coalition of countries within the Eurozone.

The analysis of the household problem is similar to that in the monetary union regime except that only a subset of households receive the money transfer in (6). To be concrete, we set, $\tau_t^{MU} = 0$ for residents in country 1 so that all money created by the single central bank is transferred to country 2 residents.

Further, we assume that monetary policy is set with the interests of country 2 only. That is, the single central bank sets money growth, denoted σ^{Euro}, to maximize the lifetime expected utility of a country 2 household.

---

1 Berg and Borensztein (2003) contains a lengthy presentation of a number of cases of dollarization.

Following the logic of the multi-currency case, the central bank representing the households in country 2 will have an incentive to create positive inflation as a means of increasing the real wealth of country 2 households relative to country 1. This is shown formally in Cooper and Kempf (2001).

Let W_i^{Euro} be the lifetime expected utility of a household in country i in the Euroization regime. As a consequence of the positive inflation in the Euroization regime, $W_2^{Euro} > W^{MU}$ since the outcome with zero inflation would be the same as the outcome in a monetary union. By the same argument, $W^{MU} > W_1^{Euro}$: the positive inflation reduces the welfare of country 1 agents relative to a monetary union.

4.1 Incentives for Exit

Here we are taking the failure of reform as a given. Cooper (2012) studies a debt crisis, a leading example of a crisis situation that would lead to reform, where a bailout and an exit option through Euroization arise jointly. Here we focus more on the Euroization dimension of the game, building on the foundations provided in section 3.

A key point of the analysis is the credibility of the Euroization option. It was argued that country 2 agents favored Euroization over continuation of the monetary union: $W_2^{Euro} \geq W^{MU}$, with a strict inequality if the optimal monetary policy in the Euroization regime entailed an inflation tax on country 1 agents. Further, since the outcome under a monetary union is more favorable than the outcome with multiple currencies, $W_2^{MU} > W^{LC}$, it is clear from the perspective of country 2, Euroization is the best outcome. That is, faced with a choice between forcing country 1 out of the monetary union, allowing country 1 to remain a full partner in the monetary union and Euroization, country 2 will choose Euroization.

Though country 1 does not have a choice in the actual game over these options, it is useful to understand its ordering of them. The cost of this inflation tax implies that country 1 agents prefer the monetary union outcome to Euroization. To this degree, pushing country 1 into Euroization is costly.

The Reform Game

What about opting out of the monetary union? As argued before, there are gains to joining a monetary union, $W^{MU} > W^{LC}$, for country 1 as well. But the inflation tax in the Euroization regime means that the welfare of country 1, W_1^{euro} falls below W^{MU}. So is it the case that $W_1^{euro} > W^{LC}$? If not, then country 1 has an incentive to drop out of the Euroization regime and to adopt its own currency.

By continuity, if the inflation rate under Euroization is not too large, then this will be preferred to the multiple currency regime by country 1. As argued earlier, the main determinant to the inflation rate will be the openness of the countries. Thus, if country 1 does not trade too much with country 2, so that $\bar{\theta}$ is close to one, then the inflation tax in the Euroization regime will not be too large and the outcome will be acceptable to country 1. Moreover, if the inflation was excessive, then the participation condition of country 1, given by $W_1^{euro} \geq W^{LC}$, would become a constraint on the choice of inflation in the Euroization regime.

There is another benefit to Euroization relative to a return to multiple currencies through complete exit. This game assumes that once a country is forced into a form of exit, there is no return. More generally, one might imagine that return to the monetary union is feasible and is more likely under Euroization than complete exit.

In addition, as emphasized in Cooper and Kempf (2001), size matters: if country 2 is large relative to country 1, then the inflation tax will not be very large. Finally, there are political costs of exit from a monetary union that could be reduced by accepting the Euroization regime. For these reasons, there is an added benefit to country 1 from accepting Euroization.

4.2 Reform Incentives

The reform stage of the game is not modeled explicitly. The point is that this "punishment" of Euroization is present following a number of different types of episodes of a failed reform. The analysis follows as long as the reform measures themselves do not directly impact the long-run values assigned to the various exit options.[2]

The incentive effects of exit come directly from its credibility. If country 1 understands that there is a credible punishment of Euroization, then this will alter its decisions regarding reform.

From the analysis, it seems as if the Euroization option is always open to existing members of a federation. What prevents its use outside of "crisis times"? The underlying assumption is that in the creation of a federation, countries choosing to join the union do so with an understanding that these measures will be used to deal with extraordinary events. Otherwise, countries may not have an incentive to join the monetary union in the first place.

5 Conclusion

In the absence of a device to commit to its choices, the member countries of a monetary union need to establish guidelines for dealing with situations requiring large reforms, such as debt crises. The lack of a credible mechanism has been made clear by the ongoing dealings with, for example, Greece. The Eurozone nations are searching for a mechanism to deal with debt crises and other failures of reform.

---

2 If there is an interaction, then the choices must be understood jointly in a more specific model setting.

The effects of a credible exit option should be clear: it creates an incentive for reform. In the current situation of Greece, a credible threat of exit will have an effect on the nature and pace of reforms. But if the talk of exit is not credible, then it has no economic effects. The value of the Euroization option is in its credibility and the resulting incentive effects.

The exit device through Euroization is partial: the country which exits retains the use of the common currency but is eliminated from policy determination. This approach avoids the need to renegotiate debt obligations in the face of a change in currencies following a complete exit.

To be clear, the punishment arises by exclusion from policy determination. This lack of representation leads to an inflation tax. While a country cannot be prevented from using the Euro, it can be prevented from participating in monetary policy decisions.

References

Berg, A., and E. Borensztein (2003): "The Pros and Cons of Full Dollarization," The Dollarization Debate, Oxford Scholarship Online Monographs, 1(9), 72-102.

Cooper, R. (2012): "Exit from a Monetary Union through Euroization: Discipline without Chaos," NBER Working Paper # 17908.

Cooper, R., and H. Kempf (2001): "Dollarization and the Conquest of Hyperinflation in Divided Societies," Federal Reserve Bank of Minneapolis Quarterly Review, 25(3).

Cooper, R., and H. Kempf (2003): "Commitment and the Adoption of a Common Currency," International Economic Review, 44(1), 119-42.

Cooper, R., H. Kempf, and D. Peled (2010): "Regional Debt in Monetary Unions: Is it inflationary?," European Economic Review, 54(3), 345-358.

8
Is Austerity Going Too Far? Structural Reforms and The Debt Trap

Pier Carlo Padoan & Paul van den Noord

Fiscal consolidation is ongoing in many countries, including in several Euro area member states. There are increasing calls to ease the pace of consolidation on the grounds that too strong a pace of consolidation, rather than strengthening debt sustainability, by lowering risk premia, could be self defeating as its negative impact on growth (both actual and potential) would more than offset credibility benefits. It could be argued that such a dilemma should be resolved empirically as whether and in which circumstances markets prefer discipline or growth. However this dilemma cannot be addressed effectively without expanding the discussion and looking more carefully at growth in a high debt environment, such as the one that many advanced countries face today (and will face for some time to come). In such an environment, the role of debt in depressing growth (and affecting risk assessment) must be taken into consideration as well as the role that structural policy can play in boosting growth and contributing to debt sustainability.

"Good" and "bad" equilibria

How should we identify the "right amount" of fiscal consolidation? One possible way is the following. Fiscal consolidation will go too far if, in a world where multiple equilibria are possible, it will push the economy towards a bad equilibrium. A "bad equilibrium" is characterized by the simultaneous occurrence, and adverse feedbacks between, high and growing fiscal deficits and debt, high risk premia on sovereign debt, slumping economic activity and plummeting confidence. Remedies to break the downward spiral are generally deemed to include financial firewalls to prevent contagion and structural reforms to boost growth or expectations thereof. As mentioned, the role of fiscal policy is less clear. Consolidation may help to put debt on a sustainable path, but negative demand effects may generate offsets or could exacerbate the downturn, add to the risk premiums, and thus accelerate the fall towards a bad equilibrium.

As a preliminary step we need to identify what is such a "bad" equilibrium and what distinguishes it from a "good" equilibrium. In another paper (Padoan, Sila and Van den Noord, 2012) we define these concepts with the help of a stylized economic stock-flow model. The simplest version of the model has two equations.[1] The first equation describes the negative relationship between public debt and economic growth (Y = output, D = real government debt and an over-dot indicates the change in the variable):

$$\frac{\dot{Y}}{Y} = a - b\frac{D}{Y} \quad (1)$$

This equation is depicted in Figure 1 as the downward-sloping straight line *RR*. *RR* stands for Reinhart and Rogoff (2010) who were the first to posit this relationship and to have tested it empirically.[2] This negative relationship can be explained by, e.g., crowding-out effects on investment or adverse expectations with regard to future taxation associated with high public debt. Growth is positively affected by the exogenous impact of structural reforms captured by parameter *a*. This growth equation can be augmented with the short-to-medium run impact of financial conditions proxied by the interest rate *r*, and the fiscal policy stance proxied by the primary deficit as a share of GDP *p*:

1 It is inspired by a model developed by Duesenberry (1958) to analyze the Great Depression.
2 See also Cecchetti et al. (2011) and Padoan, Sila and Van den Noord (2012).

$$\frac{\dot{Y}}{Y} = a - b\frac{D}{Y} - fr + gp$$

A higher interest rate depresses growth and a larger fiscal deficit supports growth.

Figure 1. Good and bad equilibrium.

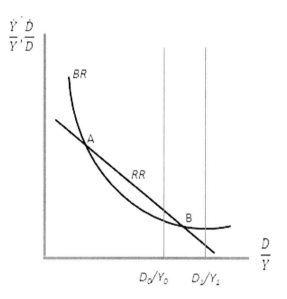

The horizontal axis measures the public debt to GDP ratio and the vertical axis the growth rates of public debt and output. *RR* is the relationship between growth and debt and *BR* the government's *budget constraint*. If the debt ratio is located right from the bad equilibrium *B*, it derails while output contracts at an accelerating pace.

The second equation is the budget constraint of the government and hence it is an identity. The budget constraint relates the primary deficit as a per cent of GDP *(p)* to the real interest rate r and real public debt *D*:

$$\dot{D} = rD + pY \qquad (2a)$$

Dividing the two sides of the equation by D yields:

$$\frac{\dot{D}}{D} = r + \frac{p}{D/Y} \qquad (2b)$$

This is the hyperbolic relationship between real growth of debt and the debt ratio depicted as *BR* (as in budget restriction) in Figure 1. As the debt ratio increases, the real growth of debt approaches asymptotically the real interest rate.[3] The intersections of the two curves correspond to, respectively, the "good" equilibrium *(A)* and the "bad" equilibrium *(B)*. If the debt ratio is located in the interval between the intersections *A* and *B* (indicated by D_0/Y_0), output growth will exceed the growth of debt and hence the debt ratio is falling, until the good equilibrium *A* is attained: the good equilibrium is stable.

However, if the debt ratio is located right of the intersection point *B* (e.g., if the debt ratio equals D_1/Y_1), the growth of debt exceeds output growth. So the equilibrium *B* is unstable. Beyond *B,* without drastic corrective action the debt ratio keeps on growing and growth keeps falling.

Finally, we can assume that the interest rate *r* responds to the (expected) growth in the debt ratio and hence on the fiscal stance and (exogenous) contagion *h*. So:

$$r = h + c\left(\frac{\dot{D}}{D} - \frac{\dot{Y}}{Y}\right)$$

This simple model allows us to consider the interaction of three policy variables: fiscal policy, financial policy (firewall), and structural policy.

For a given fiscal policy stance, a stabilizing policy (that moves the debt ratio to the left of the bad equilibrium) requires financial action to dampen contagion (and lower the interest rate) and structural policy. Here the different timing of policy is of the essence. Firewall action can be very powerful in the short term but its effects can quickly fade away if not supported by further confidence building measures as the interest rate grows with the debt ratio. In our description, a lower interest rate induced by financial policy can temporarily boost

3 The real interest rate is bound to increase if the debt ratio increases (see below), but this is not shown in this simple diagram. Also, the depicted hyperbolic relationship is only valid in this form if the primary balance is in deficit. If it is in surplus, the shape of the curve will change substantially, but will still yield a good and a bad equilibrium with similar properties as described above.

growth and keep the economy away from the bad equilibrium. But its effect is likely to fade if the interest rate fall is not made permanent by a lower debt ratio. Structural reforms can provide confidence but even more importantly can boost growth permanently. So it is essential that the window of opportunity generated by financial policy is fully exploited. It takes time for structural reform to have a full impact on growth and debt, while time is severely lacking in a sovereign debt crisis. Moreover, for structural reform to have this virtuous effect, confidence must be restored to induce the investment (in financial, physical, and human capital) needed to achieve higher growth. So the budget must be brought under control immediately through a combination of (credible) fiscal consolidation and financial backstops. The need to decrease debt is particularly relevant in the current circumstances, in which debt ratios for many advanced countries have grown significantly, and therefore the possibility that one or several countries fall into a bad equilibrium is also elevated.

A strategy that could lead to unambiguous results is to use structural reforms to boost growth and fiscal policy to pursue fiscal consolidation while financial policy could provide the initial, yet possibly temporary, benefit in terms of a confidence bridge. A decline in the debt ratio, also prompted by higher growth, would allow for a permanently lower interest rate.

This can be seen graphically. Changes in the policy variables shift the curves. Structural reforms, lower interest rates, **higher fiscal deficits** shift the RR schedule upwards and so the bad equilibrium debt to GDP ratio moves further to the right (hence a previously unsustainable debt ratio becomes sustainable, the bad equilibrium is "less destabilizing").

Lower interest rates, **lower fiscal deficits** shift the BR downwards, also making the bad equilibrium less destabilizing. However, lower fiscal deficits also bring the RR downwards, partially offsetting the positive impact of lower interest rates.

Figure 2. The impact of fiscal consolidation and structural reform (figure revised).

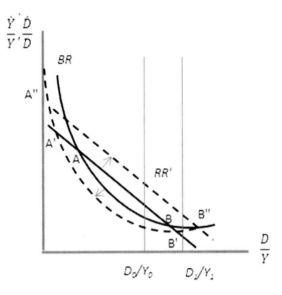

The impact of the strategy suggested above can be described as follows using Figure 2. A fall in the primary deficit and a lower interest rate shift the budget constraint down from *BR* to *BR'*. However, this affects mostly the location of the good equilibrium (which shifts from *A* to *A'*) and much less so the bad equilibrium *B* (which shifts to *B'*). The intuition is straightforward: a sustained cut in the primary deficit yields a lower debt ratio and higher economic growth in the long run, but the initial impact on debt is small. If the debt ratio turns out to be located right of the points *B* and *B'*, fiscal consolidation alone will not be an effective way to improve the debt dynamics in the short to medium run.

However, the combination of structural reform, fiscal consolidation and financial policy will likely deliver higher economic growth. Structural reform and a lower interest rate shift to the right the Reinhart-Rogoff relationship from *RR* to *RR'*, while the lower deficit would shift it to the left, so we will have to assume that this growth depressing impact is more than compensated by the growth enhancing effect of structural reforms and financial policy. The initial positive impact of a lower interest rate on growth is reinforced later by the impact of structural reforms. In this case, the bad equilibrium shifts further to the right, from *B'* to *B"*. The debt ratio D_1/Y_1 is now located left of the equilibrium and has become sustainable. The economy now tends automatically towards the good equilibrium *A"*.

How much can structural reforms actually help?

It is often argued that growth effects of structural reform will only materialize with a lag, but recent research by the OECD (2012a) suggests that this should not be exaggerated. Another counter-argument that is often heard is that the electorate dislikes structural reform and that therefore governments are unlikely to go for it. However, this reasoning underestimates the wisdom of voters and is not fully in line with the facts (Buti et al., 2010). Moreover, financial markets are likely to reward the increased growth potential of the economy which can yield positive wealth effects on demand even in the short run.

OECD work provides some evidence of the implementation and impact of structural reform. The following facts are worth mentioning. First, since the beginning of the crisis, reforms have accelerated, especially in low income countries (Figure 3), so they may be producing fruits earlier than expected. Second, structural reforms have been implemented alongside, and not as an alternative to, fiscal consolidation (Figure 4). Third, structural reforms can deliver significant output gains, especially in the Euro area (Figure 5). Fourth, reforms can have positive cross purpose impacts, e.g., product market reforms can boost labour market performance (Figure 6). Fifth, while the full benefits of structural reform materialize in the medium term, there are some short term benefits and the much feared short term adjustment costs could be overestimated (Figure 7). Sixth, structural reforms could boost growth in the Euro area also by helping current account rebalancing through their impact on savings and investment gaps in both deficit and surplus countries (Figure 8).

Figure 3. Reforms have accelerated

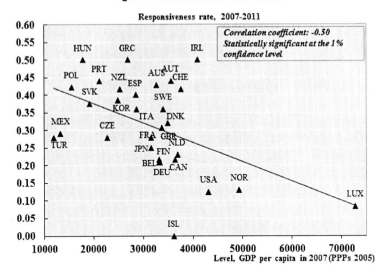

Figure 4. Reforms and fiscal consolidation

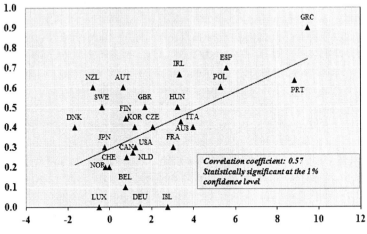

Variation in the underlying primary balance as a percentage of potential GDP from 2010 to 2012

Figure 5. Potential gains from broad reform package
(Ten years, levels in per cent)

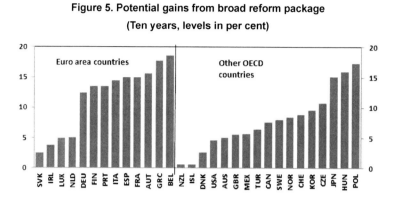

Figure 6. Change in aggregate employment rate following a "typical" reduction in initial unemployment benefit replacement rate

Years after the reform

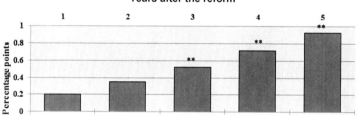

Figure 7. Change in aggregate labor force participation following a "typical" product market reform

Years after the reform

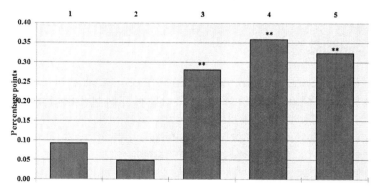

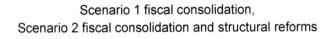

Figure 8. Changes in saving investment gaps.

Scenario 1 fiscal consolidation,
Scenario 2 fiscal consolidation and structural reforms

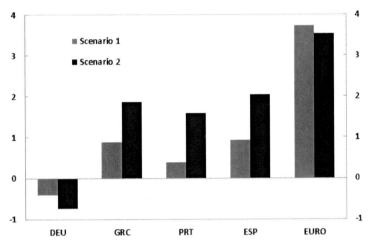

Source: Kerdrain, C., et al. (2011), "Current Accounts Imbalances: Can Structural Reforms Help to Reduce Them?" in OECD Journal: Economic Studies, Vol. 2011, OECD Publishing, Paris.

Conclusion

The contribution of structural reforms to solving the Euro area crisis should be seen in the context of the need to progress in fiscal consolidation. While growth enhancing structural reforms can clearly benefit fiscal consolidation and debt sustainability, the issue arises of the role of timing and sequencing of a policy strategy that includes fiscal consolidation, structural reforms, and confidence enhancing financial measures.

Empirical evidence indicates that, as widely expected, structural reforms bear their fruits in terms of higher output over the medium (and sometimes long) term. In addition, structural reforms become more effective when other policies are also implemented including confidence building measures. One example is product market reforms aimed at boosting investment by eliminating barriers to competition. More competition opens up new profit opportunities and thus investment, but if confidence is depressed, such as during a deep recession, even liquidity rich companies may choose the option to wait rather than kicking off investment. Also, in some cases the impact of structural reforms may be low in the short term if activity remains weak. The implication is that, at times of depressed activity, confidence building measures not only prevent the economy from falling into a debt trap but also provide a bridge between the short and the long term by enhancing the impact of structural reforms and thus facilitating the escape from the debt trap.

References

Buti, M., A. Turrini, P. van den Noord and P. Biroli (2010), Reforms and Re-elections in OECD Countries, Economic Policy, Vol. 25, Issue 61, pp. 63-116.

Cecchetti, S. G., M. S. Mohanty and F. Zampolli (2011), The Real Effects of Debt, BIS Working Papers, No 352.

Duesenberry, J. S. (1958), Business Cycles and Economic Growth, McGraw-Hill.

OECD (2012a), Can Structural Reforms Kick-Start the Recovery? Lessons from 30 Years of OECD Reform, Chapter 4 in OECD (2012b).

OECD (2012b), Economic Policy Reforms 2012: Going for Growth, OECD, Paris.

Padoan, P. C., U. Sila and P. van den Noord (2012), A Dual Equilibrium Model for Public Debt and Growth, forthcoming.

Reinhart, C. M. and K. S. Rogoff (2010), Growth in a Time of Debt, American Economic Review Papers & Proceedings, No. 100, pp 573–8.

9
The Reform of the Political and Economic Architecture of the Eurozone's Governance A Legal Perspective

Jacques Ziller

This chapter presents to economists and political scientists a legal perspective on the most recent reform of the political and economic architecture of the Eurozone's governance. The paper does not include any economic or political science perspectives; it has to be underlined that trying to conduct a "legal analysis" is something different from paraphrasing the content of legal documents. By "most recent reform," we mean the decisions made at the EU summit of 9 December 2011 and implemented by the Treaty on Stability, Coordination and Governance in the Economic and Monetary Union (TSCG) that has been negotiated from December 2011 to February 2012.[1]

---

1 Treaty on Stability, Coordination and Governance in the Economic and Monetary Union (TSCG), available on the Internet Site of the Council: http://european-council.europa.eu/eurozone-governance/treaty-on-stability

Therefore, the so-called "Six-Pack"[2] will not be analysed here – although it has entered into force on 1 January 2012 – as the related decisions have been made during the last months of 2010 and implemented by the six regulations and directive that have been presented by the Commission in early 2011, and discussed and adopted by the European Parliament and the Council in the last months of 2011. Some attention will be devoted only to one of the changes in governance introduced by the "Six-Pack," which is very interesting from a legal perspective: the shift of burden of qualified majority voting in the functioning of the Stability and Growth Pact.

Three points will be developed in order to contribute to understanding if significant changes have been introduced into the Eurozone's governance with the decisions taken on 9 December 2011. In the first section, I will explain the reasons for, and consequences of, the need for an appropriate legal basis for EU actions which derives from the choices made by European governments since the early 1950s as far as the form and instruments of integration are concerned. With the second section, I will examine whether, due to the constraints imposed by the legal bases of the economic and monetary union (EMU), it was necessary from a legal point of view to adopt the content of the decisions taken on 9 December 2011 in the form of an international treaty, the so-called "Fiscal Compact," i.e., the TSCG of 1 March 2012. In the third section, I briefly discuss the remaining constraints for the Eurozone's governance that derive from the

---

2 Regulation (EU) No 1173/2011 of the European Parliament and of the Council of 16 November 2011 on the effective enforcement of budgetary surveillance in the Euro area; Regulation (EU) No 1174/2011 of the European Parliament and of the Council of 16 November 2011 on enforcement measures to correct excessive macroeconomic imbalances in the Euro area; Regulation (EU) No 1175/2011 of the European Parliament and of the Council of 16 November 2011 amending Council Regulation (EC) No 1466/97 on the strengthening of the surveillance of budgetary positions and the surveillance and coordination of economic policies; Regulation (EU) No 1176/2011 of the European Parliament and of the Council of 16 November 2011 on the prevention and correction of macroeconomic imbalances; Council Regulation (EU) No 1177/2011 of 8 November 2011 amending Regulation (EC) No 1467/97 on speeding up and clarifying the implementation of the excessive deficit procedure and Council Directive 2011/85/EU of 8 November 2011 on requirements for budgetary frameworks of the Member States, all available on http://ec.europa.eu/economy_finance/economic_governance/index_en.htm

constraints imposed by the legal bases of the EMU. The analysis is limited to EU law; it should, however, be borne in mind that important issues of national law are being raised under the motto of democratic accountability, which are starting to be addressed by legal scholars and courts, mainly in Germany until the present time, i.e., the beginning of 2012.

1. The Need for an Appropriate Legal Basis for EU Actions

From a strict legal perspective, the European Union is not a state, it is a grouping of states based upon an international treaty for the purpose of exercising a number of delimitated functions.

In international public law and in public law, the existence of a "state" is determined by the combination of a territory, a population living on that territory, and a government that has effective and ultimate power over that territory and population. The EU does not have a territory of its own, as Art. 52 (2) of the Treaty on European Union (TEU) reminds. It says that *"The territorial scope of the Treaties is specified in Art. 355 of the Treaty on the Functioning of the European Union* [TFEU]"; according to Art. 355, TFEU the EU treaties – and the law that derives from the treaties, in the form of directives, regulations, decisions, general principles of law and the case-law of the European Court of Justice (ECJ) – apply to the territory of the member states, with a series of exceptions that are precisely delimitated in Art. 355 or in some of the Accession Treaties – for some of the States that have become members of the European Communities / European Union since 1973. The EU does not have a population of its own, as expressed in Arts. 9 TEU and 20 (1) TFEU: *"Every person holding the nationality of a member state shall be a citizen of the Union. Citizenship of the Union shall be additional to and not replace national citizenship"*; it derives from such a definition of citizenship that the EU, as opposed to a state, does not have the power to lay down the conditions and procedures according to which its citizenship is being acquired – or lost. The EU does not have a government that has effective and ultimate power over that territory and population: there is without any doubt a government of the EU, made up of its institutions, which have a number of powers to decide (competences), but there are no EU-only instruments of constraint upon individuals, groups and businesses (physical and legal persons).

Thus the EU Constitution – the founding treaties (TEU and TFEU[3], as well as the Charter of fundamental rights of the EU, and the protocols which are annexed to the treaties[4]) – cannot be understood in the same way as a federal state's constitution such as the Constitution of the United States of America of 1787 or the Fundamental Law of the Federal Republic of Germany of 1949. The EU is based upon international agreements (i.e., treaties) that are binding upon sovereign states; as long as the treaties do not specify legal rules and principles applicable to the functioning of the EU, the international law of treaties is applicable – a set of principles and rules which has been to a large extent codified by the United Nations Convention on the Law of the Treaties of 1969. One of the fundamental principles of international law is the principle of specialty, according to which organizations or bodies set up by a treaty have only the powers which they have been provided by the treaty; on the contrary, a state, in international law, has no limitation to its powers, other than the limitations they have voluntarily accepted by agreeing to international treaties. The principle of specialty is also known as the "principle of conferral," and has always been applicable to the European Communities.

The principles of conferral and of institutional balance set the boundaries that frame the actions of the European Union's institutions.

While the principle of conferral has always been applicable to the EC/EU treaties, some member state governments have insisted, referring to the constitutional treaty of 2004 and the Lisbon Treaty of 2007, that it be explicitly specified in the text of the TEU. According

---

3 One should avoid referring to numbers of articles of the 'Lisbon Treaty'; the latter was a treaty amending the existing Treaty on European Union and Treaty establishing the European Community; numbers of articles refer usually to the 'consolidated versions' of the TEU and TFEU.

4 The full coordinated text of the EU treaties, Charter and protocols is available as Consolidated versions of the Treaty on European Union and the Treaty on the Functioning of the European Union at http://eur-lex.europa.eu/JOHtml. do?uri=OJ:C:2010:083:SOM:EN:HTML

to Art. 5 (1) and (2) TEU:

> *"1. The limits of Union competences are governed by the principle of conferral. The use of Union competences is governed by the principles of subsidiarity and proportionality.*
>
> *2. Under the principle of conferral, the Union shall act only within the limits of the competences conferred upon it by the member states in the Treaties to attain the objectives set out therein. Competences not conferred upon the Union in the Treaties remain with the member states".*

According to the principle of conferral, EU institutions may only take action in areas for which they have a competence – i.e., powers to act – and according to the rules set up. In the field of economic and monetary policy, the EU indeed has such competences. The system of competences of the EU is organized in the TFEU, Art. 2 to 6. The treaties make a distinction between "exclusive competences," where only the EU may set rules, "shared competences," where both the EU and member states may establish rules, provided the latter do not contradict EU rules, and areas where the EU sets up mechanisms and actions in order to coordinate, support or complement the actions of the member states. Amongst exclusive competences we find the *"monetary policy for the member states whose currency is the Euro"* (Art. 3 (1) letter c TFEU) – or also for instance *"establishing" "the competition rules necessary for the functioning of the internal market"* (Art. 3 (1) letter c TFEU). The internal market is the most typical area of shared competences (Art. 4 (2) letter b TFEU). A specific article is devoted to the competences in matters of coordination of economic policy (Art. 5 (1) TFEU), employment policies and social policies (Art. 5 (2) and (3) TFEU). It may be worthwhile to point to the fact that the European Convention, which drafted these provisions in 2002-2003 as part of the future constitutional treaty of 2004, was proposing the same kind of wording for all three areas, i.e., "the Union" coordinates, takes measures etc. On the insistence of some government representatives, the wording chosen for economic policy is: *"[t]he member states shall coordinate their economic policies within the Union* [not the Union shall coordinate]. *To this end, the Council shall adopt measures, in particular broad guidelines for these policies.*" From a legal point of view, this difference in wording has no consequence, but it is highly indicative of the mood of many member states' governments – be they part of the Eurozone or not – with regard to giving economic policy competence to the EU.

For the rest of the principles set up in Art. 2 to 6 TFEU, it suffices to quote Art. 2 (6) TFEU, according to which *"The scope of and arrangements for exercising the Union's competences shall be determined by the provisions of the Treaties relating to each area."* The said provision basically means that one needs to look at the precise clauses of the Treaties which are devoted to a specific area.

A second principle that is highly relevant to the point which is being made in this section is the "principle of institutional balance." This principle has been applied by the ECJ since the 1950s – first in the framework of the European Coal and Steel Community[5] – when the Court has to decide on cases involving issues about which institutions can act and within which parameters. The principle of institutional balance has been written down in Art. 13 (2) TEU: *"Each institution shall act within the limits of the powers conferred on it in the Treaties, and in conformity with the procedures, conditions and objectives set out in them."* The said provision means that it is not possible for an EU institution (for instance the Commission) to act where the treaties specify that another institution (for instance the Council) shall act; it also means that each institution is bound by the procedural rules which are set up for its functioning in the treaties, be it under general institutional rules or under the special rules that are indicated for a given area in specific treaty clauses.

The combination of the principles of conferral and of institutional balance finds its expression in the "legal bases" that determine whether and how EU institutions may act in a given area.

Correctly applying the relevant legal bases is indispensable in order to allow the EU to act.

A legal basis is made of a clause or a series of clauses of the EU founding treaties; there are also further legal bases for action which

---

5 Judgment of the Court of 6 April 1962, Meroni & Co. and others v High Authority of the European Coal and Steel Community, Joined cases 21/61 to 26/61.

are set up by "secondary EU law," i.e., in directives, regulations etc. Legal bases of secondary law have to comply with treaty legal bases. The analysis of this paper is limited to treaty legal bases, as this is the central issue. There are usually four components of a "legal basis" in EU Law.

First, the clauses that constitute a legal basis indicate – with more or fewer details – the area in which the Union has a competence, i.e., may act (or sometimes has to act). According to Art. 119 (1) TFEU (*emphasis added*):

> *"For the purposes set out in Article 3[6] of the Treaty on European Union, **the activities of** the member states and **the Union shall include**, as provided in the Treaties, **the adoption of an economic policy which is based on the close coordination of member states' economic policies, on the internal market and on the definition of common objectives**, and conducted in accordance with the principle of an open market economy with free competition."*

According to Art. 119 (2) TFEU *(emphasis added):*

> *"Concurrently with the foregoing, and as provided in the Treaties and in accordance with the procedures set out therein, **these activities shall include a single currency, the euro, and the definition and conduct of a single monetary policy and exchange-rate policy** the primary objective of both of which shall be to maintain price stability and, without prejudice to this objective, to support the general economic policies in the Union, in accordance with the principle of an open market economy with free competition."*

Second, the clauses that constitute a legal basis indicate – with more or fewer details – the legal instruments to be used by the EU. There may be a specific indication of which instruments may be used, i.e., directives, or regulations, or decisions; in such a case, the institutions may not resort to another instrument (i.e., a regulation instead of a directive). There may also be more general indications, the treaty re-

---

6 Art. 3 sets the objectives of the EU. The relevant clause is Art. 3 (4), according to which "The Union shall establish an economic and monetary union whose currency is the euro."

ferring very often to "measures"; this means that EU institutions may choose between directives, decisions or regulations according to their preferences. The binding character of an instrument, as well as the need for member states to transpose the EU rules into national law (for directives), or the absence of such a need (for regulations), are indicated in the applicable general provisions of the treaties – mainly in Art. 289 TFEU. There are only a few cases where the treaties limit the choice of instruments in the field of EMU. One may quote as particularly relevant Art. 121 TFEU, which provides for the use of regulations for the multilateral surveillance procedure.

Third, the clauses that constitute a legal basis indicate the decision-making procedure which applies. In many cases, the treaty refers to the "ordinary legislative procedure," i.e., the procedure whereby the Commission presents a proposal to the European Parliament and the Council, which needs to be approved – if needed after amendments – both by the Parliament deciding by a majority of the votes cast, and by the Council deciding by qualified majority voting (QMV). If a legal basis does not refer to the ordinary legislative procedure, it always indicates exactly which institutions propose (usually the Commission) and/or decide upon an action (Council, or Council and Parliament, or Commission, or even exceptionally the European Council), and by which majority. It is particularly important to take into account whether the Parliament has a co-decision power (as in the ordinary legislative procedure) or not, and whether the Council or European Council decides by QMV or by unanimity (or by consensus, as far as the European Council is concerned). While it is hardly worthwhile trying to memorise the details of QMV, it is indispensable to understand two points: *i)* unanimity means that a single government has a veto power, which it may use to block a decision or to negotiate a specific advantage; and *ii)* QMV means that governments who want to oppose a proposal need to find allies in order to build a blocking minority which impedes the adoption of a decision.

Fourth, the clauses that constitute a legal basis indicate very often – but not always – sector specific objectives or parameters. A typical example is that of Art. 119 (2) TFEU which sets the objectives of the monetary and exchange-rate policy of the EU: *"the primary objec-*

tive of both of which shall be to maintain price stability and, without prejudice to this objective, to support the general economic policies in the Union, in accordance with the principle of an open market economy with free competition."

The consequences of disregarding a legal basis are a sufficient enough incentive for EU institutions to take those bases seriously. That is the main legal reason for reforms to be adopted by means of treaty change.

At the EU level, even if the Commission, Parliament and Council – i.e., at least a solid majority of member states – would agree on a distorted use of existing legal bases, there is always a possibility for minority member states to challenge the adopted instruments through a request for judicial review by the ECJ; and furthermore, businesses, associations and individuals may also request judicial review if they can demonstrate a strong enough interest to be protected against the consequences of an EU act. The Court may declare the relevant decision, directive or regulation as being void, thus depriving the instrument from any impact. Furthermore, member states' courts which have to give effect to an EU legal instrument in litigation may refer to the ECJ through a "question for preliminary ruling" in order to know whether the relevant EU instrument is valid under UE law. If the ECJ responds that the instrument is invalid, the member state's court will not apply the EU act to the litigation, thus depriving it of effect. This double track for judicial review has demonstrated in the past that it is a strong instrument in order to ensure compliance with the treaties, and it has greatly contributed to the functioning of the internal market. The fact that only a rather limited number of ECJ rulings declare an EU instrument to be void due to the absence of a legal basis or inadequacy of the existing bases does not mean that the remedies are ineffective; indeed, the legal services of the Commission and of the Council check the presence and adequacy of legal bases before the EU institutions adopt an instrument, and therefore only a limited number of cases, where there are different possibilities of interpretation, are left open to a challenge with courts. At member state level, there is a further possibility for individuals, businesses and groups to challenge an EU act, in those countries where a Supreme court or Constitutional court has declared that it may check whether EU institutions – including the ECJ – act beyond the powers which have been given to them by the treaties ("ultra vires"), and that the Court might therefore declare the relevant instrument not applicable in their country; this is the case of the German constitutional court. Such an "ultra vires" declaration has never been pronounced until now, but the relevant Court rulings act as a "Sword of Damocles" upon the EU institutions and member states' governments; conversely such declarations by Courts are sometimes used by a member state's government in order to impede EU action during negotiations.

If there is no appropriate legal basis in the treaties, the only possibility that remains in order to enable the EU to act is treaty amendment. Treaty amendment is far from being impossible, as demonstrated by the succession of reform treaties which have been adopted since the mid nineteen-eighties by the Single European Act signed early 1986, which entered into force on 1 July 1987; the Maastricht Treaty signed early 1992, which entered into force on 1 November 1993; the Amsterdam Treaty signed in October 1997, which entered into force on 1 May 1999; the Nice Treaty signed early 2001, which entered into force on 1 March 2003; and the Lisbon Treaty, signed in December 2007, which entered into force on 1 December 2009. There are, however, two strong limitations to treaty reform. First, treaty reform always requires the unanimity of all member states – even if the reform only applies to some of them as is the case for the Eurozone. The unanimity rule gives a very strong veto position to any member state's government that either does not agree with the content of the proposed reform or wants to use its vetoing power in order to bargain on any other topic of interest. Second, treaty reform always requires ratification according to member states' constitutional rules. This has several consequences: *i)* member state's governments are never 100% sure that they will be supported by a majority of their Parliament, especially if a reinforced majority is required for the reform of EU treaties, as happens quite often; *ii)* some member states have a set of rules which may lead to the need for a referendum, as happens for most treaty reforms with Denmark and Ireland, and as would happen with the United Kingdom since the European Union Act of 2011; *iii)* rules regarding the discretion of the Head of State to ratify a treaty or not once having the required agreement from Parliament (or through referendum) are not totally clear, as has been demonstrated by the Czech Republic with the Lisbon Treaty in 2009. Ratification rules give strong arguments to those governments who do not want to be seen as directly opposing reform, in order to oppose it indirectly or to bargain on any other topic of interest.

As a consequence of the aforesaid, from a legal perspective, it is easier for the EU to act within the boundaries set by existing legal bases, especially if the relevant legal bases only require QVM in the Council. This being said, other reasons may lead to treaty reform when it is not a necessary requirement, e.g., uncertainty about the exact limits of existing boundaries to EU action, or simply political reasons, e.g., governments wanting to send specific signals to their electorate or to the market[7].

A whole series of treaty bases for economic and monetary policy are to be found in the EU treaties[8].

The most relevant treaty legal bases for Eurozone governance are to be found in the TFEU Part III, Title VIII "Economic and Monetary Policy": Arts. 119 to 144 establish the system of governance of the Eurozone as well as the rules applying to non-Eurozone member states – i.e., a series of rules and principles relating to economic and monetary issues that apply to all EU member states, and the general principles according to which a member state which is not yet in the Eurozone may enter the EMU. As far as the UK and Denmark are concerned, they have obtained an opt-out of the EMU together with the Maastricht Treaty, and their procedures to enter the EMU are established in separate protocols, which have the same value as the treaties. Sweden, on the contrary, does not benefit in principle from an opt-out; its special position is due to the fact that – unlike other new member states – the Swedish government neglected to adhere to the exchange-rate mechanism of the European Monetary System at the moment of its accession to the EU in 1995, and thus Sweden does

---

7 See the chapter by Bruno de Witte, Treaty Games, in this book.
8 See footnote 4 above.

not comply with one of the four conditions for entering the EMU[9]. Four very important protocols complement Part III, Title VIII of the TFEU; i.e., Protocol (n° 4) on the Statute of the European System of Central Banks and of the European Central Bank; and Protocol (n° 12) on the Excessive Deficit Procedure; Protocol (n° 13) on the Convergence Criteria; and Protocol (n° 14) on the Eurogroup. The rules and principles of these texts have all been drafted by the intergovernmental conference (IGC) on the economic and monetary union of 1991 and were part of the Maastricht treaty, with the exception of the Protocol on the Eurogroup, which has codified existing practice in a protocol annexed to the Lisbon Treaty in 2007. It is important to take into account that the relevant IGC was composed mainly – at the technical level – by experts from the member states' Central Banks and Treasuries; the clauses on the European Central Bank are due to the German Bundesbank's experts.

Protocol n° 12 has a very specific feature: contrary to other protocols, it does not need to follow the usual treaty reform procedure with ratification for its amendment. According to Art. 126 (14) TFEU (*emphasis added*):

> "***Further provisions*** *relating to the implementation of the procedure described in this article* ***are set out in the Protocol on the excessive deficit procedure*** *annexed to the Treaties.*

> "***The Council shall, acting unanimously*** *in accordance with a special legislative procedure and after consulting the European Parliament and the European Central Bank,* ***adopt the appropriate provisions which shall then replace the said Protocol.***

> "*Subject to the other provisions of this paragraph,* ***the Council shall,*** *on a proposal from the Commission and after consulting the European Parliament,* ***lay down detailed rules and definitions for the application of the provisions of the said Protocol.***"

The quoted provisions of Protocol n° 12 are particularly important for the topic examined in this paper as they provide for the definition

---

9 "The observance of the normal fluctuation margins provided for by the exchange-rate mechanism of the European Monetary System, for at least two years," see Art. 140 (1) for the formulation of the rule after the entry into force of the Lisbon Treaty.

of the "reference values" for the "excessive deficit procedure," and of the concepts to be used in the application of this procedure, as well as the respective responsibilities of the Commission and of member states. The authors of the Maastricht Treaty thus prepared the ground for reforms of one of the central features of the governance of the Eurozone's economic policy: the excessive deficit control procedure, which details may be amended in the same way as a regulation requiring unanimity of the Council, and not through Treaty amendment.

2. The Treaty on Stability, Coordination and Governance in the Economic and Monetary Union of 1 March 2012 and the EU Treaty.

From the time of the preparations for the European summit of 9 December 2011, there has been talk of a "Fiscal compact" for the rules and principles which have been embedded in title III of the TSCG signed on 1 March 2012, or even for the entire treaty. This has generated and still sometimes generates a number of misunderstandings. Apart from the fact that the word "compact" is far from being precise and clear in legal terms – it may apply to a treaty as well as to any other kind of binding or even non binding instrument – the expression "*fiscal*" generates misunderstandings in those member states where the word fiscal is not perceived as "*involving financial matters*" as in the English language, but as having to do with taxation. In French, for instance, "*politique fiscale*" has always meant "tax policy," and indeed the Dutch, French, Italian, and Spanish versions of Title III "*Fiscal Compact*" of the TSCG of 1 March 2012 rightly say "*begrotingspact*," "*pacte budgétaire*," "*patto di bilancio*," or "*pacto presupuestario;*" there is no risk of misunderstanding with the German "*Fiskalpolitischer Pakt*" where the word *Fiskal* has the same meaning as the English fiscal.

The Treaty signed by 25 of the 27 EU member states contains four series of provisions.

Title I "*Purpose and Scope,*" Title II "*Consistency and Relationship with the Law of the Union,*" as well as Title VI "*General and final provisions*" contain either declaratory statements, underlining that the content of the Treaty is not in contradiction with EU law, or the usual technical clauses which one finds in a treaty. The mere fact that the treaty declares its consistency with EU law does not mean that it is indeed consistent with the obligations and limitations which the EU treaties put onto member states and EU institutions: further examination is needed and, in theory at least, nothing can impede a member state from bringing the matter to the ECJ on the basis of a procedure for EU treaty infringement. Art. 14 (2) provides for entry into force of the TSCG on 1 January 2013, provided that twelve member states of the Eurozone have ratified it; therefore, the vetoing powers embedded in the EU treaty amendment procedure are set aside. It has to be underlined that the TSCG will only be binding for those member states that will have ratified it.

Title III contains the specific rules of the *"fiscal compact,"* Title IV those for *"economic coordination and convergence,"* and Title V those for *"governance of the euro area."* From a legal perspective, only Title III contains innovations which are worth commenting on.

Compared to the existing EU treaty provisions, the "fiscal compact" provisions contain two innovations.

First, according to Art. 3 of the TSCG, budgetary deficits should be prohibited by member states' laws, and an appropriate mechanism should be included in the relevant legal provisions in order to impede government from departing from this "golden rule." Second, competence is given to the European Court of Justice to control whether a member state has infringed upon its obligation to set up and apply legislation for the "golden rule," and eventually to impose financial sanctions upon a member state that persists in infringing upon the said obligations. The purpose of this paper is not to evaluate whether the "golden rule" system is useful or whether trying to apply it is realistic, but to understand if a treaty was needed in order to impose such a rule upon the member states.

The parameters to refer to in order to understand whether a treaty was necessary in order to establish the "golden rule" and related procedures are contained in the treaty clauses and protocols indicated in the previous section, i.e., Art. 126 TFEU and Protocol n° 12 on the excessive procedure deficit.

As a point of departure, it has to be stressed that according to Art. 126 (1) TFEU *"member states shall avoid excessive government deficits,"* whereas according to Art. 3 (1) (a) TSCG *"the budgetary position of the general government of a Contracting Party shall be balanced or in surplus."* At first sight, one might say that the TFEU allows a government deficit – as long as it is not excessive – whereas the TSCG prohibits any deficit; it is possible, therefore, to argue that a treaty reform was needed in order to impose more stringent duties upon member states than those foreseen by the EU treaties in their Maastricht-Lisbon version. However, this is by far too simplistic a way of reasoning. First, one needs to take into account the entire text of both the EU treaty provisions and the "fiscal compact" of the TSCG in order to understand them; and second, those provisions have to be interpreted in the light of the EU's objective of establishing *"an economic and monetary union whose currency is the euro."*

Comparing the details of both series of provisions shows that, more important than the principle – avoiding excessive government deficits or prohibiting government deficits – the important point is to define what has to be understood under "deficit." As a matter of fact, according to Art. 3 (1) (b) TSCG, the prohibition of government deficit *"**shall be deemed to be respected if the annual structural balance of the general government is at its country-specific medium-term objective**, as defined in the revised Stability and Growth Pact, **with a lower limit of a structural deficit of 0.5% of the gross domestic product** at market prices"* (emphasis added). According to Art. 3 (1) (d), the structural deficit may go up to 1% *"**where the ratio of** the general government debt to gross domestic product at market prices **is significantly below 60% and where risks in terms of long-term sustainability of public finances are low**"* (emphasis added). On the other hand, according to Art. 126 (2) TFEU, *"The Commission shall monitor the development of the budgetary situation and of the stock of government debt"* with regard to *"reference values"* set out in Protocol n° 12. As is well known, the "reference values" chosen by the authors of the Maastricht treaty are "*3 % for the ratio of the planned or actual government deficit to gross domestic product at market prices*" and "*60 % for the ratio of government debt to gross domestic product at market prices.*"

It seems, therefore, that it might have been possible to simply change the reference values of Protocol n° 12 and the definitions included in it in order to arrive at the same result – in substance – as sought with Art. 3 TSCG. A reform of Protocol n° 12 would not have needed the usual treaty amendment procedure to be used – and it would have been more difficult for the British Prime Minister to demand that treaty reform include changing the existing legal bases for the regulation of financial services in order to replace QMV by unanimity of the Council, as David Cameron did on 9 December 2012.

Once the reference values would have been changed in the provisions replacing Protocol n° 12, it would have been possible to adopt a directive – based upon the said provisions or, alternatively, a directive adopted under the procedure of "enhanced cooperation,"[10] which is available if 9 Member states want to do so and the Commission agrees – that would have imposed the same obligations upon Eurozone member states as those imposed by Art. 3 Fiscal compact.

Second, according to Art. 126 (10) TFEU, "*The rights to bring actions provided for in articles 258 and 259 may not be exercised within the framework of paragraphs 1 to 9 of this article.*" What this technical jargon means is that neither the Commission nor member states may bring to the ECJ an action for infringement against any member state that does not comply with its duties under the "excessive deficit procedure." Art. 126 (10) does not exclude a review by the ECJ in matters of excessive deficits: it remains possible for a member state's court to make a referral for preliminary ruling to the ECJ in order to obtain an authoritative interpretation of the EU treaties and the acts adopted by EU institutions, amongst others, Art. 126 TFEU, Protocol n° 12 and the measures adopted upon basis of the cited provisions, such as the relevant Six-Pack regulations. Until now, however, there has been no situation where a member state's Court

---

10 The procedural conditions for establishing such an "enhanced cooperation" between at least 9 member states are set up in Art. 20 TEU and 326 to 334 TFEU.

was in the position of making such a referral. In the same way, if a measure adopted upon the basis of the cited provisions were to be relevant in order to solve a dispute by member states' courts, those courts could also make a referral in order to ask the ECJ whether the relevant measure is in line with treaty provisions. More important than the Court's competence is the fact that where the Commission may exercise the action for infringement (Art. 258 TFEU), it has a far more salient power to put pressure upon member states than where it can only make recommendations to the Council – as is the case under Art. 126 (1) to (9), which establish the principles of the excessive deficit procedure.

Comparing the Eurozone's governance design to the internal market's governance design, it is clear that the main weakness of the first is the fact that final decisions upon a member state's compliance with its duties is being taken by the government of the member states in the Eurozone, instead of being taken by institutions that are independent from the member states. What is at stake is neither the degree of expertise available to the Commission, to the Council or to member states' governments, nor the individual quality of Commissioners, judges or member states' ministers, it is the fact that when examining their fellow governments' performance, member states' governments have to face a conflict of interest between their short term electoral interests at home and their medium term interests as members of the EMU. Both the shift of the burden of qualified majority voting in the functioning of the Stability and Growth Pact that has been introduced by the "Six-Pack" (see below), and Art. 8 TSCG, have to be understood in the perspective of that main weakness of the Eurozone's governance design.

According to Art. 8 TSCG, the European Commission will present a report on the provisions adopted by each Eurozone member state that has ratified the TSCG in order to introduce the "golden rule" and accompanying mechanism in its legal system. If the Commission finds that a member state has failed to comply, "the matter will be brought to the Court of Justice of the European Union by one or more Contracting Parties." The reason why the TSCG does not stipulate a power for the Commission to bring the matter to the ECJ is that it would be in contradiction with Art. 126 (10) TFEU; such a change could only have been introduced by way of EU treaty amendment, with unanimous agreement of all EU member states and ratification by all of them. Art. 8 TSCG further provides that where a member state would not adopt the measures to redress its failure to comply as declared by a judgement of the ECJ, "*it may impose on it a lump sum or a penalty payment appropriate in the circumstances and that shall not exceed 0.1 % of its gross domestic product. The amounts imposed on a Contracting Party whose currency is the euro shall be payable to the European Stability Mechanism. In other cases, payments shall be made to the general budget of the European Union.*" Too much attention has been given to this latter provision in the media – and to a large extent by politicians – with statements according to which the ECJ would decide on Eurozone member states' budgetary deficits. What matters is neither the amount nor nature of the lump sum or penalty payment, but the fact that such a mechanism further reinforces the power of the Commission as an independent institution to put pressure on member states' governments that do not comply with their obligations, in the same way as with the internal market's governance design.

The "Six-Pack"[11] contains – amongst other provisions – the first serious attempt to remedy the fundamental weakness of the Eurozone's governance design that has been indicated above. To cut a long story short, instead of needing a qualified majority of Eurozone's member states to endorse a Commission's proposal of sanction on the basis of Art. 126 – as was the rule in the past – since 1 January 2012 the burden is reversed: it is not any more the Commission's responsibility to find the necessary number of governments to support its proposal of sanction, it is the responsibility of a government that disagrees with the Commission proposal to find a qualified majority of governments to oppose the proposed sanction; if no such qualified majority is found, the Commission's proposal enters into force.

In contrast to Art. 3 and 8 TSCG, the other clauses of Title III of TSCG do not introduce legal innovations with regard to existing Eurozone governance rules. Art. 4 TSCG makes an express refer-

---

11 See references in footnote 2, above.

ence to the "Six-Pack" and to the TFEU. Art. 5 TSCG foresees that a member State "*that is subject to an excessive deficit procedure* [...] *shall put in place a budgetary and economic partnership programme*," making however an express statement to the fact that "the content and format of such programmes shall be defined in European Union law" and that its implementation "*will take place within the context of the existing surveillance procedures under the Stability and Growth Pact.*" Last but not least, there is a further attempt to correct the fundamental weakness of governance design which has previously been described, in Art. 7 TSCG. According to that provision, the Eurozone's member states "*commit to supporting the proposals or recommendations submitted by the European Commission.*" Such a commitment might seem new with respect to the relevant treaty provisions, but it is immediately blunted by the following sentence, according to which "*[t]his obligation shall not apply where it is established* [...] *that a qualified majority of [the relevant governments]* [...] *is opposed to the decision proposed or recommended.*"

The new treaty's provisions on economic policy coordination and convergence and on governance of the Euro area do not introduce any significant novelty with respect to existing EU law and practice.

Without going into detail of the provisions of Title IV "*Economic Policy Coordination and Convergence*" TSCG, it may be stated that the provisions contained in Arts. 9 to 11 are not contrary to Art. 121 TFEU, which establishes the procedure for ex-ante coordination of the Eurozone's member states' economic policies. Art. 9 is anything but a precise set of objectives and procedures: it only states that the relevant member states "*shall take the necessary actions and measures in all the areas which are essential to the proper functioning of the euro area in pursuit of the objectives of fostering competitiveness, promoting employment, contributing further to the sustainability of public finances and reinforcing financial stability*"; the same may be said from Art. 10, according to which the relevant member states will "*stand ready to make active use, whenever appropriate and necessary, of measures specific to those member states whose currency is the euro, as provided for [by the TFEU.]*" The wording of Art. 11 might seem somewhat more precise in that it says that the relevant member states *"ensure that all major economic policy reforms that they plan to undertake will be discussed ex-ante and, where appropriate, coordinated among themselves. Such coordination shall involve the institutions of the European Union as required by European Union law"*; it is far less detailed, however, than the content of the "Six-Pack." Amongst other innovations, the "Six-Pack" has introduced a series of new obligations for member states to coordinate their economic policy by reviewing their draft budgets before submitting the relevant bills to their Parliaments, during the "European semester." One might say that the content of Title IV of the TSCG is more like a "press statement" than a legally binding instrument.

Title V *"Governance of the Euro Area"'* contains the provisions of the TSCG which have most necessitated negotiations at the political level, with some rude battles between Heads of State or Governments of Eurozone and non-Eurozone member states. Reading its content in the light of previous practice of European Council and Eurogroup meetings and of Protocol n° 14 on the Eurogroup, it appears clearly that the battle was about prestige, not about substance or procedure. Art. 12 goes into the details of how the relevant Heads of State or Government of Eurozone member states shall *"meet informally in Euro Summit meetings"* and how those of non-Eurozone member states will be from time to time invited to attend such "informal meetings." Obligations relative to "informal" meetings are nothing but a legal oxymoron, and at any rate it was by no means necessary to adopt a separate treaty in order to set them down; if wanted, a regulation adopted under enhanced cooperation procedures would have had the same result in legal terms.

Summing up

To sum up: an appropriate legal basis is always needed for EU actions. The only provisions of the TSCG of 1 March 2012 which needed treaty EU reform in order to be introduced are those giving the member states power to refer to the ECJ in Art. 8 TSCG. The changes introduced by the "Six-Pack" (especially when it comes to shifting the burden of QVM) are far more important from an institutional point of view than the "Fiscal Compact" Treaty.

3. The Remaining Constraints of EU Primary Law for the Eurozone's Governance.

A quick oversight of the remaining constraints of EU primary law for the Eurozone's governance is indispensable in order to underline the boundaries within which further reforms of the governance architecture and procedures could be undertaken without EU treaty change. It has to be stressed that a treaty between member states – such as the TSCG of 1 March 2012 – cannot set aside the said boundaries. Only amendments according to Art. 48 TEU can achieve such a result. In other words, qualitative changes in the Eurozone's governance that would go beyond the said boundaries need either full consensus of all the governments of EU member states and support by their Parliaments and electorates – even formally speaking, in the case of Denmark, Ireland and the UK – or a strong political commitment by those governments who would wish to go further, to start anew with the EU integration scheme, accepting the risks of implosion of the EU as it is now that such a move would imply.

Taking into account that the well known "reference values" of 3% and 60% GDP may be changed by an EU regulation or equivalent instrument that only necessitates unanimous agreement of governments at a Council meeting, the remaining constraints on the Eurozone's governance are mainly those of Art. 122 to 125 and 127 TFEU, complemented by Protocol n° 4 on the statute of the European System of Central Banks and of the European Central Bank.

First, Art. 122 TFEU only permits temporary safeguarding measures to be taken by the EU institutions and/or member states in cases of overwhelming financial or economic crises. The amendment to Art. 136 TFEU that has been adopted by the European Council on the basis of Art. 48 (6) TEU in May 2011[12] should establish a permanent legal basis for member states' actions such as setting up the "European Stability Mechanism"; this will only happen if all EU member

---

12 European Council Decision of 25 March 2011 amending Article 136 of the Treaty on the Functioning of the European Union with regard to a stability mechanism for Member States whose currency is the Euro, Official Journal of the European Union of 6/4/2011 n° L 91, p. 1.

states ratify the amendment, which is foreseen to enter into force on 1 January 2013 at the earliest.

Second, Art. 125 TFEU establishes the famous "no bail-out" clause, which is complemented by a prohibition of direct banking facilities to governments (Art. 123 TFEU) and a prohibition of privileged access to banking institutions (Art. 123 TFEU). Similar provisions are laid down in Protocol n° 4 on the ESCB and ECB. To cut a long story short, there are at least three possible interpretations of the "no bail out" clause of Art. 125 TFEU, according to which the Union and member states *"shall not be liable for or assume the commitments of [member states governments] without prejudice to mutual financial guarantees for the joint execution of a specific project."* According to a strict interpretation, Art. 125 establishes a prohibition for EU institutions and member states to guarantee directly or indirectly for the consolidated sovereign debt[13] of a member state; such an interpretation would not leave room for the actions that have been hitherto undertaken in order to help Greece, Ireland and Portugal during the financial crisis; such an interpretation is supported by an important part of German legal doctrine. According to a less strict interpretation, Art. 125 only establishes a prohibition against EU institutions and member states guaranteeing directly for the consolidated sovereign debt of a member state; it does not prohibit EU institutions or member states from lending money to a member state in order to help it finance its consolidated sovereign debt. Such an interpretation is implicitly supported by the Eurozone's member state governments and EU institutions. According to an even less strict interpretation, the purpose and scope of Art. 125 TFEU is only to protect EU institutions and member states against claims of creditors of sovereign debt of another member state; such an interpretation is only rarely put forward openly, but was clearly the major reason why Germany insisted so much upon a "no-bail out" clause being part of the Maastricht Treaty signed in 1992.

---

13 The words "consolidated sovereign debt" are used for "the commitments of central governments, regional, local or other public authorities, other bodies governed by public law, or public undertakings of any Member State" as indicated precisely in Art. 125 TFEU and comparable clauses.

In theory, only the ECJ, if asked to do so, could choose which interpretation has to prevail. There are two ways according to which the Court could be asked such a question. First, one of the EU Institutions or any member state (whether a member of the Eurozone or not) could challenge a decision of an EU institution that it would deem contrary to the no-bail out clause; any possible body with legal personality that could demonstrate a direct interest in doing so could also challenge such a decision. Nothing of the kind has happened until now, and it has to be borne in mind that an action in annulment can only be brought to the court within two months of the adoption of the challenged act. Second, a member state's action deemed to be contrary to the no bail-out clause could be challenged in two ways: *i)* the Commission or another member state could start an infringement procedure; *ii)* a national Court could decide upon a court procedure against one of its government's actions deemed to be contrary to the no bail-out clause, and the relevant court might refer the question of interpretation of Art. 126 to the ECJ. The latter type of challenge to a national court has already been triggered in Germany, where the Federal Constitutional Court has had to decide upon the German participation in the financial stability funds established by Eurozone governments in 2010. The German Constitutional Court has, however, been able to avoid referring the question of interpretation of Art. 1269 to the ECJ, and will probably do its best in the future to find ways and means of avoiding such a referral.

Third, Art. 127 TFEU and Protocol n° 4 are setting up the objectives and tasks of the ECB. Any change in these objectives and tasks would need a treaty reform according to Art. 48 TEU. The major point for legal discussion is the balance to be observed between the first primary objective – *"maintain price stability"* – and secondary objectives – *"support the general economic policies in the Union with a view to contributing to the achievement of the objectives of the Union as laid down in Article 3 of the Treaty on European Union."* Suffice it to say that, whereas there are discussions about the substance of these objectives and their balance not only between politicians, between economists, but also between legal scholars, one may easily bet that Courts, and especially the ECJ, would not enter into such a debate and would most probably state that the choices to be made are within the boundaries of discretion of the relevant institutions and authorities.

Summing up.

The only provisions of TSCG of 1 March 2012 which needed treaty EU reform are those giving the Commission (and member states) power to refer to the ECJ in Art. 8 TSCG.

The changes introduced by the "Six-Pack" (including shifting the burden of QVM) are far more important from an institutional point of view than the "Fiscal compact" Treaty; these have been made using EU secondary legislation based upon the existing clauses of the treaties.

The remaining constraints of EU primary law for the Eurozone's governance have as consequences that further significant steps towards a federal economic policy would need further Treaty reform.

10
Treaty Games - Law as Instrument and as Constraint in the Euro Crisis Policy

Bruno De Witte

1. Introduction

This paper deals with the role of law, and in particular the role of treaties, in the attempts made by EU institutions and governments of the EU member states to deal with the sovereign debt crisis during the past two years (April 2010-April 2012).[1] Once it was decided, under the pressure of events, that common policy responses were needed, the use of legal instruments came fairly naturally, as most public policies require legal change for their implementation.[2] In this particular case, though, questions arose again and again as to which kind of legal instruments should be chosen: soft law instruments (such as the Euro Plus Pact), EU legislation (such as the five Regulations and one Directive collectively known as the 'Six Pack'), or the conclusion of international treaties.

---

1 This text was completed on 2 May 2012 and does not reflect later developments.
2 This does not exclude, of course, the use of other policy instruments that do not involve legal change. To give one prominent example from the sovereign debt crisis, the policy decision of the European Central Bank to create massive lending facilities for private banks was adopted and implemented in the framework of its existing powers and did not require legal change.

The particular theme of this paper is why and how the treaty instrument (including the amendment of the existing Treaties) was chosen on four different occasions in the course of the past two years. The choice of that instrument has particular advantages and drawbacks, compared to other legal instruments, and that choice can therefore be interpreted as a policy game involving the interaction of strategic actors, principally – in this case – the governments of the EU member states. Like all games, treaty games are subject to a number of rules of the game: there are conditions to be fulfilled for states to be allowed to conclude treaties on certain subjects (in view of the constraints of their EU membership), and there are consequences that derive from opting for the conclusion of a treaty. In that respect, law has not only acted as an instrument of Euro crisis policy, pliant to the wishes and often irrational hopes of governments and EU institutions, but it has also acted, and continues to act, as a constraint for that Euro crisis policy.

The four treaties that were concluded in the context of the sovereign debt crisis are the following:

(1) A Decision of the Representatives of the Governments of the Euro Area countries of 10 May 2010 by which they agreed to set up a provisional European Financial Stability Facility (EFSF). Although this document is not called 'treaty,' it is in fact a binding international agreement and was treated as such by the national governments and parliaments.[3] This agreement immediately entered into force. The EFSF, which was based on it, took the unusual form of a company of private law based in Luxembourg, of which the 17 Euro states are the shareholders, and the company then concluded a 'framework agreement' with its 17 shareholders, defining its mandate.

(2) An amendment of Article 136 of the Treaty on the Functioning of the European Union (TFEU) to allow Euro area countries

---

3 The term 'international treaty' is, in fact, a shorthand denomination for all written agreements whereby the participating states (or international organisations) lay down legally binding obligations, whatever the actual name of the instrument. Thus, treaties can be called 'convention,' 'agreement,' 'pact,' 'charter,' or – as here – 'decision of the representatives of governments,' but they all share the same basic legal regime laid down in the Vienna Convention on the Law of Treaties.

to set up a permanent financial stability mechanism, which was adopted on 25 March 2011. This amendment is formally speaking not an international treaty but a unanimous decision of the European Council; but since its intended effect is to modify an existing provision of the TFEU, and since that modification will itself have the force of a Treaty norm, we can include it in our examination. This Treaty amendment has not yet entered into force, because it must first be approved by all 27 EU member states according to their own constitutional requirements.

(3) A Treaty establishing the European Stability Mechanism (ESM Treaty), concluded on 1 February 2012 between the 17 Euro area countries, which uses the 'permission' granted by the TFEU amendment mentioned above. The ESM is intended to replace the EFSF but the ESM Treaty had not yet entered into force at the time of writing.

(4) A Treaty on Stability, Coordination and Governance in the Economic and Monetary Union (often called 'Fiscal Compact'), concluded on 2 March 2012 between the 17 Euro area countries and 8 further EU member states. This Treaty has not yet entered into force either.

Two characteristics of the 'treaty games' appear already from this listing.

The first characteristic is that treaties are, normally speaking, two-step legal processes: they are first negotiated and signed by the state parties when they have agreed on the content, but they must afterwards be ratified by each state in order for that state to be formally bound by the treaty. This requirement allows for the text, which was negotiated by the government, to be approved by the national parliament or to be submitted to other legal checks (for example, by a constitutional court) before it becomes binding on the participating countries. The entry into force of the treaty is often made dependent on ratification by all states, but not necessarily so (numbers 3 and 4 are both exceptions to that rule, as we shall see). Also, it is occasionally possible for international treaties to enter into force immediately, without the need for prior approval by national parliaments, as was the case with number 1.

The second characteristic is the difference in the number and identity of the state parties to those treaties. Indeed, whereas the amendment of Article 136 TFEU was agreed to necessarily by all 27 member states, the Fiscal Compact was concluded between 25 EU states, and the other two agreements were concluded among the 17 Euro states only. Thus, one of the games consisted in using treaties to organise the differentiation between the Euro area states and the rest of the EU countries.

This chapter will proceed as follows. In Section 2, I will briefly recall the general role played by treaties in the European integration process, as a background to the discussion of their use in the context of the sovereign debt crisis. In Section 3, I will examine the reasons why the 'choice for a treaty' was made, on four different occasions, during the unfolding of the Euro crisis; in this context, I will also highlight the legal constraints that determine or preclude the use of the treaty instrument. In Section 4, I will examine the legal consequences that derive from the choice, in those four cases, of the treaty instrument. In Section 5, I will conclude with a general discussion of the role played by the 'treaty games' in the crisis responses of the past two years.

2. The Role of Treaties in the European Integration Process

International treaties form, on the one hand, the *very basis* of the European Union's integration process; and, on the other hand, they have occasionally been used as *ancillary instruments* of European integration, in the margin of the European Union's central institutional framework.

The basis for the EU's institutional system is formed by the so-called founding Treaties, currently named the TEU and TFEU. In that sense, the European Union remains, formally speaking, an international organisation. Although those Treaties have been frequently and profoundly modified since they were first concluded (the TEU finds its origins in the Treaty of Maastricht of 1992, and the TFEU in the Treaty establishing the European Economic Community of

1957, but both of them have been modified beyond recognition), those revisions have been marked by the rigidity of the Treaty amendment process, which requires the agreement of all the member state governments followed by the individual ratification by each of them. The failure of one or more states to ratify a treaty revision may lead to the postponement of its entry into force, as happened with the Treaty of Lisbon after the first Irish referendum in 2008, or to its complete demise, as happened after the negative referenda on the Constitutional Treaty in France and the Netherlands, in 2005. The Treaties continue to be particularly rigid instruments. They contain a wealth of fairly detailed rules constraining the day-to-day operation of the EU institutions and of the member states, and therefore the need or will to modify those detailed rules is bound to arise frequently with evolving political circumstances. And yet, such modifications are made very difficult by the unanimity rule which implies that all Treaty amendments must be agreed to unanimously by all 27 governments, and must then be approved, in one way or the other, by the domestic institutions (including, in any case, the national parliament) of each country. Therefore, the entry into force of the Lisbon Treaty in December 2009, after a cumbersome ratification process of more than two years, was marked by a huge sense of relief from the side of the EU governments, and they expressed a strong preference for not opening up new treaty negotiations in the foreseeable future.

In addition to forming the legal backbone of the European Union's operation, international treaties have also been used as ancillary legal instruments, giving legal support to the cooperation of some or all of the member states in the margins of the EU institutional framework. At the time the European Communities were created, one such agreement entered into force almost simultaneously, namely the Treaty establishing the Benelux Economic Union (1958). The EEC Treaty contained an express reference to it that basically authorized this partial agreement, whose content overlapped considerably with the EEC Treaty, as long as it went further than EEC law and none of its legal rules conflicted with EEC law. This explicit authorization is still in the Treaties today, namely in Article 350 TFEU. Later on, there were other examples, of which the most well-known were the Schengen Agreement and Schengen Convention that were initially concluded between a limited number of member states, but whose membership later expanded without ever including all the EU countries.

If one looks more closely at these partial international agreements (that is, agreements concluded between less than all the EU member states), two categories can be distinguished:

1. Special interest agreements, when some member states have a special interest in something which the others do not share. Take, for example, the protection of the environment of the Alps: only the member states whose territory is part of the Alps have an interest in concluding such an agreement, but the others do not.

2. 'Move forward' agreements that try to push forward the agenda of European integration when not all member states are ready to do so; this was the case with the Schengen treaties and this is the case now again with the Fiscal Compact. Not all countries are prepared to take this (alleged) step forward in integration, and the conclusion of a separate international agreement allows the others to circumvent this opposition.

Partial international agreements between member states of the EU are allowed, but only within the limits set by EU law obligations.[4] Briefly said, this means that such agreements may not be concluded in areas of exclusive EU competence (e.g., in the field of external trade, or of monetary policy as far as the Euro area countries are concerned), that they may not affect the normal operation of the EU institutions (this is the so-called duty of sincere cooperation) and that they may not include any provisions that conflict with EU law.

3. The Unfolding of the Treaty Games

In this section, I will examine, case by case, how each of the four international agreements came into being, and in particular how the

---

4 For a discussion of those limits, see B. De Witte, 'Old-fashioned Flexibility: International Agreements between Member States of the European Union,' in G. de Búrca and J. Scott (eds), Constitutional Change in the EU – From Uniformity to Flexibility? (2000) 31. See also the study by L.S. Rossi, Le convenzioni fra gli Stati membri dell'Unione europea (2000).

choice for an international agreement came to prevail over alternative legal instruments.

The Creation of the EFSF

When the Greek sovereign debt crisis erupted for the first time, in the spring of 2010, it triggered a twofold policy response at the European level. On the one hand, the Council of the EU adopted a Regulation establishing a European financial stabilization mechanism (EFSM) based on Article 122(2) TFEU.[5] Article 122(2), whose text dates from the Maastricht Treaty, allows the Union to grant financial assistance to a Member State that 'is in difficulties or seriously threatened with severe difficulties caused by natural disasters or exceptional occurrences beyond its control.' At the same Council session of 9 May, the ministers of the Euro area countries, wearing their intergovernmental hats, adopted a Decision in which they committed themselves to support a separate and additional loan and credit mechanism.[6] That mechanism, called the European Financial Stability Facility (EFSF), was established soon after as a so-called Special Purpose Vehicle – in legal terms, a private company established in Luxembourg but jointly controlled by the Euro area states. In terms of its lending and guarantee capacity, the EFSF, with a total amount of 440 billion Euro, far outstripped the EFSM which has an EU budget guarantee amounting to only 60 billion Euro. The operation of the EFSF was limited by the founders to a period of three years.

Why was this two-pronged approach chosen in May 2010? The main reason seems to have been that the EU-law instrument (the EFSM) was insufficiently powerful to deal with the crisis. In view of its limited and strongly earmarked budgetary resources, the European Union

---

5 Council Regulation 407/2010 of 11 May 2010 establishing a European financial stabilization mechanism, OJ 2010, L 118/1.

6 The Decision has the following baroque denomination: Decision of the Representatives of the Governments of the Euro Area Member States Meeting Within the Council of the European Union. See Council document 9614/10 of 10 May 2010, accessible on the public register of Council documents. There is a longstanding practice of government representatives 'switching hats' during a Council meeting and adopting decisions qua states rather than qua Council members, but this phenomenon is quite unusual in a context of enhanced cooperation such as this one, namely limited to the Euro area countries.

itself does not possess sufficient 'firepower' to deal with a massive sovereign debt crisis. Also, by having recourse to the EU budget, the non-Euro countries are indirectly called to fund an operation which aims at ensuring the stability of the Euro area. The United Kingdom, in particular, was less than keen to spend large amounts of EU money to support Greece; hence, the decision to 'go outside' the institutional framework of the European Union, and to build a more powerful financial guarantee instrument by means of a separate agreement between the Euro area countries themselves. However, negotiating a fully-fledged international treaty would not have been practical, in view of the urgency of the required policy response. Therefore, rather than concluding a formal treaty, the Euro states concluded what is known in the jargon of international law as an executive agreement, that is an agreement that is immediately operational upon signature by the (governmental) representatives of the states without the need to go through ratification by their national parliaments. Of course, this mechanism cannot be used to circumvent the domestic separation of powers. Therefore, it is only permissible – under the constitutional law of most European states – to the extent that no important new legal obligations or limitations of sovereignty are incurred by the agreement. In the particular case, the argument could be made that setting up the EFSF, by itself, did not create commitments for the participating states but only the actual loans made by the EFSF which could form the object of separate ex ante authorizations or ex post approvals by the parliaments, depending on the applicable rules in each state.

The Amendment of the Treaty on the Functioning of the EU

On 25 March 2011, the European Council adopted a decision aiming at the amendment of the Treaty on the Functioning of the European Union by the addition of a new paragraph to Article 136 of that Treaty. The additional paragraph, consisting of two short sentences, runs as follows:

> "*3. The Member States whose currency is the euro may establish a stability mechanism to be activated if indispensable to safeguard the stability of the euro area as a whole. The granting of any required*

financial assistance under the mechanism will be made subject to strict conditionality."[7]

Since this is an amendment of the TFEU, it can – according to Article 48 TEU – enter into force only if approved by the 27 member states of the EU according to their own constitutional requirements and procedures. The European Council, in Article 2 of its decision of 25 March, indicated that it shall enter into force on 1 January 2013, provided that all the national approval procedures have successfully been accomplished by that time. This amendment constitutes the first use of one of the two so-called simplified revision procedures that were introduced by the Lisbon Treaty.

The simplified revision procedure used on this occasion, that of Article 48 paragraph 6, has a rather broad scope. It applies to all amendments of 'Part Three of the Treaty on the Functioning of the European Union relating to the internal policies and action of the Union,' which means altogether some 171 treaty articles – but subject to one major exception: if the proposed amendment of an internal policy provision leads to an increase in the European Union's competences, then the ordinary revision procedure will have to be used instead. It might not always be clear, though, whether a proposed amendment will increase the Union's competences, so there might be some contestation in the future on whether the use of this procedure is appropriate. Upon closer examination of the procedure prescribed by paragraph 6, it soon appears that this is not really a simplified procedure at all. It is true that there is no need for a Convention or an Intergovernmental Conference to negotiate the treaty amendment; the amendment will rather be adopted directly by the European Council acting by unanimity of its members. But that decision is still subject to 'approval' by each member state under its own constitutional requirements. One may expect these constitutional requirements to involve, in most if not all member states, a consultation of the national parliament and probably also a positive vote of approval by the parliament, and nothing prevents the states from also calling a

7 European Council Decision of 25 March 2011 amending Article 136 of the Treaty on the Functioning of the European Union with regard to a stability mechanism for Member States whose currency is the euro, OJ 2011, L 91/1 of 6 April 2011.

referendum on the proposed treaty change. Therefore, this procedure has the appearance of simplicity (since it does not involve the formal conclusion of a revision treaty), but in political terms it is almost as complex an enterprise as the 'ordinary' revision procedure.

Why was this Treaty amendment deemed to be a necessary instrument of the European response to the sovereign debt crisis? From a legal point of view, there were 'constitutional' problems with the package that had been adopted previously, in May 2010. On the one hand, it was not entirely certain whether the intergovernmental measures taken by the euro countries (namely, the creation of the EFSF) complied with the TFEU rule that prohibits EU states from giving financial support to each other (the so-called 'no-bailout' rule of Article 125 TFEU). It could be argued that a mechanism of lending money subject to severe conditionality, as was put in place for Greece and through the EFSF, is not caught by this prohibition of giving direct financial support, but there were some lingering doubts about that interpretation. Moreover, the creation of the EFSF on the basis of an executive agreement, rather than a formal treaty subject to parliamentary ratification, could seem dubious from a national constitutional law perspective. As for the EU Regulation creating the EFSM, there were doubts as to its legality under Article 122(2) TFEU. In particular, it might be argued that Greece and Ireland were not facing exceptional occurrences beyond their control (as the text of Art 122 requires), since their governments had contributed to creating the sovereign debt crises which they were facing.

Those legal controversies worried the German government, since complaints had been lodged before the German Constitutional Court challenging the existing arrangements. Given the erratic record of the court of Karlsruhe, the government did not feel entirely confident about the outcome of those complaints.[8] So, it is because of the legally controversial and shaky basis of the financial stability regime created in May 2010, that the member states, later in 2010, came to envisage a TFEU amendment that would provide a firm basis for a permanent crisis mechanism replacing the exceptional and

---

8 For a discussion of the German constitutional law perspective, see D. Thym, 'Euro-Rettungsschirm: zwischenstaatliche Rechtskonstruktion und verfassungsgerichtliche Kontrolle,' Europäische Zeitschrift für Wirtschaftsrecht (2011) 167-171.

legally uncertain EFSM and EFSF. Indeed, that treaty amendment could seem to solve both legal problems mentioned above. By inserting an explicit provision in the TFEU which authorizes the Euro area member states to put in place a financial support mechanism for countries in budgetary and financial trouble, the effect of the bail-out prohibition of Article 125 TFEU would be neutralized by a complementary norm with the same treaty rank. At the same time, the intergovernmental nature of the future mechanism means that the legally 'risky' EU Regulation could be discontinued after 2013, thus cutting short the possible constitutional challenges before the German Constitutional Court or elsewhere in Europe.

The hypothesis of a limited treaty amendment had first been mooted by German chancellor Merkel in March 2010 but had been greeted with much skepticism by the other EU governments who were rather horrified by the prospect of engaging in a new Treaty revision process only a few months after the Lisbon Treaty had finally come into operation. However, in the autumn of 2010, the German government managed to convince the French government, as emerged from a joint Franco-German declaration made in Deauville, on 18 October 2010, in which the two countries considered 'that an amendment of the treaties is needed and that the President of the European Council should be asked to present (...) concrete options allowing the establishment of a robust crisis resolution framework before (...) March 2011.'[9]

Ten days later, at the European Council meeting of 28-29 October 2010, general agreement was found among all the 27 on 'the need for Member States to establish a permanent crisis mechanism to safeguard the financial stability of the Euro area as a whole' and the President of the European Council was invited 'to undertake consultations with the members of the European Council on a limited treaty change required to that effect, not modifying Article 125 TFEU ('no bail-out' clause).'[10] The last part of the sentence resulted from the discussions among the EU governments, and meant that

9 See P.M. Kaczynski and P. ó Broin, From Lisbon to Deauville: Practicalities of the Lisbon Treaty Revision(s), CEPS Policy Brief No. 216, October 2010.
10 Conclusions of the European Council of 28-29 October 2010, EUCO 25/10, p. 2.

the treaty amendment, rather than deleting the no-bail out clause, would take the form of a separate rule to be put alongside that clause. Most importantly, the formulation adopted by the European Council expressed a preference for a crisis mechanism to be established by the member states of the Euro area rather than by the European Union itself. This choice paved the way for the use of the simplified revision procedure of Art 48(6). Since the amendment would relate to the 'internal policies' part of the TFEU and since it would not increase the competences of the Union, the conditions for the use of the simplified procedure of Article 48(6) TEU were met.

Following the political agreement of 28-29 October, a draft text of the amending Decision was prepared for adoption by the next European Council meeting on 16-17 December.[11] This draft Decision then formed the basis for the consultation of the European Parliament, the Commission and the European Central Bank, as prescribed by the text of Article 48(6) TEU.[12] When examining the draft European Council decision, the European Parliament proposed some changes which aimed at inscribing a complementary role for the European Union institutions in the text of the new Article 136, in particular by stating that the principles and rules for the conditionality of financial assistance under the mechanism should be determined by an EU regulation adopted under co-decision.[13] This, however, would have implied that the Treaty amendment would have conferred new competences on the European Union and, hence, the simplified revision procedure would no longer have been available. The European Council, at its March 2011 meeting, decided not to modify a word of the draft decision which it had adopted in December 2010 and not to mention the EU institutions at all, but instead the European

---

11 Conclusions of the European Council of 16-17 December 2010, EUCO 30/10, Annex 1.
12 Consultation of the Commission and the EP is required in all cases of recourse to the simplified revision procedure of Art 48(6). Consultation of the ECB is required by Art 48(6) only 'in the case of institutional changes in the monetary area.'
13 For the text of the amendments proposed by the EP, see the annex to the Resolution of the European Parliament of 23 March 2011, *Amendment of the Treaty on the Functioning of the European Union with regard to a stability mechanism for Member States whose currency is the euro.*

Council adopted 'further particulars' relating to the future ESM[14] which provide for a close involvement of the Commission in the ESM's eventual operation. The Commission would be called to act as an 'agent' of an intergovernmental cooperation system.

The ESM Treaty

The choice of establishing the permanent stability mechanism by means of an international treaty followed logically from the TFEU amendment discussed above. The fact that the amendment indicated that the mechanism would be established by the Euro states (and not by the EU itself) left no other choice than the use of an international treaty. To that extent, the choice for the international treaty instrument needs no further explanation. What is surprising, however, is the sequencing between the two operations. Since, at least for the German government, the TFEU amendment was to be a precondition for the lawful creation of the permanent mechanism, one could have expected that the treaty establishing that mechanism would be adopted only after the TFEU amendment would have safely passed the national approval hurdles and been ready to enter into force. But this is not what happened. On the contrary, the adoption and ratification of the ESM Treaty have taken place in parallel with the ratification of the TFEU amendment.

The very same European Council meeting of March 2011 at which the TFEU amendment was adopted also saw the adoption of the main lines of the future mechanism. It was confirmed, in the Conclusions of that European Council meeting, that the ESM would be established by means of a treaty among the Euro-area Member States as an intergovernmental organization under public international law with its seat in Luxembourg.[15] Shortly afterwards, negotiations started on the text of the treaty setting up the ESM. A first text was agreed to in June 2011, and was subsequently twice revised due to the unfolding of the crisis. Eventually, the latest version signed in March 2012 by the 17 governments of the Euro area,[16] was opened

---

14 Those further particulars are called the 'Term sheet on the ESM' and are published in Annex II of the European Council Conclusions of 24-25 March 2011.
15 Conclusions of the European Council meeting of 24-25 March 2011, p. 22.
16 For the text of this treaty, see www.european-council.europa.eu/media/582311/05-tesm2.en12.pdf

up for ratification by each country according to its internal arrangements, and this process is now in full swing. Given the proximity in
time and subject matter with the Fiscal Compact, most of the Euro
countries' parliaments decided to examine the two international treaties as a single political package.

The Fiscal Compact

This treaty intends to reinforce the financial stability of the Euro
area through a stricter coordination of the national budget policies,
including the definition of benchmarks for structural deficit and
debt-to-GDP ratio, and a judicial enforcement mechanism for non-
compliance with such benchmarks. The Fiscal Compact requires a
legal commitment by each State Party to a balanced budget and the
provision, in the event of significant deviations, of an automatic correction mechanism to be implemented at the national level.[17]

There was, arguably, no strict need to adopt a new treaty to implement what is contained in the text of the Fiscal Compact. Most of
what it contains in terms of economic governance at the European
level could have been adopted through enhanced cooperation within
the EU or by means of a modification of Protocol No. 12 on the excessive deficit procedure. The treaty confirms the creation of the Euro
Summit and also provides for a new body, the Meeting of the Heads
of State or Government of the Contracting Parties, whose membership will reflect the number of states that will eventually ratify the
Fiscal Compact, but whose role is limited to loosely monitoring the
implementation of the Fiscal Compact. Those bodies will operate in
an informal manner. No new hard governance mechanisms are introduced at the European level. The core of the new treaty and its real
novelty, also in terms of democratic practice, lies elsewhere, namely
in the introduction of the 'golden rule': the obligation to introduce
into national law (preferably constitutional) the new budgetary limits defined in Article 3, para. 1, in particular a 'structural' deficit not
exceeding 0.5% of the GDP. Again, this could have been achieved
legally speaking by means of EU legislation, if necessary adopted
by means of the 'enhanced cooperation' mode of decision-making

17 The text of this treaty can be found on www.european-council.europa.eu/
eurozone-governance/treaty-on-stability

in which not all EU states must participate. However, it was made very clear by the German government (that acted once more as the agenda-setter for this treaty), in the course of the autumn of 2011, that the circumstances required nothing less than a treaty. Compared to EU legislation, a treaty could seem to have two advantages: first, it could be adopted more quickly, since it only requires an agreement between the member state governments without the need to involve the Commission and European Parliament as the EU legislative procedure does. And secondly, a commitment to budgetary stability seemed more solemn and more permanent if contained in a treaty which cannot be 'bent' later on, whereas EU legislation was more liable to be 'softened.' Therefore, making a treaty seemed to be the appropriate symbolic message of strong resolve which the unruly financial markets required in the autumn of 2011.

The kind of treaty norm that the German government, and later also the French government, had in mind was a formal amendment of the TFEU like the one adopted in March 2011 (on which, see above). But this would have required the unanimous agreement of all EU member states. At the December 2011 summit, as is well known, the UK government refused to agree on such a TFEU amendment given that the (unrelated) conditions which it had put forward had not been accepted by the other governments. During the European Council meeting itself, the other governments, led by the French-German tandem, decided instantaneously to 'exit' from the EU institutional framework, and to go for a separate international agreement instead, so as to circumvent the British veto. They did not take time to consider whether, given the impossibility of a TFEU amendment, the wisest course might have been to adopt EU legislation through enhanced cooperation, rather than take the risk of engaging in this new and unpredictable treaty game.[18] Indeed, negotiating an international treaty may be a quick process (25 EU states did rapidly agree on the text of this Fiscal Compact in the following month), but it does not benefit from the special qualities of EU law and its entry

---

18 Various legal and policy options had been put on the table of the European Council by its President in his note of 6 December 2011, Towards a Stronger Economic Union – Interim Report, but the one option he did not mention was the conclusion of a separate international agreement outside the EU framework! For an evocation of the political circumstances of the December meeting of the European Council that eventually led to the choice for a separate treaty, see 'The European Union and the euro – Game, set and mismatch', The Economist 17 December 2011, 43-46.

into force is fraught with difficulties. This leads us to the question of the legal consequences following from the choice for an international treaty, which we will consider in the next section.

4. Legal Consequences of Treaty-Making

Inside or Outside the EU Legal Order

The EU legal order is formed by the basic treaties (the TEU and TFEU), and by the so-called secondary law adopted by the EU institutions, that is all the legal acts (whether they are called directives, regulations, decisions, guidelines, recommendations, etc…) that are adopted by the institutions of the EU in accordance with the Treaties and that embody the European Union's policies. Those legal acts are adopted in accordance with the procedures fixed by the Treaties, and their legal effects are determined by those same Treaties as interpreted by the Court of Justice.

The advantages of 'stepping outside' the EU legal framework, and concluding a separate international agreement (as has happened three times in the context of the euro crisis), are readily apparent. By concluding a separate agreement, its signatories can bypass veto positions for single countries that may exist under EU law. Thus, the decision – taken at the European Council meeting of December 2011 – to abandon the plan to negotiate an amendment of the TFEU and instead conclude a separate international agreement, offered the immediate benefit of circumventing the veto expressed by the UK government. The main disadvantage of the non-EU treaty route is, of course, that the special qualities of EU law are lost, namely the relatively democratic and transparent mode of decision-making (at least if compared to purely intergovernmental decision-making), and the capacity to make the rules 'stick' by means of a relatively efficient judicial enforcement system.

The main legal condition for the conclusion of such separate agreements is that their content should be compatible with EU law. The Fiscal Compact offers such a conflict rule in its Article 2(2): 'The provisions of this Treaty shall apply insofar as they are compatible with the Treaties on which the Union is founded and with European Union law.' This is a mobile conflict rule: it recognizes not only the primacy of EU law as it stands today but also as it might become in the future: if, for example, new provisions of secondary EU law will be enacted that conflict with the Fiscal Compact, they will prevail.

There is much controversy about the possibility to 'borrow' the EU institutions under an international agreement. There is a major difference to be made, in this respect, between the Court of Justice and the other institutions. Article 273 TFEU allows the member states to submit to the Court of Justice, "under a special agreement between the parties," "any dispute between Member States which relates to the subject matter of the Treaties." The subject matter of the Fiscal Compact is indeed closely connected to the TEU and TFEU, and Article 8(3) of the FCT is expressly declared to be a 'special agreement' in the sense of Article 273 TFEU, so that the 'use' of the Court of Justice to enforce the international law obligations contained in the Fiscal Compact is justified. Similarly, in Article 37(3) of the ESM Treaty, it is stated that disputes between ESM member states about the application of the Treaty shall be submitted to the Court of Justice of the European Union.

But how to justify the involvement of other EU institutions than the Court, which occurs to a limited extent in both the ESM Treaty and the Fiscal Compact? According to Article 13(2) TEU, the EU institutions shall act within the limits of the powers given to them under 'the Treaties' (meaning the TEU and the TFEU, and no other treaties). This would be a strong textual argument for the view that it is not possible to give any new competences to the Commission, the Parliament and the Council under separate international agreements. One way, though, to make sense of this is to distinguish between 'competences' and 'tasks.' What Article 13 TEU seeks to convey is that the competences of the institutions are fixed by the treaties; it does not exclude that extra tasks may be given to the institutions as long as those tasks fit within their competences. To explain this difference, a parallel can be made with secondary EU legislation, by which new tasks are often given to the Commission and the Council, e.g., to further implement a piece of legislation. Those tasks fit within the general constitutional mandate of those institutions but they are extra tasks, in the sense that they are not specified in so many words in the Treaties but are being gradually defined as EU law develops. In the present case, this gradual development occurs not through secondary legislation but through a separate international agreement. Now, do those extra tasks defined by the ESM Treaty and the Fiscal Compact fit within their constitutional competences, as defined by the TEU and TFEU? This would indeed seem to be the case: within the context of their competences in the field of Economic Union, as recently fleshed out by the 'six-pack' legislation, the institutions will also perform the tasks which are attributed to them under the ESM Treaty and the Fiscal Compact.[19]

The Ratification Requirement

Most treaties must, after their signature, be separately ratified by each participating state. This is not a whimsical complication, but a consequence mandated by the national constitutional law of most states. Indeed, most European constitutions nowadays require that international treaties of some importance must be approved by the national parliament before the government can actually declare that the state will be bound by the treaty; this is to avoid the government undermining the parliament's legislative powers 'through the backdoor' by agreeing to legal obligations or transfers of sovereignty through the negotiation of an international treaty.

This requirement weakens the effectiveness of the treaty instrument, since its effects are delayed in time. Also, it remains uncertain whether the original agreement that led to the signature of the treaty will stick, or whether one or more of the signatories will be unable to honour their pledge through their failure to ratify the treaty. The reason for the failure to ratify might be the refusal by the national parliament to approve the treaty, but there can be other reasons as well. The content of the treaty may require a constitutional amendment in one or other countries, which may entail the mandatory organisation of a popular referendum; this is happening in Ireland with the Fiscal

---

19 For further discussion of those legal issues, see 'Editorial comments – some thoughts concerning the Draft Treaty on a Reinforced Economic Union,' Common Market Law Review (2012) 1-14.

Compact: its ratification is considered to require an amendment of the Irish constitution and hence the organisation of a referendum which will take place on 31 May 2012. Or ratification of the treaty may be stopped by a decision of the national constitutional court, as was attempted in Germany. Or there may be a change of government after signature, and the new government may be unwilling to proceed with ratification of the treaty text as it stands; this could happen with the Fiscal Compact in France where presidential candidate Hollande has announced that he would request *une renégociation,* which he could try to force upon the other signatory states by refusing to ratify the current text.

We find ourselves now in the middle of the ratification process for three of the four instruments: the amendment of article 136 TFEU, to be approved by all 27 member states; the ESM treaty, to be ratified by the 17 euro states; and the Fiscal Compact, to be ratified by 25 states. Given the proximity of their subject matter, it is likely that parliamentary debates and votes will run in parallel. For example, the Slovenian parliament ratified the Fiscal Compact and the ESM Treaty on the same day of 19 April 2012.[20]

The hazardous nature of the national ratification process is well known from earlier revisions of the EU Treaties. The ratification of the Treaty of Maastricht, the Treaty of Nice, the Constitutional Treaty and the Lisbon Treaty were all very laborious; three of them required a repetition of a popular referendum in one country, and the Constitutional Treaty never came into being because of ratification problems. As regards revisions of the founding Treaties (TEU and TFEU), the ratification by every single member state is a precondition for their entry into force, which gives each country a veto right, although the effectiveness of that veto depends also on political factors such as the size of the country: when France and the Netherlands proved unable to ratify the Constitutional Treaty, that treaty was abandoned; but when Denmark proved unable to ratify the Maastricht Treaty, and Ireland unable to ratify the Nice Treaty and Lisbon Treaty, in each case those countries were 'invited' to try again after

20 See www.sloveniatimes.com/parliament-ratifies-fiscal-compact, consulted on 24 April 2012.

having obtained some limited political concessions.[21] The same difficulty applies to the current amendment of Article 136 TFEU. Even though it took place by means of the so-called simplified revision procedure – that is, by means of a European Council decision rather than a formal treaty – the separate approval by each of the 27 member states is still required, so that this Treaty change is at the mercy of an incident in one or other member states. The United Kingdom has made European Treaty revisions even more fragile than before after the adoption of the European Union Act 2011, which makes any Treaty revision subject to a popular referendum except if that revision has no major consequences for the country. But the amendment of Article 136 TFEU, since it refers to future action undertaken by the Euro area countries alone, has no immediate consequences for the UK, and therefore the UK government decided that it could be ratified without the organisation of a referendum.

Separate international agreements, which do not involve an amendment of the TEU and TFEU, can define alternative requirements for their entry into force. Not only can such agreements be concluded among fewer than all the EU states, but they can also provide for their entry into force even if not all the signatories are able to ratify. The Fiscal Compact offers a spectacular example of this flexibility in that it provides that the treaty will enter into force if ratified by merely 12 of the 25 signatory states, provided that those 12 are all part of the Euro area. The fact that the authors of the Fiscal Compact moved decidedly away from the condition of universal ratification for its entry into force has created a 'ratification game' which is very different from that applying to amendment of the European treaties, where the rule of unanimous ratification gives a strong veto position to each individual country.[22] Here, instead, the cost of a negative decision cannot be 'externalized' to the other countries, and would moreover mean that the country cannot benefit from the potential

---

21 See G. de Búrca, 'If at First You Don't Succeed: Vote, Vote Again. Analysing the Second Referendum Phenomenon in EU Treaty Change,' Fordham International Law Journal (2010) 1472-1489.
22 For a discussion of those differences, see C. Closa, 'Moving Away from Unanimity. Ratification of the Treaty on Stability, Coordination and Governance in the Economic and Monetary Union', RECON Online Working Paper 2011/38.

support of the European Stability Mechanism.[23] The ESM Treaty, as well, has removed the veto power at least of the smaller Euro states by providing that it will enter into force if ratified by states that, together, contribute 90% of the funds for the Mechanism. In this way, the larger countries (who contribute more than 10% each) still have a 'ratification veto,' but the smaller Euro states, such as Estonia, Slovenia, Greece or Portugal, do not.

Conclusion

The 'treaty games' examined in this paper describe the strategic interactions between the national governments of the EU states (with other actors, such as the EU institutions, playing interesting minor roles) that have led them – in the course of their responses to the Euro crisis – to resort to the conclusion of international treaties as an appropriate response. They did so on four occasions, each of which must be understood in its particular political and legal context. Still, some general conclusions can be drawn from the observation of those treaty games.

The first observation is that treaties appear to provide flexibility in crisis response. They allow the governments to act quickly by deciding on the adoption of new binding rules without being 'hindered' by the supranational institutions of the EU or by the cumbersome decision-making procedures that apply for the adoption of EU law. That flexibility may seem so tempting that governments may fail to give sufficient weight to the risks and costs involved in using the treaty instrument, namely the danger of introducing rules that are inconsistent with EU law (which would be unlawful), the risk that entry into force may be delayed or derailed by the failure of one or more states to ratify, and the cost of setting aside the democratic qualities of EU law-making and the judicial control powers provided by EU law. In adopting the four international agreements, the governments have tried to use that flexibility and to avoid those risks and costs as best they could. As a result, though, the international treaties which they have made are much less ambitious, in their con-

---

23 The linkage between ratification of the Fiscal Compact and benefiting from ESM support is expressly made in both the preambles of the ESM treaty and of the Fiscal Compact.

tent, than what was trumpeted to the public. The Fiscal Compact, in particular, is likely to be more important in symbolic political terms than as an efficient legal instrument of economic governance. The main game of economic governance will – most likely – continue to be played, despite those international treaty diversions, within the European Union's institutional framework.

11
The United Kingdom and the Eurozone: How to Co-exist

Charles Goodhart

The Eurozone will need major reform and reinvention if it is to survive. The present crisis has revealed all too clearly both the political and the economic flaws of the original Maastricht Treaty. On the political front, decisions remain in the hands of the national political leaders, especially those from the largest countries. They are constrained by local political pressures to view the issues through national, rather than European, viewpoints. Meanwhile the European leaders, Barroso and van Rompuy, have no power, no democratic mandate, and little influence. I attach, as Appendix 1, a long passage from a recent paper by George Soros on this subject.

On the economic front, austerity without growth is a recipe for depression, despair and growing social and political dissonance. Something will crack, probably first in Greece. The proposals for achieving faster growth, e.g., structural reform, would help in the longer run, but would do little, if anything, to restart growth in the short run.

Under these circumstances, there are probably three possible medium/longer term outcomes. The first (A) is that, with or without a crisis, the Eurozone reinvents itself as a viable currency union. This requires a major move towards political, fiscal and financial centralisation. The second (B) is that the Eurozone breaks up, but the European Union maintains the single market and free movement of capital and labour. The third (C) is that both the Eurozone and the EU collapse in a welter of recrimination and a recrudescence of protective nationalism.

I shall discuss the role of the UK in each case, taking these three options in reverse order.

But, first, it may be helpful to record the historical roles of England and Scotland separately. England (and Wales) are, of course, an integral part of Europe. But the English have never seen their destiny as solely a European country; rather they have always seen themselves as an Atlantic power, with interlocking circles of interest, involving the north Atlantic on one hand and the Commonwealth on the other, as well as Europe. A figurative illustration of how the English tend to see their position in the world is shown in Figure 1. As such, it has always been the historical objective of the English leadership to prevent a dominant power taking root on the Continent. Often they have been successful in this; sometimes they have failed. Since we are meeting in Italy, I could mention the failure of the British, notably Queen Boadicea, to stop the Roman legions; Mrs Thatcher may even have seen herself as a reincarnation of Boadicea. It is in accord with its historical role that the English are averse to a federal state developing on the Continent.

In contrast, the Scots have always been much closer to the Continental powers, notably France, seeing in Brussels or Paris a useful counterweight to domination from London. If it had not been for the collapse of RBS and HBOS, with these two banks becoming wards of the British taxpayer, an independent Scotland would probably have sought to join the Euro immediately, should independence be achieved. [Incidentally, the Shetland Islands see domination from Edinburgh as unfavourably as the Scots see domination from London. Some of the oil is not Scottish, but Shetland's. The Shetland's allegiance could go to Norway, or London, rather than Scotland;

whether the Scottish regiments would invade Shetland with kilts fly-
ing to enforce their subjugation would have to be seen.]

Anyhow, this historical background may help to explain the position
which the English have traditionally adopted in their relationship
with the Continent. Let me now revert to the three options for the
future of the Eurozone that I have set out, and how the English (but
not the Scots) might react.

Figure 1

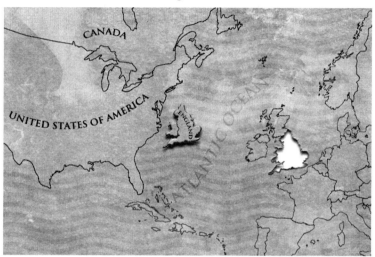

C. Complete Collapse and Break-up

This would, of course, be a disaster, and would be seen as such by
most people in the UK, if only because the immediate economic
implications would be so dire. But since the UK has integrated less
than the Continental countries, the adjustments – social, institutional, political and economic – would be less wrenching for the UK
than for the Continental countries. Moreover, the UK would cease
to be an outsider, and would become a major player in a devastated
scenario. This would be a total disaster, but one that would be less
horrific for the UK than for its neighbours.

B. Collapse of Euro-zone but Retention of Single Market

In many respects this would be the outcome that the UK wanted, and expected to happen, so long as the EU remained a confederation of separate sovereign states, rather than becoming a single Federal state. The problem with this is, not the British, but the French position. The French tend to argue that a single market, without tariffs, etc., is inconsistent with the members of that market having flexible exchange rates, which they can influence, e.g., by intervention or monetary policies (e.g., QE), to gain an 'unfair' advantage in trade. Thus they believe that a single market, (at least among equals, since they explain away the North American Free Trade Agreement (NAFTA) as a function of the overwhelming relative size of the USA), requires a single currency.

Thus the continuation of a single market, in a context where many, or most, of the members of that market did not operate a single currency would seem to require some centralised oversight, and a degree of control, over policies, especially monetary policies that could directly influence relative exchange rates. This would presumably include rules to prevent direct intervention on foreign exchange markets and rules requiring monetary policy measures to be only used for internal price stability. All this could be monitored by the European Commission and breaches could be punished by allowing other countries to impose countervailing tariffs.

As noted earlier, the UK would have no particular problem with such a system; indeed, it would welcome it.

A. The Eurozone Transforms into a Federal Country

What the minimum conditions – political, social and economic – that are necessary for a viable single currency area are remains a subject of dispute and discussion, (n.b., the optimum currency area literature was really an unhelpful distraction). On the political front, I would argue that a single currency area requires central political leadership, with elections to such positions giving a democratic mandate.

This immediately raises a large question. If the political leadership is primarily for the members of the single currency union, it cannot be elected by non-members, e.g., the UK. The European Union institutions are currently European-wide. The political requirements of a currency union imply institutions coterminous with the boundaries of that union. So, almost all the EU institutions would have to bifurcate, with a tight effective, currency-zone core, and a much looser relationship between the single currency core (Federal) states and a penumbra of separate currency countries.

The UK would strongly dislike this outcome since it would entrench and emphasize the insider/outsider split. The UK would probably do what it could to sabotage such an outcome despite it being the logical implication of a successful transition to a single currency, more centralised Eurozone system.

The economic requirements of moving towards a more centralised Euro-state include shifting more fiscal powers to the Federal centre. An earlier outline of what this might entail was set out in the EC Commission paper, 'Stable Money, Sound Finances,' *European Economy* (1993), on which I served as an external expert. This included a semi-automatic fiscal stabilisation mechanism to support regions badly hit by an asymmetric shock. This should also give the federal centre power to tax and power to borrow. And supervision, resolution and bail-out funding arrangements for cross-border Eurozone financial institutions, above a certain size, would probably need to be centralised.

Again, the UK would want to distance itself from a system in which fiscal and financial control powers could be imposed on the UK from a more powerful Euro-centre. But it would also be hesitant about encouraging and allowing a more completely unified and integrated Euro-system to spring up on the Continent from which it was excluded. So UK public opinion and politics would continue to be split and divided. Assuming that a much more unified European system could be established and did appear successful, a sizeable proportion of people in the UK would want to join for all the standard well-known reasons. But, equally a sizeable proportion of UK Eurosceptics would fight to the bitter end to prevent the, by now much greater, transfer of sovereignty to the federal European centre.

The thesis here is that a successful single currency area in Europe would require a much greater centralisation of powers in a federal centre – political, fiscal and regulatory – than heretofore. If this were to be achieved, it would leave the UK both marginalised and divided. The UK hopes that the continuing strength of nationalism in continental countries, plus UK opposition, will stymie any such effective shift of powers. If so, the fall-back position would be a single market, but without a single currency, except perhaps for a greater D-mark area, comprising perhaps Austria, Denmark, Finland and the Netherlands, as well as Germany.

We shall see.

Appendix[1]

The euro crisis is particularly instructive in this regard. It shows that policies that could have worked at one point of time are no longer sufficient at the next one. It also demonstrates the role of imperfect understanding and misconceptions in shaping the course of history. Since the euro crisis is currently exerting an overwhelming influence on the global economy I shall devote the rest of my talk to it. I must start with a warning: the discussion will take us beyond the confines of economic theory into politics and social philosophy. It will provide an excellent illustration of the reflexive interaction between imperfect markets and imperfect regulators. That is an interaction that goes on all the time while bubbles occur only infrequently. This is a rare occasion when the interaction exerts such a large influence that it casts its shadow on the global economy. How could this happen? My explanation is that there is a bubble involved but it is not a financial but a political one. It relates to the political evolution of the European Union and it has lead me to the conclusion that the euro crisis threatens to destroy the European Union. Let me explain.

In my theory a boom bust process or bubble has two components: a trend that occurs in reality and a misconception relating to that trend. In the boom phase the European Union was what the psychoanalyst David Tuckett calls a "fantastic object" – unreal but immensely attractive. It was the embodiment of the open society – an association of nations founded on the principles of democracy, human rights, and rule of law in which no nation or nationality would have a dominant position.

The process of integration was spearheaded by a small group of far sighted statesmen who practiced what Karl Popper called piecemeal social engineering. They recognized that perfection is unattainable; so they set limited objectives and firm timelines and then mobilized the political will for a small step forward, knowing full well that when they achieved it, its inadequacy would become apparent and require a further step. The process fed on its own success, very much

1 George Soros, "Remarks at the Institute for New Economic Thinking Annual Plenary Conference," Berlin, Germany, 12 April 2012.

like a financial bubble. That is how the Coal and Steel Community was gradually transformed into the European Union, step by step.

Germany used to be in the forefront of the effort. When the Soviet empire started to disintegrate, Germany's leaders realized that reunification was possible only in the context of a more united Europe and they were willing to make considerable sacrifices to achieve it. When it came to bargaining they were willing to contribute a little more and take a little less than the others, thereby facilitating agreement. At that time, German statesmen used to assert that Germany has no independent foreign policy, only a European one.

The process culminated with the Maastricht Treaty and the introduction of the euro. It was followed by a period of stagnation which after the crash of 2008 turned into a process of disintegration. The first step was taken by Germany when, after the bankruptcy of Lehman Brothers, Angela Merkel declared that the virtual guarantee extended to other financial institutions should come from each country acting separately, not by Europe acting jointly. It took financial markets more than a year to realize the implication of that declaration.

The Maastricht Treaty was fundamentally flawed, demonstrating the fallibility of the authorities. Its main weakness was well known to its architects: it established a monetary union without a political union. The architects believed however, that when the need arose the political will could be generated to take the necessary steps towards a political union.

But the euro also had some other defects of which the architects were unaware and which are not fully understood even today. First of all it failed to take into account the fallibility of the architects: there is neither an enforcement mechanism nor an exit mechanism and member countries cannot resort to printing money. This put the weaker members into the position of a third world country that became over-indebted in a hard currency.

The Maastricht Treaty also assumed that only the public sector is capable of producing unacceptable imbalances; the market was expected to correct its own excesses. And the Maastricht Treaty was supposed to have established adequate safeguards against public sector imbalances. Consequently, when the European Central Bank started operated it treated government bonds as riskless assets that banks could hold without allocating any capital reserves against them. This encouraged commercial banks to accumulate the bonds of the weaker countries in order to earn a few extra basis points. This caused interest rates to converge which, contrary to expectations, led to divergences in economic performance. Germany, struggling with the burdens of reunification, undertook structural reforms and became more competitive. Other countries enjoyed a housing boom that made them less competitive. Yet others had to bail out their banks after the crash of 2008. This created conditions that were far removed from those prescribed by the Maastricht Treaty with totally unexpected consequences. Government bonds which had been considered riskless turned out to carry significant credit risks.

Unfortunately the European authorities had little understanding of what hit them. They were prepared to deal with fiscal problems but only Greece qualified as a fiscal crisis; the rest of Europe suffered from a banking crisis and the divergence in competitiveness also gave rise to a balance of payments crisis. The authorities did not even understand the nature of the problem, let alone see a solution. So they tried to buy time.

Usually that works. Financial panics subside and the authorities realize a profit on their intervention. But not this time because the financial problems were reinforced by a process of political and social disintegration. While the European Union was being created, the leadership was in the forefront of further integration; but after the outbreak of the financial crisis the authorities became wedded to preserving the status quo. This has forced all those who consider the status quo unsustainable or intolerable into an anti-European posture. That is the political dynamic that makes the disintegration of the European Union just as self-reinforcing as its creation has been.

At the onset of the crisis a breakup of the euro was inconceivable: the assets and liabilities denominated in a common currency were so intermingled that a breakup would have led to an uncontrollable meltdown. But as the crisis progressed the financial system has been progressively reoriented along national lines. This trend gathered momentum in recent months. The LTRO enabled Spanish and Italian banks to engage in a very profitable and low risk arbitrage in the bonds of their own countries. And the preferential treatment received by the ECB on its Greek bonds will discourage other investors from holding sovereign debt. If this continued for a few more years a break-up of the euro would become possible without a meltdown – the omelet could be unscrambled – but it would leave the central banks of the creditor countries with large claims against the central banks of the debtor countries which would be difficult to collect.

The Bundesbank has become aware of the danger. It is now engaged in a campaign against the indefinite expansion of the money supply and it has started taking measures to limit the losses it would sustain in case of a breakup. This is creating a self-fulfilling prophecy. Once the Bundesbank starts guarding against a breakup everybody will have to do the same. Markets are beginning to reflect this.

Without it, the Eurozone's "fiscal compact," agreed last December, cannot possibly work. The heavily indebted countries will either fail to implement the necessary measures, or, if they do, they will fail to meet their targets because of collapsing demand. Either way, debt ratios will rise, and the competitiveness gap with Germany will widen.

Whether or not the euro endures, Europe is facing a long period of economic stagnation or worse. Other countries have gone through similar experiences. Latin American countries suffered a lost decade after 1982, and Japan has been stagnating for a quarter-century; both have survived. But the European Union is not a country, and it is unlikely to survive. The deflationary debt trap is threatening to destroy a still-incomplete political union.

This is a dismal prospect. There must be a way to avoid it – after all, history is not predetermined. Right now Europe hangs together out of grim necessity. That is not conducive to a harmonious partnership. The European Union had been a "fantastic object", a desirable goal, when it was only an idea, but it turned into an objectionable imposition when it became a reality. The only way to reverse this seemingly inexorable fate is to recreate the European Union as a fantastic object worth striving for. The European Union has the makings of an open society that could be a model for the rest of the world. All it needs to do is to recommit itself to the principles of open society and that requires the authorities to recognize their mistakes and correct them. Angela Merkel has shown some signs of doing so but the German authorities, notably the Bundesbank and the constitutional court are dead set on enforcing laws that have proved to be unworkable. This has turned statutes that were meant to be stepping stones into immovable rocks that stand in the way of finding a solution. I believe a solution can be found even at this late stage but it will require a change of heart by the German public.

I cannot propose a cut-and-dried plan, only some guidelines. First, the rules governing the Eurozone have failed and need to be radically revised. Defending a status quo that is unworkable only makes matters worse. Second, the current situation is highly anomalous, and exceptional measures are needed to restore normalcy. Finally, new rules must allow for financial markets' inherent instability.

12
European Union and Eurozone: How to Co-exist?

Brigid Laffan

Introduction

The global financial crisis and the manner in which it manifested itself in the Euro area from autumn 2009 onwards is in the process of transforming the European Union. This crisis, like all crises, will leave a distinctive political, institutional and governance legacy. The contours of that legacy are evident in broad outline. A new EU is being formed with the Euro area at its core. This has implications for the dynamic of European integration and for the 27 member states that make up the Union. Differentiated or flexible integration, a feature of the EU from the 1970s onwards, is and will be a more pronounced feature of the EU that is emerging. An *avant garde* or *kerneuropa* may consolidate within the EU. An *avant garde* implies that there are countries left behind, a rear guard. The rear guard may catch up (multi-speed flexibility) or the Union may consolidate into two or more tiers (vertical) or a hard inner core with outer circles (concentric circles). It is as yet unclear if the Euro area will become the 'hardest of hard cores.' The aim of this chapter is to (a) provide an overview of the evolution of differentiated integration in the EU, (b) analyse developments within the Euro area in the context of differentiated integration, and (c) address the impact of developments in the Euro area for the co-existence of those both inside and outside the single currency.

Section I: Differentiated Integration

The European Union is characterised by deep diversity. Although the EU was confronted with managing diversity from the outset, successive enlargements and an ambitious widening of the scope of integration have undoubtedly brought the dynamics of difference sharply into focus. A bewildering array of terms – two-speed Europe, multi-speed Europe, two-tier, à la carte, variable geometry, flexible integration, graduated integration, core Europe, avant garde Europe, concentric circles, and hub and spoke integration – have been deployed as metaphors for differentiated integration both by academics and practitioners at different times in the evolution of the Union[1] (Stubb 1996, 1997; Holzinger and Schimmelfennig 2012). The terminological debate and the battle of ideas about concepts of differentiated integration reflected real concerns and dilemmas confronting the EU and its member states (Andersen and Sitter 2006). The multiplicity of terms and the underlying concepts highlight the challenge of responding to diversity in the Union on terms conducive to all. Behind the Euro-jargon were varying conceptions of the future of the Union and different responses to the challenge of diversity (De Neve 2007, Emmanouilidis 2007). A discussion of flexibility and differentiation emerged for the first time in the 1970s but became and remained a key issue on the European agenda from the end of the 1990s onwards. Attention to differentiation sought to respond to three interrelated dilemmas. First, how to structure the Union to achieve a balance between the unity of the system and the assurance of sufficient flexibility to allow for varied levels of engagement. Second, how to deepen the level of integration in the face of opposition from some member states who were unwilling to go further. Third, how to address the problem of the unable, due to the different capacities of the member states. Addressing the challenge of the unwilling and unable lay behind much of the debate on differentiated integration. The political discussion of differentiation intensified during periods of treaty change and in anticipation of or in response to enlargement. Provisions for enhanced co-operation were formally inserted in the Treaty of Amsterdam (1997) and altered in

---

1 Stubb (1996) lists 30 different terms that are broadly covered by the concept of differentiated integration.

the Treaty of Lisbon (2009) to make it less demanding to use these treaty provisions. The Amsterdam provisions were never used but the Lisbon provisions were deployed for the first time in 2011.

A distillation of the various concepts of differentiated integration suggests that they vary across a number of significant dimensions. Stubb classified the concepts on the basis of three dimensions; time (two-speed, multi-speed), space (two tier, hub and spoke, concentric circles) and matter (different policy areas) (Stubb 1996, 1997). Holzinger and Schimmelfennig (2012) identified six dimensions; namely, permanent versus temporary differentiation, territorial versus purely functional differentiation, differentiation across member states or multi-level differentiation, differentiation within or outside the EU treaties, decision-making at EU level or regime level, EU member states exclusively or the involvement also of non-member states or areas (Holzinger and Schimmelfennig 2012, 297). A combination of two of the dimensions identified by Stubb (1996) – time and space – combined with two of the dimensions identified by Holzinger and Schimmelfennig (2012) enables us to capture the character of differentiation within the EMU. (See Figure 1.)

EMU represents one of the most important policy areas not shared by all member states and the Euro crisis has accentuated the importance of the Euro club. The significance of membership, non-membership, pre-ins and opt-outs has been highlighted by the crisis because the Euro states have had to deepen the level of integration within the Euro area, add new institutions and additional policy instruments.

Section II: Developments within the Euro area

The duration and intensity of the crisis within the Euro area resulted in a sustained focus by the European Council, the Eurogroup, the ECB, the Eco-Fin Council and the Commission on Crisis Management since 11 February 2010. Since then, regular and emergency European Council and Eurogroup meetings have been almost entirely devoted to the crisis. A marked feature of the crisis was the importance of bilateral meetings between the German Chancellor and French President in preparation for meetings of the 17 or 27.

Figure 1: EMU-Differentiated Integration

Dimensions of Differentiation in EMU	Time	Space	Decision making within the EU treaties or regime	Within or outside the EU treaties
	11 euro members 1999	UK opt out negotiated as part of TEU 1992.	Legal and institutional provisions for governing the euro were contained in the TEU.	Treaty on European Union (TEU), Maastricht 1993. Lisbon Treaty 2009.
	Greece 2001	DK opt-out negotiated as part of the Edinburgh Agreement but pegged to euro and a member of ERM II.	Eurogroup was established in 1997 by the European Council. Has had a permanent elected chair since 2004. Protocol on the Eurogroup appended to the Lisbon Treaty.	Outside the EU Treaty Framework: *Treaty on Stability, Coordination and Governance of EMU* known as the Fiscal Compact signed 2nd March 2012, 25 member states.
	Slovenia 2007	Sweden has a de facto opt out as it has declared that membership of ERM II a precursor to the euro is not under consideration.	Eurogroup issued its first HoSG (Heads of State/Government) statement on 11th February, 2010 in response to the Greek crisis.	
	Cyprus and Malta 2008	All other states are obliged to join the euro when they meet the criteria established in the TEU. This requires them to be members of ERM II		
	Slovakia 2009			
	Estonia 2011			

Captured by the term Merkozy, the leaders of the two largest Euro area economies worked closely together to manage the crisis. Addressing the interrelated problems of the loss of market access for three Euro states (Greece, Ireland and Portugal), contagion to other states and problems in the European banking system have stretched the EU's political capacity to its limits. Since Spring 2010, the Euro states and the ECB operated under constant pressure from the financial markets and rating agencies. The latter sent strong signals to the Euro area and in turn wanted a convincing narrative from the HoSG

(Heads of State/Government) and the ECB that they were capable of responding to the problems.

Policy responses in the Euro area were designed both to address the immediate crisis (crisis management) and ensure that the Euro area was not confronted with a crisis of this severity again (crisis prevention). Key actors in the Euro area engaged in a combination of 'puzzling,' 'powering,' 'persuading,' and 'masking,' as they sought to address the crisis. The 'puzzling' involved the definition of the crisis, its attendant problems and potential policy solutions and 'powering' related to the mobilisation of resources and support for policy action. 'Persuasion' was required to convince key Euro states that action was needed in the first place and was later evident throughout the crisis given the political constraints on key actors. 'Masking' the hidden face of power was evident in the manner in which the crisis was identified as a sovereign debt crisis and not also a banking crisis. Crises accentuate power differentials within a consensus system such as the EU and Euro area. The ECB and the Euro HoSG were the dominant institutions in the policy process. Neither the Commission nor European Parliament played a central role. The responsibilities of the Commission were widened during the crisis but not its agenda setting role.

Within the Euro HoSG, Germany was the swing state. No action could be taken without its agreement and it had veto power over the deployment of policy instruments. As the largest economy in the Euro area, its influence was decisive. Germany's dominance in the management of the crisis stemmed both from its economic weight and performance and its embedded preferences on monetary policy and the role of the central bank. Moreover, the German Chancellor faced a number of domestic constraints that influenced the timing and content of policy responses. Chancellor Merkel was concerned from the outset that any rescue or new policy instrument within the Euro area might face a challenge at the German Constitutional Court. Hence legal cover was a major concern. The federal character of the German state meant that elections were a perennial feature of the political system; the calendar of state elections played into federal politics in Berlin. As the EU has become more politicised, elections in Germany matter more than they did in the past. Once Germany conceded that there would have to be intervention in Greece, it was determined to mould the crisis response in a manner that was aligned to its preferences. France found itself in a subordinate role within the Franco-German tandem.

The second consequence of the crisis was to emphasize the difference between Euro members and non-members. The 'ties that bind' will bind more tightly and there will be considerably more intrusion into the budgetary affairs of the Euro states. Fear of being left behind and left outside led six non-Euro states to join the Competitiveness Pact and eight states to sign the Fiscal Compact. Non-Euro states anticipate joining the Euro at some future date or at least do not want to be sidelined. Regardless of when a state joins the single currency, future membership bids will receive serious scrutiny prior to membership. The experience of the crisis has underlined the damage that a weak link within the Euro area may cause. The standing of the United Kingdom was altered by the actions of David Cameron at the December European Council. His refusal to agree to treaty reform under the auspices of the existing treaties forced the other member states to negotiate a treaty outside the EU's legal framework. The Fiscal Compact is a classical international treaty that does not rest on the existing European treaties although it is designed as a bridging treaty. One significant feature of the treaty is that it will come into operation once ratified by twelve states. This would not have been possible within the treaty framework as unanimity is the decision rule on treaty change within the EU.

A third consequence of the crisis was the further deepening of the link between European integration and the single currency. Throughout the crisis, the HoSG reiterated their determination to do whatever was necessary to protect the Euro and the financial stability of the Euro area. This was not mere rhetoric but a determined commitment to protect the single currency as the core of European integration. The 2010 December European Council emphasized that 'The euro is and will remain a central part of European Integration.' This then leads to the issue of what else the Euro states will have to do to address the design faults in the Euro and resolve the crisis. The range of potential policy options includes the partial mutualisation of debt, fiscal transfers, a bank resolution mechanism, a financial transaction tax and further policy coordination in the budgetary and fiscal spheres. If the Euro area evolves into a transfer union, however disguised, there will be pressure for further political integration. The relative stabilisation following the LTROs in January 2012 did not address the underlying problems in the Euro area as the crisis reignited in April 2012 with Spain under particular pressure in the bond markets. This suggests that further integration including the use of enhanced cooperation is likely.

Section III: Co-existence within the Euro area and between the Euro area and the 27

On the face of it, it could be argued that the Euro area is just one example of differentiation in the EU, not unlike Justice and Home Affairs or defence policy. In other words, the Euro area is just another club in a club of clubs. This however is to underestimate the manner in which the crisis has already transformed the dynamic of the EU and the Euro area. All of the Euro states, including Germany, have learnt that the Euro created a very high level of interdependence and vulnerability among sovereigns and banks across the Eurozone. The experience of contagion and the potential for further contagion has stoked fears that the exit of any one state or the abandonment of the Euro may lead to a systemic implosion of the European and global financial system. The sheer uncertainty of what might happen pressurises Euro area states to continue muddling through the crisis in an effort to prevent an implosion at all costs. Fear of the likely impact on European integration of a Euro break-up makes the EMU club the pre-eminent club or core of the EU. But it is a club that is deeply fractured. The nature and depth of the crisis has generated profound tensions and conflict within the Euro area between creditor and debtor states. Trust has weakened and resentment has built up on both sides. The stakes are high as the central issues turn on the question of who bears the losses for the public and private excesses of the 2000s and who carries the cost of adjustment. Notwithstanding agreement on the Fiscal Compact, the politics of the Euro area have become more strident. The framing of the crisis as a sovereign debt crisis has imposed the largest adjustment costs on the debtor states; however, the creditor states have exposed themselves to potential future losses depending on the outcome of the crisis. Policy making on the Euro crisis has been characterised by a high level of informal politics, led by the Franco-German tandem.

Informal bilateral politics have been a pronounced feature of the dynamic of integration from the outset. States, large and small, engaged in multiple bilateralism to collect intelligence about the preferences of partners, to influence positions and to prepare for formal negotiations. The Franco-German couple has been a feature of European integration from the outset. As the two largest states, they have considerable structural power within the system and their ties were formalised in the 1963 Elysée Treaty. France and German officials maintained very close working ties regardless of the relationship between the two senior office holders. In this crisis, bilateral meetings between Chancellor Merkel and President Sarkozy were a pronounced feature of the informal politics of the crisis. Joint meetings, photo opportunities and press conferences were central to the script of crisis management. Their meetings set the agenda and determined the available policy options. The role of their joint meetings was to ensure that both states 'sang from the same hymn sheet' as any policy response at a minimum required their agreement and they had different preferences about how to address the crisis and the timing of intervention. France supported more active intervention in the crisis from the outset and was prepared to support a Greek bailout at a much earlier stage than Germany. France saw the crisis as an opportunity to revive its long held preference for enhanced 'economic governance' within the Euro area whereas Germany was committed to the independence of the ECB. Germany had a preference for the highest level of automaticity in sanctioning countries that breached agreed fiscal targets whereas France fought for more time before sanctions were adopted. Germany wanted the IMF as an integral part of any rescue; France wanted the EU to handle the crisis on its own.

As the crisis persisted, a shift in the balance of power occurred. The bilateral meeting, the walk on the beach, held at Deauville on the

18th of October 2010, was a turning point in the response to the crisis. While the two leaders were meeting in Deauville, the Finance ministers were meeting in Luxembourg to work out what would happen to the bail-out fund (EFSF) once it had run its course. An email was received from Deauville outlining agreement between the two principals. This was done without consulting the other member states or the ECB. The content and the way the deal was struck was a strong signal of how the Euro crisis would be handled thereafter and the growing ascendency of Germany. The Deauville deal consisted of three elements. First, Germany agreed that the sanctions regime in the budgetary sphere would be less automatic than it had wanted. This represented its last major concession to France in the crisis. Second, a permanent bail-out mechanism would be established following treaty change. France did not at this stage wish to reopen the treaties but Chancellor Merkel wanted to put a future bail-out fund on a sound legal footing. Third, France agreed to Germany's preference for private sector involvement in any future bailouts. Private sector bondholders would have to accept a reduction in the money they were owed. The latter decision had a profound impact on the crisis by further undermining investor confidence in the risks attached to government bonds in the Euro area. This had an immediate impact on the markets and the loss of confidence in the bonds of peripheral Euro area states has continued. Euro area sovereign bonds, once considered a very safe asset, were further undermined by the decisions taken in Deauville. The Deauville agreement was watered down by the December 2010 summit and later abandoned, but serious damage was done to the Euro area's sovereign bond markets from which they have not recovered. The decision by the two HoSG trumped the formal decisionmaking processes of the EU and caused considerable anger at the Eco-Fin meeting in Luxembourg when the Finance Ministers and the President of the ECB heard of the Deauville agreement. President Trichet accurately predicted the market response.

Following Deauville, the agenda and policy responses in the 'E' pillar were driven by Germany. This alteration in the power dynamic within the EU will have lasting effects. Regardless of who wins the French presidential election, the French President is weaker than at any time since the foundation of the EU. Germany has become the foremost leader of the Union and the Euro area. This is not a comfortable position for Germany but one that the German state elite must grapple with. France has to accept that its relative power position and standing is weakened. Italy and Spain face difficult years of fiscal consolidation but can play a role in reframing the agenda in Europe. The UK has placed itself in a position of limited influence, particularly on economic governance and future developments within the Euro area. Poland as a non-Euro state will strive to ensure that there is no rift between the ins and the outs and that there are no further barriers to membership of the Euro. The voice and presence of small and medium sized states is undermined when informal politics assume centre stage and when solutions are pre-cooked prior to full meetings of the European Council without the involvement of the Commission. The small states must ensure that they do not become the silent parties at the table and must insist on procedures and transparency at meetings of the European Council or Eurogroup. Small states have a shared interest in ensuring that they have adequate voice and representation in the Union and Euro area.

The institutional and legal legacy of the crisis is a further enhancement of the HoSG, Eurogroup and ECB, on the one hand, and a Fiscal Compact that lies outside the formal treaties, on the other. The Fiscal Compact makes provision for enhanced governance in the Euro area. It institutionalises the Euro Summit and the election of a President of the Euro Summit at the same time as the election of the President of the European Council. This implies that it is likely that both offices will be held by the same person which, in-turn, implies that the President of the European Council will be drawn from Euro area states. The treaty specifies that at least once a year, the HoSG of states not in the Euro will be invited to attend the Euro Summit if they have ratified the Fiscal Compact. The treaty makes provision for the development of budgetary committees of national parliaments, and, under Article 10 of the Fiscal treaty, envisages the greater use of enhanced cooperation. Under the current provisions, a minimum of nine states may use the EU institutions to engage in enhanced co-operation applying only to the participating states. Given the inclusion of a reference to enhanced cooperation in the Fiscal Compact, the clear intention is to use these provisions for the Euro area. A hardening of the boundaries between the 'ins' and the 'outs' makes co-existence more challenging between those in the Euro and outside given the pressure on the Euro area to deepen integration.

The emergence of an *avant garde* with the Euro as the core of European integration has the potential to solidify into a two-tier and not just a multi-speed EU. The pressure to maintain the Euro with all of its 17 members implies a further deepening of integration among the Euro states. Deepening may manifest itself in debt mutualisation (Eurobonds) and fiscal transfers to those states, particularly Greece, that are experiencing a prolonged recession. Greece, and perhaps one or two other states in the Euro, is not solvent and will have difficulty returning to the financial markets. Any deepening of integration in this direction would have to be accompanied by greater political integration and further surveillance across the member states. Deepening would serve to further harden the boundary between the Euro area and the other member states. If, however, the Euro manages to weather the storm, it will be possible to enlarge its membership when the outs have achieved the Maastricht criteria. Scrutiny of prospective members will be far more stringent than in the past. An avant garde Europe is one in which those outside the Euro may be marginalised and experience a weakening of influence. The fact that 25 states signed the fiscal compact underlines the fear of those outside concerning their influence in the system. The new member states in East Central Europe see Euro membership as part of their future within the Union. The UK appears particularly isolated, which is not good for those states wishing to see some balance to the Franco-German motor.

Co-existence between the Euro area and the EU 27 may depend on the development of a shared policy platform and a reassertion of the underlying norms of EU membership. The EU works best when it has a practical policy programme to address. The single market provides the glue that holds the EU together. All member states are committed to the internal market and all are involved. It is the one club that all member states partake in. Those outside the Euro area, particularly the UK, have always stressed that the single market is sacrosanct and that developments within the Euro area cannot be allowed to undermine the internal market. A growth strategy for the 27 is the most likely candidate for the development of a shared policy platform. The EU 27 faces challenges of competitiveness given global developments. The Euro area and the remaining member states need growth to ensure that the strains that have been experienced over the last three years are overcome. Austerity policies without growth are self-defeating for the Euro area and the EU 27. Thus, the internal market and the search for growth offers the best platform policy for co-existence between the Euro area and the EU. The Europe 2020 Strategy with its focus on structural reform is not a growth strategy for the next five years. Europe is falling behind in the digital market and faces considerable barriers to achieving a Digital Single Market by 2015.

Prior to the March 2012 European Council, the HoSG of twelve member states sent a letter entitled 'A Plan for Growth in Europe' to the President of the European Council. It was noteworthy for its content but also the fact that it was sent by a group of states that were members and non-members of the Euro. The two large states represented on the list, Italy and the UK, were joined by the Netherlands, Estonia, Latvia, Finland, Ireland, the Czech Republic, Slovakia, Spain, Sweden and Poland. This was a deliberate coordinated attempt to shift the EU agenda from austerity to growth and from the Euro area exclusively to the EU 27. For Italy, it served the Monti strategy of reframing the EU agenda to focus on growth and for the UK it represented an effort to regain some leverage at the table following the December European Council meeting. The letter was also a reminder to the Franco-German core that there were limits to its domination of the agenda and to the presence of a *de facto* if not *de jure* directoire in the Union. The combination of two large states and a number of medium and small states underlined the importance of alternative coalitions within the EU. That said, the policies and approaches of the 'big three' will have a major impact on the evolving dynamics in the Union.

The French preference is one that favours a 'hard core' Euro area driven by the Franco-German motor based on intensive intergovernmental and trans-governmental cooperation with the weak involvement of EU institutions. This is designed to enable France to disguise its weakness within the Euro area. In other words, France has invested heavily in the Franco-German relationship. It does not appear to have considered a counter-strategy of leading a coalition of Mediterranean states as a means of rebalancing the Euro area agenda away from coordinated austerity towards slower fiscal adjustment and growth. Would a Hollande Presidency consider such a strategy or is the institutionalised coordination reflex with Germany so embedded that it precludes such a strategy? The UK on the other hand finds itself outside the 17 and the 25 in a more isolated position than it would wish within the EU. It has a profound interest in getting the internal market on the agenda both for reasons of growth and presence. Paradoxically, this means that the UK should actively champion the role of the supranational institutions as the Commission is central to progress in the internal market. Germany does not wish to see a closed hard core EMU and has begun to acknowledge that growth is vital to the Euro and EU. It is also committed to the maintenance of the Euro area but not as a closed system. Traditionally a supporter of the supranational institutions, Germany has over the last ten years displayed a weaker commitment to the role of the Commission. In her speech at the opening of the Academic Year 2010 in Brugge, Chancellor Merkel distinguished between the 'community method' with the Commission at its core and the 'Union method' for those areas that involve member state coordination. A commitment to the 'community method' would have to underpin progress on the single market agenda. A platform including a serious focus on the internal market and growth would serve to bring the EU 27 together in a shared project. In addition, mutual co-existence within the EU would benefit from a reassertion of the fundamental norms of membership. The core norms are:

- Open rather than closed differentiation: this means that when non-members are ready to become members of the Euro area, the system remains open;
- Equality of access to the institutions and involvement of the core institutions in all areas of differentiated integration;
- Access for all member states to information and knowledge of what is happening in all policy fields (Gillespie 2012).

Unless the EU 27 agree to a policy platform that all member states engage with and there is constant vigilance concerning the underlying norms of EU membership, an avant garde Euro area may solidify into a tiered rather than a multi-speed EU. There remains considerable uncertainty about the future trajectory because of the continuing strains within the Euro area.

References

Andersen S.S. and Sitter N., 2006, 'Differentiated Integration: What is it and How Much Can the EU Accommodate?', European Integration 28:4, 313-330.

De Neve J.-E., 2007, 'The European Onion? How Differentiated Integration is Reshaping the EU,' European Integration 29:4, 503-21.

Emmanouilidis J. A., 2007, Institutional Consequences of Differentiated Integration, Bertelsmann Group for Policy Research, Working Paper.

Gillespie P., 2012, The Euro Crisis: Ins and Outs-Multispeed Europe, Discussion Paper, IIEA: Dublin.

Holzinger K. and Schimmelfennig F., 2012, 'Differentiated Integration in the European Union: Many Concepts, Sparse Theory, Few Data,' Journal of European Public Policy 19:2, 292–305.

Stubb, A., 1996, 'A Categorization of Differentiated Integration,' Journal of Common Market Studies 34:2, 283-95.

Stubb A., 1997, 'The 1996 Intergovernmental Conference and the Management of Flexible Integration,' Journal of European Public Policy 4:1, 37-55.

13
The Euro Area Crisis and Implications for the Relation Between The EU and The Euro Area

Guntram B. Wolff

This chapter reviews major challenges for the Euro area, discusses recent initiatives and the way forward in particular as regards Euro area vs non-Euro area EU member relations. The Eurozone faces three major challenges: (1) high private and/or public debt in some of its parts together with competitiveness adjustment needs that in some countries have barely started, (2) a weak growth outlook, and (3) continued banking sector fragility that together with sovereign stress feeds a negative feedback loop. The Euro area has taken many significant measures to overcome these problems including the six-pack, the fiscal compact, the EFSF and the ESM, which are discussed briefly. Significant risks remain. The slow real economic adjustment and the largely unaddressed banking-sovereign fragility are the largest concerns. Solving the banking-sovereign fragility will involve more Euro area integration. This will pose challenges to the relationship with non-Euro area countries. EU countries outside of the Euro area will either want to (1) leave or join the Euro, (2) get protection clauses to safeguard their vital economic interests, or (3) insist on regulatory flexibility.

The Euro area faces severe challenges. The ongoing crisis clearly exposes the failure of the Maastricht architecture for Economic and Monetary Union (EMU). Central to this failure is the lack of any fiscal capacity for the Euro area and the strong intervention rights in national policy-making that go along with central authority. Banking resolution and supervision remain largely national and need to be integrated at a Euro area level to ensure stability. More specifically, the Euro area faces three major challenges.

First, it is confronted with very high private and public debt levels in some of its parts, and a formidable adjustment challenge. The debt is not only domestically held. In Spain, Portugal and Greece, debt owed to creditors outside of the country is above 80 percent of GDP (see Ahearne and Wolff, 2012). Repaying external debt while at the same time being obliged to reduce prices to become competitive and export more to repay for the external debt is extremely difficult. In fact, historical lessons show that even the external interest burden can become difficult to shoulder.[1] Figure 1 summarises the difficulty of internal devaluation in the Euro area.

Figure 1: Changes in Real Effective Exchange Rate (REER) (Intra*) in Terms of Unit Labour Cost (ULC) and Consumer Price Index (CPI) 2007-2011

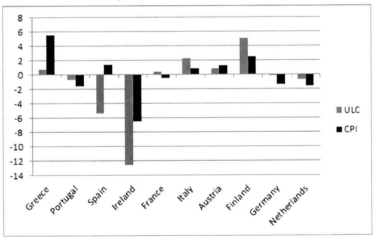

Source: EUROSTAT, * Intra refers to the REER relative to 16 euro zone trading partners.

---

1 John Maynard Keynes wrote extensively about the problem of external debt payments at a different time and in a different context, but his lessons remain valid today.

Broadly speaking, since the onset of the crisis, price adjustment has been modest or absent in most Euro-area countries. Greece continued to lose price competitiveness, as did Italy, even though in the last 6-12 months some adjustment is visible. Germany, in turn, did not change its relative position and its competitiveness remains unchanged. Spain, and in particular, Ireland, have become more competitive. Similarly, current-account divergence has reverted since the beginning of the crisis, but significant differences in deficits and surpluses remain, with Greece still running a current account deficit of 10 percent and Germany continuing to have a surplus of 5 percent.

Real macroeconomic adjustment in EMU is proving very difficult. In fact, comparing the adjustment with the adjustment of countries outside the Euro area shows that adjustment is much slower than in the Euro area (Darvas and Pisani-Ferry, 2011). The question is why this is the case. The most plausible explanation is that ECB financing and financial support in the form of financial assistance programmes is given. This sustains domestic demand and reduces price adjustment needs. In fact, one of the striking features of the Greek economy is that, despite all the fiscal austerity enacted, Greece is still running a current account deficit of almost 10 percent (in 2011).

Second, economic growth in the Euro area as a whole, and in particular in the so-called periphery, is very weak. Growth forecasts have been revised downwards. None of the four big Euro-area economies, i.e., Germany, France, Italy and Spain, are projected to grow more than 1 percent in 2012, according to European Commission forecasts. Periphery growth is particularly low and in some cases even negative.

Third, European Banking Authority stress tests have not restored trust in the Euro area banking system. We have seen the build-up of such negative feedback loops from an increasingly fragile sovereign to an increasingly fragile banking system and this is illustrated in the Figure below. Purely national strategies will fail to stop this banking fragility. Angeloni and Wolff (2012) discuss the fragility of the banking sector in more detail. National finance ministries in the periphery, in particular, cannot credibly prevent deposit runs or withdrawals of funds from banks located in their countries by themselves, as they are too small and may lack access to markets to borrow at good rates.

Figure 2: Correlation between sovereign and banking credit default swaps

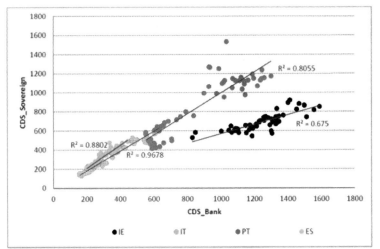

Source Bruegel calculations with data from Datastream and Macrobond.
Note: Weekly averages from January 2011 to February 2012. Banking CDS by country are calculated as weighted averages of CDS of the individual banks considered for each country. The graph for Greece is not displayed since it is characterised by hyperbolic pattern. The same graphical result holds not only for periphery countries but also for stronger EU economies such as Germany and France

During 2011, Euro area leaders took a number of significant steps to overcome these problems. At the last summit, leaders agreed on tougher and more biting fiscal rules, which are to be mostly implemented at a national level. This will help to increase fiscal discipline and thereby help to prevent problems of the kind currently seen in Greece from happening again. Such measures will also, to some extent, be helpful in increasing investors' trust in a country's political ability to repay debt. At the same time, the new fiscal rules are felt to be too restrictive in many countries, thereby undermining their credibility.

In exchange for more commitments to fiscal discipline, significant rescue funds have been put in place, including the EFSF, ESM and more resources for the IMF.

But major challenges for the Euro area remain, in particular as regards the real economic adjustment, the growth agenda and the right institutions to deal with the fragility of the EMU banking sector. Stepping up the Euro area's institutional framework also means that a serious debate about the democratic foundations of the new framework will be needed.

First, a Euro-area growth strategy is missing but is urgently needed. Without significantly higher economic growth in southern Europe, debt dynamics in combination with price adjustment needs will jeopardise sustainability. At the regional and national levels, reforms need to focus on improving supply-side conditions for business, including better administration, governance and rule of law, as well as significantly better education and innovation systems. The key reform needed is one that improves the conditions for exports. An economy with an external debt overhang needs to export to generate growth and to adjust. Price and wage adjustments are necessary in that regard.

At a Euro area level, the macroeconomic policy mix needs to be appropriate. Monetary policy alone may prove insufficient to boost demand in the face of a severe downturn. Therefore, a Euro area level tool to boost demand may become necessary. After all, it should be remembered that federal states such as the US have strong anticyclical fiscal policy at the federal level, while, at the state level, balanced budget rules render public budgets pro-cyclical. In the Euro area, the new fiscal rules – if successful – will reduce anti-cyclical fiscal policy action, which is currently already limited due to market pressure.[2] Currently, the Euro area is not equipped with an appropriate tool for exercising anti-cyclical fiscal policy beyond the automatic stabilizers. It is advisable to think about putting in place a strong Euro area tool for such purposes, for example, in the form of a means for a Euro area investment project financed with project bonds.

Second, the integrated Euro area banking system needs an integrated and powerful banking supervision and resolution authority backed by sufficient means to prevent bank runs (see also Marzinotto, Sapir and Wolff, 2011). The current system centered on national su-

2 Henning and Kessler (2012) make this point as regards the building of the US federation in the last 200 years. Bruegel fellows have repeatedly made this point in the Euro area context.

pervisors and national fiscal resources is clearly fragile. A true Euro area deposit insurance corporation (EDIC) that would ultimately be backed by the Euro area taxpayer may become necessary and would increase stability. This EDIC would have the power to supervise, control and if necessary resolve all systemically important banks in the Euro area.

Third, a solution for dealing with debt overhang is needed. Ultimately, if debt levels are too large to be repaid from purely national resources, financial assistance is needed and a framework for orderly restructuring needs to be in place. The current structure around the ESM may prove insufficient in terms of size, decision-making mechanism and set-up for dealing with a crisis in one of the larger Euro area countries. It may therefore become necessary to pool all Euro area public debt. To issue such common debt, a common treasury with tax-raising powers appears necessary.[3]

The ECB has strongly intervened recently and has prevented sudden stops by replacing private with ECB funding of banks (Merler and Pisani-Ferry, 2012). However, a lot of liquidity is hoarded in the deposit facility of the ECB, in particular from banks in the north (Pisani-Ferry and Wolff, 2012) (see Figure 3). The ECB thereby has become a financial intermediary between the north and the south of Europe. Part of the additional liquidity was used by banks to buy government bonds, and this has led to a reduction in the interest rate of government bonds of the South. So far, however, there is relatively little evidence of a turnaround in credit conditions.

The ECB faces a dilemma. It needs to increasingly ask whether its financing of current account deficits is justified. This essentially depends on an assessment of the solvency of the economy and the borrowers of ECB liquidity. If the ECB were to lend to insolvent banks against insufficient-quality collateral, it would take risks on board that could possibly lead to a fiscal transfer from some countries to

---

3 Currently, the interest cost of all Euro-area debt is 3.7 percent of Euro-area GDP. The Euro-area finance ministry would thus need tax-raising power of at least 4 percent of Euro-area GDP to credibly take on all debt. National taxes could be reduced by a similar amount so that the overall tax burden for the average Euro-area citizen would not change.

others. As long as there is no political support for it, the ECB cannot step into the role of a common treasury that would usually be tasked to provide such fiscal transfers if needed. The absence of a common treasury renders ECB action less effective as investors understand that fiscal support is missing. In that sense, ECB policy cannot solve and has not solved some of the underlying problems.

Figure 3: Use of ECB Deposit Facility - EU Rmm (June 2007 - 16th February 2011)

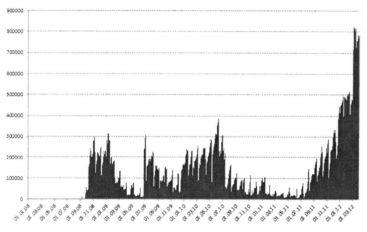

This brings me to my last point: the question of EU vs Euro area, which is discussed in detail in Pisani-Ferry, Sapir, and Wolff (2012). A robust new framework for banking supervision and resolution will require significant integration steps. The economic logic suggests that this will mostly happen at the Euro area level. This will have significant implications for non-Euro area member states. The more the Euro area integrates politically, the more it will be able to dominate decision making in the EU. This may render the EU less attractive to countries outside the Euro area, which may then quickly face the choice of joining the club or leaving. A third way would be to stay inside the EU but demand strong safeguard clauses to protect vital interests against the Euro area majority. Finally, EU members outside the Euro area may wish to negotiate in certain economic areas opt-outs to be able to set rules and standards themselves. In the short run, the strong degree of financial integration of Euro area members with non-Euro area members will require a high level of information sharing, as is already done in the ESRB and the EBA.

In summary: solving the Euro area crisis will require more integration steps, in particular in the financial and banking field. This is likely to prove a significant challenge for the Euro area-EU relationship.

References

Angeloni, Chiara and Guntram Wolff, 2012, "Are Banks Affected by their Holding of Government Debt?," Bruegel Working Paper 2012/7.

Ahearne, Alan and Guntram Wolff, 2012, "The Debt Challenge in Europe," Bruegel Working Paper 2012/02.

Darvas, Zsolt and Jean Pisani-Ferry, 2011, "Europe's Growth Emergency," Bruegel Policy Contribution 2011/13.

Henning, Randy and Martin Kessler, 2012, "Fiscal Federalism: US History for Architects of Europe's Fiscal Union," Bruegel essay.

Marzinotto, Benedicta, André Sapir and Guntram Wolff, 2011, "What Kind of Fiscal Union?," Bruegel Policy Brief http://www.bruegel.org/publications/publication-detail/publication/646-what-kind-of-fiscal-union/

Merler, Silvia and Jean Pisani-Ferry, 2012, "Sudden Stops in the Euro Area," Bruegel Policy Contribution 2012/6.

Pisani-Ferry, Jean, André Sapir, and Guntram Wolff, 2012, "The Messy Rebuilding of Europe," Bruegel Policy Brief 2012/01.

Pisani-Ferry, Jean and Guntram Wolff, 2012, "Propping up Europe?," Bruegel Policy Contribution 2012/7.

14
About Hollande and Holland

Wolfgang Münchau

Today, I would like to offer some thoughts on France and the Netherlands – Hollande and Holland. As far as Hollande goes, I am, perhaps uncharacteristically, optimistic. I consider his likely impact on France as relatively neutral, but on the Eurozone as very positive. I am also encouraged by the protest in the Netherlands against what I can consider a seriously misguided fiscal adjustment programme.

Hollande

The financial markets have reacted negatively to Francois Hollande's first round victory because they did not see it coming. I recall a fund managers' poll a couple of weeks ago, according to which a majority believed Sarkozy would win. They clearly have been reading the wrong newspapers, or the wrong commentators. Sarkozy's loss has been well flagged for anyone who has bothered to look.

It is governments that lose election, not oppositions that win it. And this old adage holds true here. The French despise Sarkozy. He is simply not presidential. Hollande is the anti-Sarkozy, a little dull, but honest. An intensely political man, for sure, but not somebody who makes cynical short-sighted policy proposals.

No dullness though, when it comes to the Eurozone. Hollande is the best hope we have to challenge the toxic consensus that lies at the root of the persistent failure of crisis resolution. As a journalist, I like to think in terms of narratives, and especially self-perpetuating narratives. The German narrative, which is also the narrative of the Eurozone dominant centre-right political class, is that the way to fight the crisis is through a combination of fiscal discipline and structural reforms. I think this narrative is flawed because it does not take into account the interaction between austerity and growth, and the interaction of simultaneous public sector deleveraging and private sector deleveraging.

The centre right is firmly in power almost everywhere. All the large and many of the smaller Eurozone countries have governments led by centre-right political parties. Angela Merkel is without a doubt the leader of the centre-right. The centre-right has always expressed a preference for inflexible fiscal rules, despite the experiences we have had with such rules, and the experience we are going to have with the rules this year and next.

The main reason why I am positive about the likely electoral success of Francois Hollande is not because I think his policies will work. It is because he is a narrative-buster. He will challenge Merkel because he will tell a different story. It is no accident that Mario Draghi proposes a growth compact at exactly this time. That initiative is not going to make much real-world difference. But Europe's elite are beginning to recognise that they need another story. And Hollande will be the main political narrator of that story.

As for the fiscal pact, I don't think Hollande is going to veto it, or seek changes to its mechanisms. This is a shame because I believe the fiscal pact needs such changes, especially to the rule that member states are almost certainly not able to fulfill: the 1/20 debt reduction rule, which requires that a country cut 1/20 of its excess debt over the 60% rule each year. In Italy's case, that's 3%, plus whatever it takes to stabilise the debt levels at current levels, and an additional 3 to 4%, depending on your assumptions about growth and interest rates. That means Italy would need to run a primary surplus of 7-8%

for about a generation. I think that Mario Monti was totally irresponsible when he signed the pact, and failed to point out this little detail to his countrymen.

There is no way that the EU is going to meet the 2013 deficit target. Italy and Spain, but also the Netherlands, and many other countries, are on a trajectory for a big overshoot of their respective deficit targets. The conservative narrative of the crisis is about to meet its nemesis, and for that reason a change in narrative is timely.

Unfortunately, Hollande's position is not quite as radical as it appears. He is not going to stop this insanity. All he will do is add some growth components to the pact – a redefinition of structural funds, a long overdue rebooting of the European Investment Bank, but nothing that stops the austerity madness, which itself will be the biggest impediment to growth. At best, he might get some flexibility clauses. But it is the whole point of the pact to deny such flexibility. The Eurozone is thus setting itself up for another treaty that is not going to work. After two stability pacts, the so-called "six pack," this will be pact number four that is destined to fail, and this will be quite soon. It will cause further damage to the credibility of the Eurozone.

What about Hollande's likely management of the French economy, which is not a first order issue of the Eurozone crisis right now, but has the potential to become one if things go wrong? I think his proposal to raise the income tax rate to 75% is as politically smart as it is economically irrelevant. It is surely better to tax excessively high incomes than to tax financial transactions. But hardly anybody will end up paying this, so there is a lot of political symbolism involved. This is a tax applied mostly to employed bankers and CEOs, as entrepreneurs will find ways to circumvent it easily and legally. There will be quite a bit of tax avoidance through emigration. We are already seeing an increase in property prices in Brussels – at least in the very high end of the market – which is directly related to Hollande's threat. The economic impact of this measure will be too small to register.

Holland

The impact of a Hollande presidency will probably be felt outside France more than inside France. The first country that may catch the Hollande virus is Holland. The most self-righteous of the Eurozone member states was last week on course to miss the 3% deficit target, after the populist Geert Wilders withdrew his support for the budget measures. The government of Liberals and Christian Democrats had until last week relied on the eccentric Wilders for their majority. He withdrew his support, which triggered the collapse of the government, and with it new elections in September. In the meantime, the government managed to agree to an austerity budget with some of the centrist opposition parties.

Wilders has his own reasons for his decision. He is not known for his astute understanding of economic issues. But as much as I hate to say it, he is right on the substance. There is absolutely no need for the Netherlands to pursue a policy of austerity at a time of economic weakness, given the room for manoeuvre the country still has due to a relative low debt-to-GDP ratio, and absurdly high current account surplus. Economically, I would welcome a more moderate form of budgetary adjustment. The opposition Labour Party agrees, and has called for a trajectory towards a 3.6% target for 2013.

Meanwhile, Geert Wilders has now discovered the Eurozone as his favourite campaign issue (ahead of immigration), which will invariably push the rest of the centrist parties into a difficult super-Grand Coalition in favour of austerity, with the extremist parties favouring a more gentle fiscal approach. This is politics gone crazy – and it may bring some nasty surprises. We have learnt from the Dutch referendum on the Constitutional Treaty that one should not underestimate the Dutch popular resistance against what is perceived to be European authoritarianism. Furthermore, if Wilders goes anti-European, and seems to succeed, it is possible that the governing parties will promise a referendum on the fiscal pact simply to take the wind out of his sails. The message would be: you can still vote for a nice and normal democratic party, and still have the chance to vote against the pact. If this is the case, I would predict a solid No majority against the fiscal pact. So this is one to watch out for.

Hollande, Holland and the future of the Eurozone

The diffuse message we are getting from voters is that they are not happy with the political management of the crisis. The voters are not experts, and why should they be? Steve Jobs once said it is not the job of the consumer to know what he wants to consume. This is the same in crisis resolution. The people want the crisis solved. It is the job of politicians to solve it. And they throw out the ones who don't. We already have enough fallen political victims to consider the set-up of a large memorial in Brussels in their memory. I count nine heads of state and government who have lost their jobs – Sarkozy included. And I think our ability to solve the crisis will depend on whether Angela Merkel will join him on our hypothetical memorial. Hollande alone is not going to provide a sufficiently strong (though still welcome) corrective. A change of leadership in Germany and France within a year of each other would be a different matter altogether. Before I get carried away, let me say that at this stage this looks unlikely, because Merkel's ratings, unlike Sarkozy's, have been consistently high. I am clearly not a fan, but she is not a monster. But I believe that despite her current popularity, her political fortunes may change as the crisis gets worse, which will expose her piecemeal style of leadership for what it is.

Even if Germany were to change in lockstep with France, we will still not get an immediate crisis resolution. But the narratives will change, and that impact cannot be overestimated. It means, for example, that eurobonds or bank resolution regimes may no longer be a taboo subject.

My reading of what happens in France and the Netherlands is very different from that of the financial markets. I welcome Hollande, and I welcome the likely insurrection that awaits in the Netherlands, though clearly I would prefer if it did not come in the form of a repugnant populist. Derailing the official crisis resolution strategy is a necessary, but not a sufficient condition for success. We have to stop blind austerity, we need a functioning resolution system for the banks, and we will ultimately also need eurobonds. That's simply not possible to do with the centre right. Forget the Nixon in

China effect. The centre-right cannot deliver this. They have been in power for too long, and have wasted time on economically illiterate pacts, on insufficiently flexible firewalls, and the micromanagement of the "voluntary" private sector participation in Greece, which will almost certainly turn into a near-complete default at one point.

I have a final concluding thought. Hollande and Holland are both a reminder that we should not take things for granted. The crisis is truly dynamic. Macroeconomists are right when they point out that the current level of interest rates, private sector deleveraging, public sector austerity, and crisis resolution constitute an inconsistent set. "What is unsustainable, will stop," Herb Stein once said. While this statement is plausible, even true, it is entirely useless in our case because it does not tell us what to do. I cannot rule out a break-up – though I think this would be a cataclysmic event nobody in their right mind would wish for. I remain convinced that this is highly unlikely. Before it will come to this, the politics is likely to shift, and the election of Hollande, if indeed he is elected, will be a reminder that this story is more open-ended than some of the determinists may think.

15
Europe's Tragedy Nears the End of Act One, but the Drama Continues

Janet Kersnar

More, not less reform: That's what Europe needs if the Euro stands a chance of survival, according to experts from a range of fields at a workshop held on April 26 in Fiesole, Italy. Titled, "Governance for the Eurozone: Integration or Disintegration?," the workshop took place as Greece and a number of other European communities are at a breaking point, squeezed by austerity and an uncertain economic recovery. Against that backdrop, the workshop, which was co-organized by the Wharton Financial Institutions Center, among others, evaluated the steps that EU members are taking to combat a potential unraveling of the union.

What a difference a year can make. When a group of European Union experts met at a workshop in Italy's Tuscan hills in the spring of 2011, the center of attention was Greece and its ever-growing sovereign debt crisis. Could it, should it, default on debt repayments? And what would happen then? The delegates wondered whether the result might be a meltdown not just of the Greek economy but of Europe as a whole.

Flash forward a year, and Greece is still a hot topic. EU experts gathering in Italy at this year's workshop focused on the region's other crisis-ravaged economies: Spain, Portugal, Ireland, Italy and Belgium.

'New EU Emerging'

According to Brigid Laffan, a panelist, "a new EU is emerging from the crisis." As the European politics professor at Ireland's University College Dublin asked, "The question is how much more do the Eurozone states have to do in order to save the Euro?"

Plenty, it seems. Against a backdrop of what Laffan called "the politics of austerity" -- in which German Chancellor Angela Merkel and former French President Nicholas Sarkozy called the shots -- a number of experts at the workshop said they see a need for more, not less, integration across the EU. That integration, they noted, goes well beyond the EU-wide fiscal discipline debates taking place today, to address the region's economic imbalances that are believed to be behind many of its current woes.

Two things are increasingly clear, according to Franklin Allen, finance professor at Wharton, echoing the discussions he co-chaired at the workshop, which was held at the European University Institute (EUI). First, "that there is not nearly enough concern for the human cost of the policies that they are trying to pursue" -- unemployment in the Eurozone is now around 11%, with around 50% of people under 25 in Spain and Greece jobless. Second, that there is "a low likelihood that they will succeed in anything over the next several years."

That may feel like an eternity for Europeans who have already endured enough hardship -- and precipitous drops in their standards of living -- since the crisis began in 2007 and deep government spending cuts took hold. As Charles Goodhart, emeritus banking and finance professor at the London School of Economics, noted at the workshop, "Austerity without growth is a recipe for depression, despair and growing social and political dissonance." Just ask the Greeks.

Big Tradeoffs

One of the biggest events since last year has been that Greece has indeed defaulted -- albeit in a de facto way, with a so-called "public-sector involvement" debt swap in which the creditors taking part faced losses of more than 50% of their principal.

It was, perhaps, not a bad thing. "It showed you could have a default without Armageddon," said Allen. "The official [European Central Bank] view, and that of many people, argued that if Greece defaulted, it would be like the world ending. But that wasn't true.... That was a big positive."

Even so, Greece continues to muddle through the crisis under the 130 billion-Euro rescue package put together by the the European Central Bank (ECB), the EU and the International Monetary Fund (IMF). Greeks have had to undergo a series of adjustments in order to receive that bailout while its economy languishes. Indeed, Bloomberg reported May 15 that Greece's economy contracted 7% in the fourth quarter of 2011, compared with a year earlier, "when the country was already deep into recession." Overall unemployment is three times higher than it was before the crisis at 20.9%, homelessness is on the rise and almost half of all homeowners say they will not be able to make their mortgage payments this year, Bloomberg also reported.

Following what turned out to be a chaotic, anti-austerity national election on May 6, leaving an indecisive victory, the Greeks continue to struggle with a troubled economy. The new interim government in place until June elections did not immediately rule out a second -- and this time, a hard -- default, reneging on agreements to pay 436 million Euros to bondholders who shunned the first debt swap earlier this spring. The payment, however, was made, thus avoiding the possibility that Greece would be cast out of the Eurozone.

Greece is hardly alone. With the help of new mechanisms, including the European Financial Stability Fund (or the EFSF, set up last year by Eurozone countries to provide loans to cash-strapped members) and an array of social and economic reform measures, policymakers in Spain and the Eurozone's other "periphery" countries, too, have spent the past year trying to fix their broken economies -- amid lots of controversy.

The question policymakers should be asking, but too often aren't, is, "Are there financial backstops that provide enough time and incentives that will allow structural reform?" noted Pier Paolo Padoan, deputy secretary-general of the Organisation for Economic Co-operation and Development, during a presentation at the workshop. "If there's a negative answer to that question, you're in trouble."

Determining how fiscal austerity -- requiring national governments to keep budgets under control and maintain tax revenues -- can go hand in hand with growth is a tall order. The fear in some circles is that the impact of austerity may, in fact, be worse than that of any current or future economic downturn. What national policymakers need to question is whether fiscal consolidation will lead to "a good equilibrium between public debt and growth," Padoan said.

French President-elect François Hollande believes it cannot; Merkel does. "We in Germany are of the opinion, and so am I personally, that the fiscal pact is not negotiable. It has been negotiated and has been signed by 25 countries," Reuters quoted Merkel as saying following Hollande's election. "We are in the middle of a debate to which France, of course, under its new president will bring its own emphasis. But we are talking about two sides of the same coin -- progress is only achievable via solid finances plus growth."

Is this impasse cause for despair? Not according to Padoan. Timing -- in terms of when such reforms take place during an economic cycle -- is important, as is market confidence that the reforms make sense, even if the full impact is not realized for the next 10 to 25 years. Padoan pointed out that the pace of reform -- "has been accelerating. Why is this good news? Not because it generates pain, but because the time when we will start to see the benefits is closer than you think," he said.

The hope is that the Eurozone's so-called periphery countries will regain the competitiveness they lost in recent years. In his presentation, Frank Smets, research director general at the ECB, explored the damaging effect that the rise of unit labor costs has had on countries such as Ireland. "On average, it was [in these countries] 1% to 2% higher than the market over this period, much higher than Germany, for example, which had one of the lowest increases in unit labor costs," he said.

One Bank, Many Mandates?

Another striking aspect in the debates about the Eurozone crisis has to do with the many institutions involved and which of those has the responsibility, and credibility, to knock the crisis on its head. Arguably the most intriguing institution in that regard is the ECB.

Just what is the ECB's role in this crisis? According to workshop participants, its role in the banking sector is more straightforward. Since the crisis began, the ECB has opened a spigot of lending to support banks in Greece and other nations. Europe's banks -- even those with relatively healthy balance sheets -- have helped themselves to the ECB's cheap money (three-year bank refinancing known as the Long-Term Refinancing Operation). Sometimes they have been tapping the ECB to rekindle their own lending in the hope that their loans to retail and wholesale customers will help local economies, or purchase sovereign debt. But more often, banks are using those loans to prop up their own businesses as new, more stringent regulations kick in, requiring them to keep higher amounts of capital in reserve for a rainy day. Meanwhile, consumer demand and productive capacity are so slack that it is questionable whether there would be much demand for loans by businesses even if the funds were fully available.

But does the ECB have a responsibility to go further by remaining as it has been recently -- a lender of last resort to provide financial stability and prevent countries like Greece from going bankrupt? It's a different matter with countries, participants at the workshop noted. For one thing, countries have a wider range of levers to pull, including raising taxes, than banks do if their coffers run low. For another, the EFSF, and the future European Stability Mechanism slated to succeed the EFSF, can play that role. "The ECB cannot solve solvency issues [of countries]," stated Guntram Wolff, deputy director of Bruegel, a Brussels-based think tank.

But the argument is far from straightforward. In a paper presented at the workshop titled, "The European Central Bank: Lender of Last Resort in the Government Bond Markets?," Paul De Grauwe of the London School of Economics, noted, "Failure to provide lending of last resort in the government bond markets of the monetary union carries the risk of forcing the central bank into providing lending of last resort to the banks of the countries hit by a sovereign debt crisis. And this lending of last resort is almost certainly more expensive." Indeed, his research found that bank liabilities in the Eurozone were about 250% of GDP in 2008, while the Eurozone's government debt-to-GDP ratio was about 80%.

As he put it, the ECB is like "a fireman who has the means to catch the arsonist before the fire." The ECB is the only institution capable of stopping the Eurozone implosion but it doesn't want to do it. Until this changes, he stated, "the Eurozone will walk from one crisis to another."

Much Talk, Little Action

It is not only the institutions, but also the leaders behind the crisis that are cause for concern. Assessing the political landscape of the Eurozone, Russell Cooper, economics professor at the European University Institute, said Merkel and the other crisis kingpins, "talk and they talk and they talk. That's not the issue. The issue is credibility."

The truth is that's there is a woeful lack of solidarity among leaders in the EU, as the workshop's panelists and delegates pointed out. National interests have and will get in the way, noted Goodhart of the London School of Economics during his discussion about the U.K.'s role in the EU.

"My country will try to prevent centralizing rules," he said. "It may well be that any move to a central currency will be stymied. Anyone wanting one will have to assume that the U.K. government will nix it."

Could this now change? With Germany dominating crisis negotiations -- with France in tow -- other countries have been marginalized, Laffan observed. For now, "nothing can happen unless Germany wants it to happen. It can determine the pace of response, and which policy solutions are used. That is why we can see no transfer union [allowing governments to move payments among themselves] and, to date, no eurobonds [which proponents say would allow Eurozone governments to issue jointly guaranteed bonds that do not differentiate between the creditworthiness of the issuers]."

Now that France has seen a change in leadership, "might it not be a good time for the country to look at the reflex action that it has had toward that relationship? Could France, post-Sarkozy, with Italy and the U.K., create not an alternate coalition, but at least another coalition?" Laffan asked. "France has a really serious decision to make as to how it projects itself and positions itself."

Summing up a widespread view at the workshop, Laffan noted that the tragedy that is unfolding across Europe is "probably only looking at the end of the first act. The drama is going to continue."

Appendix
Introduction to the Stability and Growth Pact*

Victor Ngai

One commonly cited cause for the crisis in the Eurozone is high levels of deficit and debt in numerous European countries following the creation of the single currency. The global financial crisis exacerbated the problem, with debt loads soaring in the "peripheral" countries and their effect spreading across the Eurozone.

The question arises as to whether there was a failure in Eurozone governance and in the implementation of fiscal limits in European Union (EU). The problem of high deficits and debt was in fact foreseen by the drafters of the Maastricht Treaty, who sought to create a common currency that was as stable as the Deutsche Mark. So the foundations for the establishment of the Euro were laid out in the Treaty, where certain convergence criteria were defined, most notably limits on government finances, which had to be satisfied by a member state before it was to be admitted to the third stage of the monetary union. To this end, all EU countries worked for several years to stabilize inflation, lower government spending, reduce debt and avoid devaluation of the currency, in order to achieve the convergence criteria. By 1999, deficit and debt levels declined in most EU countries, and eleven countries qualified for the Euro.

---

*The full version of this paper can be found as part of the Working Paper Series on the Wharton Financial Institutions Center web site: http://fic.wharton.upenn.edu/fic/papers/12/12-10.pdf

As the launch of the new currency neared, there were discussions to implement a formal framework to maintain fiscal discipline once countries adopted the Euro, as they were no longer bound by the convergence criteria in the Maastricht Treaty. Under the Treaty, all member states of the EU were required to "avoid excessive deficits" but with few specific stipulations for its enforcement.[1] The Treaty also grants power to the European Commission, the EU's executive body, and to the Economic and Financial Affairs Council (ECO-FIN), made up of economic and finance ministers from member states, to monitor deficit and debt levels and to issue warnings and impose fines as necessary.

The idea of a more detailed set of procedures to handle excessive debts, or a "Stability Pact," was proposed by German finance minister Theo Waigel in the mid-1990s. Germany had long maintained a policy that emphasized price stability, which had been an important part of the German economy's strong performance. The German government hoped to ensure the continuation of that policy, which would limit the ability of governments to exert inflationary pressures on the European economy.

The intent of putting in place the Maastricht convergence criteria and a Pact to enforce fiscal discipline was to maintain economic stability within the EU and avoid large divergences across countries that would disadvantage fiscally prudent countries such as Germany. Given the variability of national budgets and the lack of formal budget limits on member states after the adoption of the single currency, and in order to reassure critics of the Euro and financial markets, regulations on public finances became indispensable to the functioning and stability of the Euro, so as to avoid spillover effects on all Eurozone countries. Since countries needed to forego control of monetary and exchange rate policies, countries were presumed to gravitate towards the use of fiscal policy and fiscal deficits to manage macroeconomic shocks. Financial mismanagement in a country could reduce market confidence and lead to higher borrowing rates for all countries. Or worse, debt-ridden countries could overspend

---

1 Article 104c, Maastricht Treaty; renumbered Article 126 of Treaty on the Functioning of the European Union (TFEU).

to a point where they could demand support from other countries. Excessive debt cannot be financed in public markets and can lead to monetary financings by central banks.

The resulting agreement, the Stability and Growth Pact (SGP), was introduced in 1997 as Council regulations,[2] and was designed to strengthen fiscal discipline on deficits and debt levels of member states. Rather than as part of a formal treaty, the SGP was EU secondary law and thus part of a set of European regulations and directives that applied to all member states and was set up to complement the creation of the single currency. Elaborating and supplementing the general provisions in the Maastricht Treaty, the SGP had the purpose of maintaining and enforcing low budgetary deficits in the Economic and Monetary Union (EMU). The SGP was thus intended to safeguard "sound public finances"[3] and ensure that Member states having adopted the Euro and met the Maastricht convergence criteria would continue to observe them.

The Stability and Growth Pact

As in the Maastricht Treaty, the two major criteria that member states must respect under the SGP are:

1. Annual government deficit not exceeding 3 percent of Gross Domestic Product (GDP)

2. Government debt not exceeding 60 percent of GDP, or diminishing and approaching that value.

The SGP became the rule-based framework to coordinate national fiscal policies in the EMU. The Pact has two components: a preventive arm and a corrective (dissuasive) arm.

Based on the concept of "multilateral surveillance" as established in the Maastricht Treaty,[4] the preventive arm requires member states to submit annual stability programs (for Eurozone countries) or convergence programs (for countries outside the Eurozone) to the Com-

2 Council Regulations 1466/97 and 1476/97, Council Resolution 97/C236/0-02.
3 Article 3a [TFEU Article 119].
4 Article 103 [TFEU Article 121].

mission and the Economic and Financial Affairs Council (ECO-FIN), showing how they plan to achieve or safeguard sound fiscal positions to meet their budgetary objectives. The Commission then assesses these programs and ECOFIN gives an opinion on them and may make its recommendations public.

The preventive arm includes two policy instruments:

First, in addition to the existing GDP deficit limit of 3 percent, the preventive arm also requires countries to strive for a medium-term objective (MTO). In the original agreement from 1997, countries were urged to attain a common "close-to-balance or in surplus" position to deal with normal cyclical fluctuations, with deficit no larger than half a percent of GDP over the cycle to remain in compliance. This allowed member states a sufficient cyclical safety margin when automatic stabilizers are operated in an economic downturn.

Second, ECOFIN can issue an early warning to prevent the occurrence of an excessive deficit. With the use of official policy advice, the Commission, through ECOFIN, can directly address policy recommendations to a member state with regards to the broad implications of its fiscal policies. ECOFIN can make a recommendation to a member state to take prompt corrective measures if the excessive deficit persists or worsens. The preventive arm had little prominence and did not gain much attention in public debates.

The dissuasive or "corrective" part of the Pact governs the Excessive Deficit Procedure (EDP) created by the Maastricht Treaty.[5] The SGP specifies triggers to the EDP and if it is decided that the deficit is excessive in the meaning of the Treaty, ECOFIN issues recommendations to the relevant member state, providing guidance and a timeline to correct the excessive deficit. ECOFIN abrogates the EDP decision when the excessive deficit is corrected by the member state. If ECOFIN believes that the member state has failed to comply with the recommendations, it can trigger further steps in the procedures such as requiring publication of information, demanding a non-interest bearing deposit with the EU, or imposing a fine on the

---

5 Article 104c [TFEU Article 126].

country. However, since ECOFIN is composed of ministers from member states, the credibility of the framework is reduced since they are reluctant to impose serious sanctions on other member states.

The 2005 Reform

Germany, which was much more insistent on maintaining fiscal discipline than other countries, turned out to be one of the first countries to violate the SGP. In 2002, Germany avoided an early warning from the Commission for failing to adhere to the deficit criterion in the SGP and approaching the 3 percent limit for its deficit by striking a deal with ECOFIN. In January 2003, ECOFIN issued an early warning to France to urge it to balance its budget. In November 2003, the Commission presented its findings to ECOFIN, stating that both Germany and France had not taken adequate steps to reduce excessive deficits.

ECOFIN decided not to proceed with action against France and Germany by holding the EDP in abeyance.[6] Political pressure from these two countries led to the effective suspension of the Pact and the EDP was formally suspended in December 2004.

Romano Prodi, then President of the European Commission, called the SGP rules "stupid" for being too rigid at a time of economic downturn.[7]

The reform of the fiscal regime was subsequently announced in March 2005, with more "flexibility" for countries to account for running large deficits but the form of the original SGP remained mostly unaltered. Reference values were left untouched since they were part of the Treaties and discretionary powers were extended. The most important changes include revised medium-term objectives (MTOs) that account for national differences, as well as clarification of "exceptional and temporary" excesses and "other relevant factors."

---

6 This decision was later declared by the European Court of Justice (ECJ) in July 2004 to be an inadmissible decision since it was not preceded by a Commission proposal.

7 *Le Monde*, October 18, 2002.

Compared to the original SGP that purported to enable the Commission and ECOFIN to react quickly to deteriorations in fiscal policies and to impose sanctions within a year, the 2005 "reformed" SGP loosened the escape clauses, lengthened deadlines for taking action, and expanded the circumstances under which longer adjustment periods are permitted. These parameters include the behavior of the cyclically adjusted budget, the level of debt, the duration of the slow growth period and the possibility that the deficit is related to productivity-enhancing procedures. No EDP procedure will be launched if the excess of the government deficit over the 3% of GDP reference value is considered temporary and exceptional and the deficit remains close to the threshold.

Deficit and Debt Levels, 1995-2007

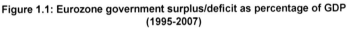

Figure 1.1: Eurozone government surplus/deficit as percentage of GDP (1995-2007)

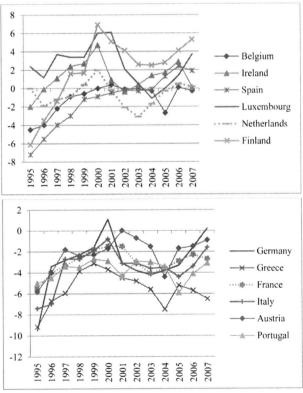

Source: Eurostat

From 1995 to 2007, only Luxembourg and Ireland managed not to exceed the 3% of GDP deficit threshold throughout the entire period. Nonetheless, before the creation of the Euro in 1999, with the exception of Greece, eleven countries sufficiently brought down their levels of deficits below the 3% reference value to meet the convergence criteria. Notably, Finland made substantial efforts to improve its deficit levels. Ireland, which was a country later hit severely by the sovereign debt crisis, held surpluses for almost the entirety of this period and fully complied with the deficit rule. Meanwhile, Germany and Spain made substantial efforts to have fiscal surpluses but several countries, including Greece, Italy, France and Portugal, maintained high deficit levels, especially after their admission to the Eurozone.

By the end of 2004, only half of the Euro area countries had fiscal positions that could be deemed as "close-to-balance or in surplus," defined as a minimum one-half percent cyclically adjusted deficit. These countries included Belgium, Finland, Netherlands, and Spain. Countries such as France, Germany, Greece, Italy, and Portugal remained far off from their objectives. As a result, these countries ended up posting deficits in excess of 3 percent that pushed them close to triggering the Excessive Deficit Procedure.

Enforcement of the SGP was made more difficult by the fact that several countries, including Greece, Italy, and Portugal underreported their deficit numbers to the European Commission. When the numbers were later revised by Eurostat, the problem was revealed to be more serious, and could possibly have disqualified some countries from joining the Euro because of the high level of deficits.

With respect to debt levels, Belgium, Italy, and Greece had the highest debt loads. Belgium and Italy showed substantial improvement over the period from 1995 to 2007, justifying their claims that they were actively reducing their debt to fulfill the Maastricht convergence criteria and SGP limits. However, Greek debt levels did not seem to decline and increased by about 10 percentage points over the period. Ireland, Spain, Netherlands, and Finland had declining levels of debt since the introduction of the single currency and consistently kept it below 60% of GDP until 2007. On the other hand, countries such as Germany, France, Austria, and Portugal maintained debt levels around the 60% of GDP specified by the Maastricht Treaty. Portugal, although having fulfilled the criterion before its admission, had its debt levels climb steadily, with 60% surpassed in 2004 and further increases following.

Figure 1.2: Eurozone government gross debt as percentage of GDP (1995-2007)

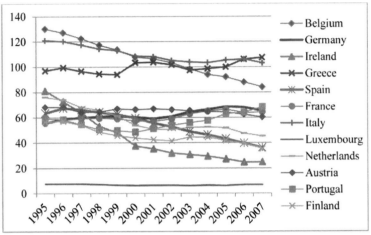

Source: Eurostat

Overall, the Maastricht convergence criteria had a positive influence for many countries such as Italy, which attempted to bring down its debt and deficit levels prior to joining the Euro, and have maintained consistent levels after adoption. However, with the different set of incentives under the Stability and Growth Pact, there was no significant improvement in deficit and debt levels in many countries. Even though there was a rebound in deficits and debt levels after the 2005 reform of the SGP, most countries' finances did not diverge widely. Countries like France and Germany did not improve their debt levels to bring them into line with the SGP, while countries such as Ireland actively brought them down to healthy levels. Comparing budgetary stabilization efforts before and after the Euro, and comparing the change between the Eurozone and the rest of the OECD, the Eurozone countries did not perform better, suggesting that the SGP has had a limited effect.[8]

---

8 Wyplosz, C. (2006). European Monetary Union: The dark sides of a major success. Economic Policy, 21(46), 207-261.

Why the SGP was ineffective

The enforcement mechanisms that support the SGP can help explain why adherence to the Pact was limited in many countries. The responsibility for enforcing fiscal limits in the SGP fell on two players. The first was the European Commission and ECOFIN. The second was the financial markets, which had the power to affect interest rates on government bonds, thereby signaling its level of confidence with a country's public finances.

In the years following the enactment of the SGP, enforcement was lax due to the lack of financial sanctions imposed on countries despite the inability of many countries to comply with targets, most notably France and Germany. Imposition of sanctions required consent of ECOFIN, composed of national ministers of finance and where France and Germany held a large portion of votes. In other words, member states could easily overturn mechanisms that they devised when their deficit and debt levels did not fall under the previously agreed levels.

When France and Germany decided to impose a looser interpretation of the SGP in 2003 to avoid sanctions, the SGP was no longer fully operative, this being only four years after the establishment of the single currency. Many warnings and reports were issued by the European Commission on countries' fiscal policies but no action was taken by ECOFIN. Prior to the crisis, an official early warning was issued to France in 2003 only after the 3% of GDP deficit threshold was breached, but not to Germany, Portugal, and Italy, for which the Commission recommended early warnings. Since European institutions were not directly elected, it was also difficult to impose sanctions on national governments that were popularly elected. No fines have ever been imposed on a member state, despite the power of ECOFIN to do so under the dissuasive arm of the SGP.[9]

By 2011, all Eurozone countries had been involved in the Excessive Deficit Procedure (EDP). Although the Commission still argued

9 In March 2012, ECOFIN threatened to suspend Hungary's access to development funds for 2013, which would be reversed if Hungary shows improvement in reducing its deficit level.

that the SGP was a framework by which member states could return to sound fiscal policies, few countries adhered to the Commission's recommendations. In addition, since 23 of 27 EU countries were subject to the EDP and many of the EDPs were launched in 2009, the likelihood of any sanctions imposed by ECOFIN on an individual member state was significantly reduced. The inability to enforce automatic sanctions, as Germany had demanded before the introduction of the SGP, is a limit that renders enforcement against countries with excessive deficits or debt difficult.

The political architecture that underlies the SGP could provide an explanation as to why the fiscal rules were not fully enforced. An important factor was creative accounting, notably by Greece, to hide large deficits, leaving the problem undetected for years. National leaders are accountable to their electorate, from whom they face possible political sanction, and this leads to a general bias towards deficits and debts. Incentives for adherence are thus much weaker at the European level, especially for large countries that have substantial political influence in the EU. An additional factor is a moral hazard problem where the lack of a significant interest rate risk premium meant that the costs of profligacy were small and were shared with the rest of the Eurozone.

Deficits and Debt Levels during Sovereign Debt Crisis

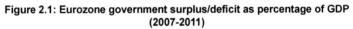

Figure 2.1: Eurozone government surplus/deficit as percentage of GDP (2007-2011)

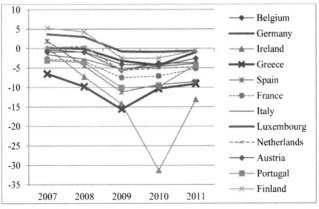

Source: Eurostat

Traditionally fiscally conservative countries, such as Germany, Luxembourg, Austria, and Finland, managed mostly to avoid large fiscal deficit until they faced the full brunt of the financial crisis that started in 2007. By 2009, these countries had hit the deficit range, but managed to maintain near the 3% reference value for deficit levels. In the rest of the Eurozone, with the exception of Greece, most countries managed to maintain their deficit levels low in 2008. By 2009, only Belgium, Netherlands and Italy kept their deficit levels under 5% of GDP, while the rest of the group fell into deficits at or near 10% of GDP. Notably, due to the bailouts of financial institutions by the government of Ireland, the deficit there dipped to 31.3% of GDP.

Furthermore, the assessment of structural balance was often deficient in the first decade of the Euro, and in addition to the fact that the effect of changes in the output gap on tax revenues was often incorrectly estimated, there was little attention paid to changes in government revenues that were due to asset cycles in the financial and housing markets, rather than to the general economic cycle. When the crisis hit, countries lost important sources of revenue from those markets and were left with a larger deficit than they otherwise would have had.

Figure 2.2 Eurozone government debt as a percentage of GDP (2007-2011)

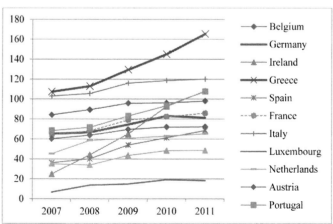

Source: Eurostat

Belgium, Greece, Italy, and Portugal, which already had high debt-to-GDP ratios before the crisis, had debt levels increase dramatically during the period, with Greece ending up with a value greater than 160%. An interesting case, however, was that of Ireland. It performed relatively well with the SGP targets prior to the crisis, yet when under pressure to save failing financial institutions, it was forced to be indebted at much higher levels, reaching over 100% of GDP by 2011. The rest of the original monetary union members saw a steady climb in debt ratios and, with the exception of Finland, went above the targeted 60% of GDP reference value.

Given the economic downturn and the push for stimulus, countries in general ignored the limits set by the SGP as most believed that they were facing one of the worst economic recessions since the end of the Second World War, which would qualify as an "exceptional and temporary" situation.

In the midst of a debt crisis, with bond yields increasing rapidly, the European Commission and ECOFIN did not make an attempt to sanction any country for ignoring the SGP targets, as most of them had breached them. As the debt level for countries such as Greece continued to climb, there were no significant institutional attempts to pressure the Greek government to reverse the change. As bond yields escalated in the market, countries continued to be hit hard with large borrowing costs, at the risk of defaulting.

One of the original intentions of the SGP was to enforce strict fiscal rules and promote prudence in government finances during most of the economic cycle, so that in "exceptional" circumstances, countries would be able to run deficits without falling away from its Medium Term Objective (MTO). Indeed, the global financial crisis had serious repercussions in Eurozone economies and it is questionable whether the SGP could have prevented the precipitous rise in debt levels in cases such as Ireland, a country that was in full compliance with the rules prior to the crisis. However, the general lax enforcement of the SGP in the years before the sovereign debt crisis made any quick return to sustainable deficit and debt levels difficult. This major shortcoming of the SGP meant that its credibility was questioned as countries grappled with the effects of the sovereign debt crisis, where Eurozone countries were widely criticized for their finances.

Market enforcement

Figure 3.1 Ten-year Government Bond Yields for EU-12 (1992-1999)

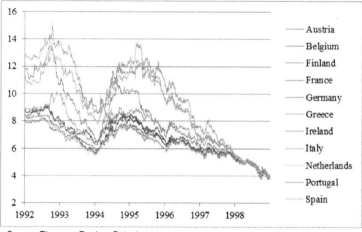

Source: Thomson Reuters Datastream

Figure 3.2 Ten-year Government Bond Yields for EU-12 (1999-2011)[10]

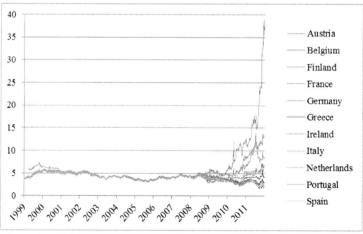

Source: Thomson Reuters Datastream

---

10 Luxembourg was excluded since the country only began issuing ten-year government bonds in 2010.

As much as the Maastricht convergence and the subsequent Stability and Growth Pact were political agreements among member states, the success of the monetary union depended partly on acceptance in the financial markets. The EU needed to assure investors of the benefits of a common currency and member states needed to convince markets that the default risk of their sovereign bonds declined as a result of joining the Euro.

After the formation of the single currency, interest rate spreads on long-term government bond yields between Germany and other Eurozone countries were narrow and almost constant, reflecting confidence in the market that participation in the Eurozone reduced the risk of default substantially even in countries that formerly had high levels of government debt and deficit. In addition, financial investors perceived the Commission to be a credible enforcer of SGP rules, which would assure the viability of the Euro. Even when deficit levels diverged between countries before the sovereign debt crisis, bond yields demonstrated little movement away from the Eurozone average. The deficit and debt levels were effectively not enforced in any significant way in the financial markets, allowing countries such as Greece to borrow at substantially much lower rates than they otherwise would have been able to.

Market responses to changes in deficit and debt levels after 2008 were much more pronounced, and many of the changes in bond yields were disproportionate to the relative changes in debt levels. In other words, markets treated the effectiveness of the SGP differently before and after the beginning of the sovereign debt crisis. Interest rates for Greece, Portugal, Italy, and Ireland increased substantially with the sovereign debt crisis. Rapidly rising borrowing costs have in all likelihood made meeting the SGP thresholds even more difficult, as seen with the remarkable increases in debt for Ireland and Greece since the sovereign debt crisis.

In fact, Eurozone countries faced less market discipline than those outside the Eurozone.[11] While arguably beneficial to provide more flexibility during economic cycles, the relaxed enforcement of SGP

11 Eichengreen, B. (2005). Europe, the euro and the ECB: Monetary success, fiscal failure. Journal of Policy Modeling, 27(4), 427-439.

rules undermined the effectiveness of the targets, and when an economic recession hit, the countries had little room for maneuver to prevent falling into excessive deficit and debt levels.

Lasting reform to the SGP?

As the sovereign debt crisis heightened after 2009 and bond yields rose to substantial levels for several countries that were considered to have poor finances, European leaders sought to reassure the financial markets of their determination to maintain sound finances in the future and of their commitment to the continuity of the single currency. Given the limitations of the existing SGP, the EU attempted to reinforce it by launching the "Six-Pack," which is a legislative package of six legal acts (five regulations and one directive) that entered into force on December 13, 2011.

On March 2, 2012, 25 EU countries agreed on an intergovernmental treaty, titled the Treaty on Stability, Coordination and Governance in the Economic and Monetary Union, commonly referred to as the Fiscal Compact or the Fiscal Stability Treaty. When ratified, the Treaty would enshrine budget and debt limits into their respective constitutions, with legally enforceable penalties for violators.

The Euro had symbolized a new stage in European integration and the monetary union was to be the demonstration of the success of EU cooperation. A thorough evaluation of the inefficacies of the current SGP would be helpful to bring about a response for a permanent, viable system that is effective at both political and market levels in committing Eurozone countries to enact fiscal policy that will bring stability to the Euro and bring growth to the European economies.

Note: Color versions of all graphs in this publication are available for download at:
http://www.eui.eu/Personal/Carletti/
http://www.eui.eu/DepartmentsAndCentres/Economics/SeminarsEvents/Conferences/
GovernancefortheEurozoneIntegrationorDisintegration.aspx
http://finance.wharton.upenn.edu/FIC/FICPress/goveuro.pdf

DEPARTMENT OF ECONOMICS

Governance for the Eurozone: Integration or Disintegration?

Workshop organized by Profs. **Franklin Allen, Elena Carletti** and **Saverio Simonelli** in the framework of the PEGGED project (Politics, Economics and Global Governance: The European Dimensions)

Co-organized by
Department of Economics,
Global Governance Programme (GGP),
Robert Schuman Centre for Advanced Studies ,
Wharton Financial Institutions Center

Sala Europa, Villa Schifanoia
Via Boccaccio 121, 50133 Firenze

Programme	**April 26, 2012**

9.30-10.15   Registration and coffee

10.15 – 10.30   Welcome by EUI President **Josep Borrell**

10:30 – 12:00   Panel 1: Public financial institutions

    a) The role of the European Central Bank
    b) The structure of the EFSF/ESM
    c) What are the fiscal boundaries for central banks in the Eurosystem?

                  Chair: **Elena Carletti** (European University Institute)

Participants: **Antonio Borges** (Catolica-Lisbon School of Business and Economics)
                  Paul De Grauwe (LSE)
                  Friedrich Kübler (Johann-Wolfgang-Goethe University & University of
                  Pennsylvania)
                  Frank Smets (European Central Bank)

12:00 – 13:00   Keynote Lecture: **Richard Portes** (London Business School)

13:00 – 14:30   Lunch at Villa Schifanoia

Villa San Paolo
Via della Piazzola 43, 50133 Firenze, Italia • **Tel.** +39 055 4685 033 • **Fax** +39 055 4685 902 • www.eui.eu

European
University
Institute

14:30 – 16:00   **Panel 2: The reform of the political and economic architecture**

    a) Reform of the growth and stability pact
    b) Enforcement mechanisms
    c) Liquidity provision and financial regulation with risk of sovereign debt default

        Chair: **Franklin Allen** (Wharton Financial Institutions Center)

Participants: **Leszek Balcerowicz** (Warsaw School of Economics)
        Russell Cooper (EUI)
        Pietro Carlo Padoan (OECD)
        Jacques Ziller (University of Pavia)

16:00-16:30   Coffee break

16:30 – 18:15   **Panel 3: European Union and Euro zone: How to coexist?**

    a) Informal role of stronger states
    b) A two tier Europe
    c) Role of countries outside the Eurozone and European institutions

        Chair: **Saverio Simonelli** (European University Institute)

Participants:

        Bruno De Witte (Maastricht University)
        Charles Goodhart (London School of Economics)
        Brigid Laffan (UCD)
        Guntram Wolff (Bruegel)

18:30   Reception and Dinner at Villa Schifanoia

Dinner speaker: **Wolfgang Münchau** (Eurointelligence)

This conference is financed by the PEGGED Collaborative Project.
The PEGGED Collaborative Project is funded by the European Commission's 7th Framework Programme for Research. Grant Agreement no. 217559.

CPSIA information can be obtained at www.ICGtesting.com
Printed in the USA
BVOW012235220712

295858BV00003B/3/P